The Human Person and a Culture of Freedom

Edited by
Peter A. Pagan Aguiar and
Terese Auer, O.P.

Forward by
Alice Ramos
With an introduction by
Francis Cardinal George, O.M.I.

AMERICAN MARITAIN ASSOCIATION
Distributed by The Catholic University of America Press
Washington, DC 20064

Library of Congress Cataloging-in-Publication Data

The human person and a culture of freedom / editors, Peter Pagan and Terese Auer ; foreword by Alice Ramos ; introduction by Francis Cardinal George.

p. cm. -- (American Maritain Association publications)

Includes bibliographical references and index.

Summary: "Collection of essays on the metaphysical underpinnings of intellectual and individual freedom within a civic-political order or cultural milieu"--Provided by publisher.

ISBN 978-0-9669226-7-7

1. Christianity and politics--Catholic Church. 2. Liberty--Religious aspects--Catholic Church. 3. Theological anthropology--Catholic Church. 4. Christian sociology--Catholic Church. 5. Maritain, Jacques, 1882-1973. 6. Catholic Church--Doctrines. I. Pagan, Peter, 1961- II. Auer, Terese, 1954-

BX1793.H86 2009

123'.5--dc22

2008048792

Manufactured in the United States of America

Distributed by The Catholic University of America Press
620 Michigan Avenue, N.E. /240 Leahy Hall
Washington, DC 20064

PUBLICATIONS OF THE

AMERICAN MARITAIN ASSOCIATION

General Editors: Anthony O. Simon (1990 – 2004)

Michael D. Torre (2009 -)

Jacques Maritain: The Man and His Metaphysics
Edited by John F.X. Kansas, 1988
ISBN 0-268-01205-9 (out of print)
Distributed by the University of Notre Dame Press

Freedom in the Modern World: Jacques Maritain, Yves R. Simon, Mortimer J. Adler
Edited by Michael D. Torre, 1989, Second Printing, 1990
ISBN 0-268-00978-3
Distributed by the University of Notre Dame Press

From Twilight to Dawn: The Cultural Vision of Jacques Maritain
Edited by Peter A. Redpath, 1990
ISBN 0-268-00979-1
Distributed by the University of Notre Dame Press

The Future of Thomism
Edited by Deal W. Hudson and Dennis Wm. Moran, 1992
ISBN 0-268-00986-4
Distributed by the University of Notre Dame Press

Jacques Maritain and the Jews
Edited by Robert Royal, 1994
ISBN 0-268-01193-1
Distributed by the University of Notre Dame Press

Freedom, Virtue, and the Common Good
Edited by Curtis L. Hancock and Anthony O. Simon, 1995
ISBN 0-268-00991-0
Distributed by the University of Notre Dame Press

Postmodernism and Christian Philosophy
Edited by Roman T. Ciapolo, 1997
ISBN 0-8132-0881-5
Distributed by The Catholic University of America Press

The Common Things: Essays on Thomism and Education
Edited by Daniel McInerny, 1999
ISBN 0-9669226-0-3
Distributed by The Catholic University of America Press

The Failure of Modernism: The Cartesian Legacy and Contemporary Pluralism
Edited by Brendan Sweetman, 1999
ISBN 0-9669226-1-1
Distributed by The Catholic University of America Press

Beauty, Art, and the Polis
Edited by Alice Ramos, 2000
ISBN 0-9669226-2-X
Distributed by The Catholic University of America Press

Reassessing the Liberal State: Reading Maritain's Man and State
Edited by Timothy Fuller and John P. Hittinger, 2001
ISBN 0-9669226-3-8
Distributed by The Catholic University of America Press

Faith, Scholarship, and Culture in the 21st Century
Edited by Alice Ramos, and Marie I. George, 2002
ISBN 0-9669226-5-4
Distributed by The Catholic University of America Press

Jacques Maritain and the Many Ways of Knowing
Edited by Douglas A. Ollivant, 2002
ISBN 0-9669226-4-6
Distributed by The Catholic University of America Press

Truth Matters: Essays in Honor of Jacques Maritain
Edited by John G. Trapani, Jr., 2004
ISBN 0-9669226-6-2
Distributed by The Catholic University of America Press

The Human Person and a Culture of Freedom
Edited by Peter A. Pagan Aguiar and Terese Auer, O.P., 2009
ISBN 978-0-9669226-7-7
Distributed by The Catholic University of America Press

DEDICATION

This volume is dedicated to

Our Lady,

Spouse of Eternal Love,

Mother of Incarnate Truth

ACKNOWLEDGMENTS

I am delighted to take this opportunity to thank the many persons, including the various authors represented within these pages, who contributed in one way or another to the completion of this long-awaited volume. I am especially indebted to Sr. Terese Auer, O.P., who gave generously of her time, and without whose professional collaboration the publication of this collection would have been delayed considerably longer. I must also express my sincere gratitude to Mother Ann Marie Karlovic, O.P., for permitting Sr. Terese to serve as the volume's coeditor. I thank the Dominican Sisters of the Congregation of St. Cecilia and Aquinas College for their spiritual and material support of my ongoing professional involvement in the American Maritain Association's scholarly activities. I am deeply grateful to the Vice President of the American Maritain Association, Dr. Gavin Colvert, for his valuable technical assistance in producing both the volume's index and the camera-ready version of the manuscript. I thank Sr. Mary Angelica Neenan, O.P., for sharing her keen artistic sensibilities and recommendations on cover design. I thank Dr. Michael Torre, the series' general editor, for his positive encouragement and helpful suggestions during the closing stages of the editorial and publication process. Finally, I am grateful to my wife, Karen Ann, and to our five children for their Christian patience, support, and generosity in allowing me to devote so many hours to academic endeavors such as this.

Peter A. Pagan

CONTENTS

PART III
CHURCH AND STATE: RELIGIOUS FREEDOM IN THE PUBLIC SQUARE

PART IV
THE DIGNITY OF HUMAN LIFE AND FREEDOM

FOREWORD

In his address to the United Nations over ten years ago, John Paul II exhorted men and women throughout the world to build in the new millennium "a civilization worthy of the human person, a true culture of freedom."[1] The decline in moral and spiritual values both in America and in Europe attests to the urgent need for cultural renewal. We are presently facing not only the threat of terrorism and of fanaticism, but also the challenges to humanity arising from unprecedented technological power.[2] The future of humankind and of the world stands in peril unless theoretical and practical wisdom is forthcoming. Concerted efforts by people of good will to provide this wisdom are, however, being made, and so there is hope that we can build a better world.

The quest for freedom is one of the distinctive features of our time. Men and women throughout the world have taken "the risk of freedom" in order to lead a life in keeping with their dignity as human persons.[3] The twentieth-century philosopher Jacques Maritain, whose work is indebted to Thomas Aquinas and whose influence is evident in the personalist thought of John Paul II, describes the human person in words taken from Aquinas: "The person signifies what is most perfect in all nature–that is, a subsistent individual of a rational nature."[4] According to Maritain and the tradition in which he philosophized, human persons are like God in that they have the powers of reason and free will and can thus determine themselves. The great dignity of human persons resides in their freedom, in that capacity for self-determination or self-mastery, whereby they are able in a sense to make or mold themselves, to

---

1. Address to the Fiftieth General Assembly to the United Nations Organization, New York, October 5, 1995. See the Vatican website.

2. On the great moral challenges of biotechnology, see Leon Kass, "How Brave a New World?" 2007 commencement speech at St. John's College, in Annapolis, Maryland.

3. See John Paul II's address to the United Nations, October 5, 1995.

4. Jacques Maritain, "The Individual and the Person," in *The Social and Political Philosophy of Jacques Maritain*, eds. Joseph W. Evans and Leo R. Ward (New York: Charles Scribner's Sons, 1955), p. 4. See also Thomas Aquinas, *Summa Theologiae* I, q. 29, a. 3, resp.

perfect themselves, and to perfect the world in which they live. When persons act contrary to their dignity and greatness as free beings, then they act slavishly. We are no doubt witnesses to the myriad forms that slavish action can take, whether by means of drugs, sex, the cult of bodily beauty and of physical comfort and well-being, to the detriment of the care of the rational soul.

Authentic freedom cannot be detached from the quest for truth. When freedom is severed from the truth about the human person, then it degenerates into license or into the will to power. History, past and present, provides us with abundant examples of how lawless freedom or absolute autonomy creates havoc in the lives of individuals and in political life. As John Paul II put it: "Freedom has an inner 'logic' which distinguishes it and ennobles it: freedom is ordered to the truth. . . . Far from being a limitation upon freedom or a threat to it, reference to the truth about the human person–a truth universally knowable through the moral law written on the hearts of all–is, in fact, the guarantor of freedom's future."[5]

Since there is such an intimate connection between freedom and the truth about man, we shall find that false freedoms have their origin in false anthropologies. John Paul II recognized that rival versions of politics and culture always start from a particular conception of the human person. Nowhere is this more evident than in contemporary public debates regarding freedom and rights. As Mary Ann Glendon, Harvard Professor of Law, has shown, these debates generally make use of either the libertarian or the dignitarian modes of discourse.[6] In the libertarian context, rights are generally formulated without reference to limits or to responsibilities; although libertarian freedom has a procedural framework, it lacks a specific normative framework. On the other hand, the dignitarian mode of discourse found, for example, in the Universal Declaration of Human Rights or in the social doctrine of the Catholic Church, sees rights as

---

5. See John Paul II's address to the United Nations.

6. In this brief discussion of the libertarian and dignitarian traditions, I am making reference to a more detailed account which appears in Professor Glendon's contribution to a seminar on John Paul II's address to the United Nations. The seminar was held at the Trusteeship Council Chamber of the U.N. on May 8, 1996. Professor Glendon's statement is found on the website of the Holy See Mission.

both safeguarded by fair procedures and as grounded in a normative structure based on personal dignity. In the dignitarian tradition, the uniqueness of each individual is acknowledged, but importance is also given to the ways in which the individual is constituted by his relations to others; individual persons and groups have responsibilities as well as specific rights.

While both of these traditions may be subject to deformation, it is the libertarian tradition in particular which has given way to debased versions: from the debasement of libertarian freedom we have crude power politics, materialism, and hedonism. Reference can also be made to utilitarianism, skepticism, and relativism, which in the final analysis deny the existence of common truths and thus attack the foundation of universal rights. We need to search for the distinct conception of the human person that underlies these different conceptions of rights and freedom. According to Professor Glendon, "That search, in the case of debased libertarianism, leads to 'radically autonomous man,' in the case of utilitarianism, to 'economic man,' and in the case of relativism to 'plastic man'–who, having no nature of his own, can morph into an infinite variety of forms."[7]

Given the connection between freedom and truth, it is evident that a freedom which is not anchored in the truth about the human person will not be used responsibly and will harm both the individual person and society. Furthermore, the dissociation of freedom from truth makes intercultural dialogue on rights impossible. Unless the quest for freedom is grounded in a continuous search for truth, it becomes impossible to discuss the human future intelligibly. At the heart of all wisdom traditions there is the conviction of a common humanity, of a common moral order, that is the basis for our reflection and deliberation about the human future. We must appeal to that "moral logic which is built into human life."[8] John Paul II expressed it best when he said: "The universal moral law written on the human heart is precisely that kind of 'grammar' which is needed if the world is to engage this discussion of its future."[9] Our discussion of the future and

7. Ibid.

8. See John Paul II's address to the United Nations.

9. Ibid.

the destiny of humankind can be intelligible because we do not live in an irrational world nor is human life meaningless.

We need a vision of the human person which is more profound and holistic than any of the reductionist anthropologies mentioned above, a vision of the person which recognizes, as Maritain and Aquinas and others have maintained, the inestimable dignity and value of each human life. In consonance with this conception of the person, John Paul II's anthropology presents the human person "as a creature of intelligence and free will, immersed in a mystery–['the mystery of God']–which transcends his own being and endowed with the ability to reflect and the ability to choose–and thus capable of wisdom and virtue."[10] It is precisely these God-given capacities for wisdom and moral virtue, together with divine providence, that will enable us to bring about "a true culture of freedom." Beyond all the cultural differences, there is in effect "a fundamental commonality,"[11] an intelligible human nature shared by all peoples, which makes possible dialogue between individuals of different lands. If persuasion by means of reasoned dialogue is to succeed the "violent coercion" of the twentieth century,[12] then appeal must be made to the nature of the person, with its internal moral law and objective demands, as the foundation for universal human rights.

The vision of the human person presented by John Paul II has been called a "transcendent humanism" and stands in sharp contrast to what has been termed an "atheistic humanism" or an "exclusivist humanism."[13] Not only does the latter exclude from public life all transcendent moral reference points, as is evident in the present cultural crisis of Europe, but it also expresses a truncated version of human reason, what Cardinal Ratzinger, now Pope Benedict XVI, has

---

10. Ibid.

11. Ibid.

12. Ibid.

13. On "atheistic humanism" see Henri de Lubac, *The Drama of Atheist Humanism*, trans. Edith M. Riley, Anne Englund Nash, and Mark Sebanc (San Francisco: Ignatius Press, 1995). On "exclusive humanism" see Charles Taylor, *Sources of the Self: The Making of the Modern Identity* (Cambridge, Massachusetts: Harvard University Press, 1989), and on "transcendent humanism" see my article entitled "Foundations for a Christian Anthropology," *Anthropotes*, no. 2 (1989), pp. 225-257.

called the "mutilation of reason."[14] By limiting reason to the empirical realm, to scientific reason, no reasonable access to religion and to an objective or public morality is possible. In an "exclusivist humanism," therefore, reason is no longer considered as that human capacity to know the truth of things, including moral truth; it is no longer *capax entis, capax Dei*, capable of knowing the whole of being, which is intelligible, and also capable of knowing God. We thus need to reaffirm reason's capacity to attain the truth, for, as we have seen, human freedom and its responsible use depend on truth.

By broadening the concept of reason, by opening it to the divine, and more specifically to the God of the *Logos*, we will be able to enter into a "dialogue of cultures" and thus work toward ending the many forms of violence perpetrated against the human person.[15] The rediscovery of reason's metaphysical reach and of a "transcendent humanism" is vital if we wish to create "a civilization worthy of the human person, a true culture of freedom."

ALICE RAMOS

St. John's University

---

14. Joseph Ratzinger, *Christianity and the Crisis of Cultures* (San Francisco: Ignatius Press, 2006), p. 43. See also George Weigel's essay entitled "Is Europe Dying? Notes on a Crisis of Civilizational Morale," on the website of the American Enterprise Institute.

15. See James V. Schall, *The Regensburg Lecture* (South Bend, Indiana: St. Augustine's Press, 2007), which also includes in the appendix the lecture given by Pope Benedict XVI at the University of Regensburg, September 12, 2006.

INTRODUCTION

Pope Benedict XVI often brings his listeners to the question of truth, no matter the subject under discussion, because he knows that the search for objective truth not only trains the mind but also frees the will. The discovery of truth brings the searcher out of purely individual experience into the realm of the communal and, at the deepest level, the universal. The mind's assent to truth becomes the will's surrender to a person, when ultimate truth is identified with Jesus Christ, crucified and risen from the dead for the salvation of the world. True freedom, therefore, depends on knowing the truth, both in concept and in encounter. The Pope speaks often about the relation between truth and love, between truth and justice, between truth and peace, but most persuasively he teaches about the relation between truth and freedom.

Jacques Maritain considered over many years the nature of freedom in order to reach the truth about it in all its dimensions. He thought and wrote from a philosophical perspective, one in which rational discourse was open to faith but not defined by it. The chapters of this book explore various dimensions of Maritain's thought, sometimes pushing it into areas he himself did not exhaustively explore. In these few pages, I would like to present three notions of freedom analyzed variously in Maritain's work, reflecting on them in a historical context he anticipated but did not live to see fully developed.

In our world and our time, the very idea of freedom is contested. On the one hand, the new militant and scientific atheists base themselves on a highly reductive view of what we human beings can know, and they have convinced themselves and a significant number of others that the iron laws of physics determine all things, leaving no room for freedom. On the other hand, broad groups of what we shall call here, for the sake of simplicity, postmodernists, reject all definite knowledge and the kind of systematic closure the scientists claim to possess, in favor of what is absent, marginal, overlooked, incomplete, paradoxical, and uncanny. Freedom itself is too strong a term for them. Still, they also usually talk a lot about discourses of power, seeking to wrest power away from dominant groups for themselves and others without being able to say definitively on their own grounds why it is wrong or improper that some groups have power and others do not. Right and wrong are, after all, normative concepts that have to be explained and justified and not simply asserted. Freedom of the most radical sort seems to be possible in this radical problematizing of all settled truths, though it is a freedom that is fundamentally empty. The postmodern destruction of truth does not allow for a really significant free act. All action, in that way of thinking, is and can only be a creative performance whose meaning has always already been deconstructed before it even occurs. Caught between iron scientific determinism and gossamer deconstructive performance, the idea of freedom has no natural contemporary home.

It should come as no surprise that, if the idea of freedom is so troubled in our time, the reality is not doing very well either. Many problems we currently face show obscure but deep and real connections between determinism and radical autonomy, though it would be a long task to trace out all those connections. The new atheists seem to think their own work is all-encompassing truth and denounce the continuing persistence of religion in the most rabid terms: child abuse, mind control, and the root of all evil. These are strong words for a phenomenon that ought to be looked upon serenely as just one among many of the universe's necessary outcomes since, on their own principles, nothing escapes scientific determinism. Religious believers can plead: the universe made me do it. Our diverse group of postmodernists speaks in very similar terms, if to different purposes. They simply add the scientific worldview to the other forms of allegedly oppressive truth claims in the somewhat desperate hope of thereby opening up possibilities for freedom. But the obvious self-contradictions of both schools demand some kind of pragmatic effort to rescue human concerns and permanent value from antecedent errors. It is largely because of this situation that coarse utilitarian ethics have entered so prominently into some of the most sacred precincts of human life.

These and many other phenomena lead us to believe that we need a different analysis of what freedom is in itself and the forms it ought to take in a society, like our own, that claims to value human freedom. We did not get to our present position by chance. It's possible to see behind the situation outlined above one set of consequences of Kant's view of human beings and the world. In his system, the world is everything we can analyze scientifically, and human freedom lies in distinguishing sharply between what is natural and what is human. Our two main modern camps are Kantian schismatics, each taking one half of the great man's system and trying to build a whole philosophy out of it by ignoring the other half, which each believes is no longer intellectually tenable. To a certain extent, each is right: the scientists have their fingers on a significant truth when they dismiss notions of a human freedom that is alleged to exist entirely separated from nature. That was a weakness in Kant, and it remains a weakness for all ways of thinking that posit the human being as a kind of ghost in a machine. The postmodernists do not bother so much about consistency, because they believe that truth is a construct anyway, even scientific truths, which are not exhaustive and are as incoherent as any other totalizing claim. For them, the machine itself is a ghost, or at least a mirage, and it is dangerous to take it as real.

The problem here cannot be solved by refinements in one camp or another, and, in the meantime, the Western peoples who learned from the Bible their respect for the human person, for the centrality of moral choice, and for the liberty of God's children find that even the secular spin-offs of that tradition are less and less plausible. We need to turn to a way of thinking that restores our belief in these notions, and for that we need a different starting point and a way of proceeding that will do full justice to the physical world of nature and the characteristically human things that are connected to that world, but not reducible to or separable from it. Above all, we have to make sure that the tremendous growth in our knowledge of nature and our advances in developing the technological ways to put nature to human uses do not entirely eclipse the other dimensions of our lives, dimensions like understanding, creativity, will, that have made the scientific discoveries possible in the first place.

Sometimes this problem is presented as the need to find a place for a vigorous humanism in our conception of the world. That is certainly true, but at the same time humanism itself can have just as reductive an effect as the false scientific knowledge and postmodern deconstruction noted above. In historical fact, deconstruction in a broad sense has replaced in many colleges and universities the study of the human things and, as a result, has prevented our swelling population of college graduates from knowing very much about the rich humanistic tradition, to say nothing of the religious and theological principles on which it stands. Many of those graduates, of course, possess a robust common sense that leads them into important truths beyond their formal studies. But it is not a good thing for a free society to depend on freelance sanity while its official institutions of higher learning are inculcating what is sometimes simply insanity. We can and must do better in conveying the central human things that, under God, help make and keep us truly free.

For some time in the nineteenth and twentieth centuries, humanism was often presented as something by its nature opposed to Christianity. The failures of the Christian churches and faith communities to keep up with social problems in this world and, perhaps, an overemphasis on the next world contributed to this false opposition. Properly understood, however, Christianity is not opposed but is indeed the source of some of the values that the Enlightenment recovered in a one-sided way for Western civilization. For example, the sacredness of the human person and the rights of conscience are indispensable notions for the development of any sort of humanism. But apart from Christianity, which enriches them and keeps them in a wider context, even these humanistic notions can go wild, when they do not simply decay for lack of a living root in a deeper reality. In the twentieth century, some people thought Marxism was a kind of humanism that would free large swaths of workers from bondage to capital. In fact, Marxism created a worse bondage for those very workers and literally rode roughshod over human rights and conscience, killing 100 million people in the gulags, forced famines, Cultural Revolutions, and other modern inventions supposed to advance the most far-seeing vision of a truly human and free life. Nazism, too, presented itself as a kind of humanism that would restore the natural vigor of the German people, and it killed 40 million along the way. In these two examples, one international, the other national, we see two glaring instances of what happens when certain "humanistic" principles are emphasized to the neglect of other truths.

Many peoples like to think of themselves as superior to these murderous regimes because they have had no similar bloodbaths and have succeeded reasonably well in guaranteeing rights of conscience and respecting the dignity of the human person. But in the United States, Canada and Western Europe, we have probably aborted more children than Communism and Nazism produced victims in the camps and purges. We say we believe in the dignity of every person, unless that person happens to be living in the womb or nearing the end of life, frail, unproductive and burdensome to family and society. As the population of almost all the Western nations grows older because falling birth rates are failing to offset deaths, we are likely to see rather nasty pressures on the elderly to unburden us through physician-assisted suicide or, if the elderly resist, perhaps through mandated euthanasia. All this has come about because of distortion of the meaning of freedom of choice and of human dignity, both of which we need to look at more carefully if we do not intend to repeat the evils of which we are already aware, or to create even worse horrors that we cannot yet imagine.

In considering various understandings of freedom, the most prominent is freedom of choice. Freedom of choice has become nearly a shibboleth in the United States and in Europe, as if the bare exercise of the human capacity to choose was an unqualified good, without looking at what is specifically chosen. This kind of freedom, a capacity built into human nature, is necessary if there is to be any ethical life at all in a free society such as we all claim to cherish. But a good portion of what governments do is to protect us from the choices that others make. Our armed forces confront terrorists and armed enemies abroad; our police apprehend and detain thieves, rapists, murderers, white-collar criminals at home; our justice system tries to adjudicate between parties in civil conflicts who make contending claims of harms done. The baseline freedom of choice that inheres in all human beings is not something we celebrate or defend when it is used to improper ends. Freedom is a means to an end, a good end, and we rightly value it personally and socially as a good that makes a responsible and creative life possible. But not all realizations of chosen possibilities are desirable or even tolerable in any society.

Many people might follow the arguments about freedom thus far, but then draw back and object: you are talking about legislating morality. Since we do that all the time with regard to non-controversial questions like assault, robbery, and homicide, there is no reason to be shy about saying openly that, yes, we are talking about legislating morality. What else would we legislate? The real objection some have about legislating morality, of course, is whether the state should be able to curtail the freedom to divorce, to abort, to engage in homosexual relations, to marry a person of the same sex, to use certain drugs, and other matters which were formerly often crimes and are currently being redefined by some in our society as fundamental rights. This is not the place to go into those specific issues, but it is clear that humans have a natural freedom that makes them able to choose these things; whether a society or a moral system should give its blessing to those activities, however, is debatable. Just because there is a difference of opinion about some matters does not mean we cannot make public decisions about them. A good society will make a number of delicate judgments about contested questions. It cannot be prohibited from making such judgments with the simple invocation of freedom of choice.

We need to look further into the notion of freedom of choice, because it may help us towards a better understanding of freedom's prerogatives and its responsibilities. The present volume is highly valuable precisely because it directs our attention to several ways in which Jacques Maritain offers a much richer and fuller appreciation of what freedom means. He identifies a second meaning of freedom once common to the moral philosophy of the past, but which has largely dropped out of common discourse: the freedom that is mastery over ourselves. Since philosophy began in ancient Greece, there has been a dictate of common sense that, without the ability to order and control the desires we find in ourselves towards a variety of things, so-called freedom sinks into mere impulse and chaos. With Kant in the eighteenth century, a gap opened up between human nature and human will. Kant puts aside all those inclinations that might lead us towards right action, such as love, affection, delight, wonder and so forth, because they form no part of the ethical will as such. Properly used, this insight has some value. But if it is taken to mean, as Kant and many Kantians have meant it over the years, that a pure sense of duty is all that matters in the moral life, then it cannot help but lead to moral resentment for the great majority of people who do not find in themselves an ability to follow duty rigorously, or to moral Phariseeism for the few fortunate enough to be able to act without serious disturbance from passions or temptations. In short, this is not a picture of freedom useful for the human race as we know it.

That is why in the Aristotelian and Thomistic tradition such a large role is allowed to virtue. A virtue, we have been taught, is a habit that perfects a human power. In other words, by repeatedly choosing what is right, our fundamental capacity for free choice begins to create a second nature, as it were, a settled disposition to act well in certain circumstances. Just as a musician by repeatedly practicing a set of notes becomes capable of playing something he could not before, so the ethical actor extends his initial, free capacities by repeated acts of choosing the good. Notice that this habituation to right action is not the creation of a mechanical response to choices offered, which has nothing truly to do with the ethical will strictly speaking. It is one of the duties of the ethical will to develop such habits. There are passages in Kant's works that acknowledge such second-order duties, and Kant's own life in its legendary regularity shows his living out such virtues himself. It is unfortunate that Kantianism and all modern ethical theories that neglect the empowering dimension of good habits have in the process taken away the normal path to ethical rectitude and virtuosity as well. Few are the persons in any generation who have the naked will power to confront all ethical challenges without long periods of habituation in virtue, whether that occurs by design or implicit practice. A mere intention to be free is not sufficient to secure a free life.

But there is a third level of freedom in our tradition that goes beyond even the bare freedom of choice and the virtuous life. If freedom of choice is the most basic condition of all human freedom and virtue is the perfection of several dimensions of our moral life, these are both only means to an end, what has sometimes been called terminal freedom. Maritain argues that it is only at this level of disciplined freedom that we can invoke the ancient notion of a free person as autonomous, in the true sense of this much abused term. Clearly, autonomy of this kind is almost at the polar opposite of what is often meant by autonomy in contemporary debates. The proper use of autonomy refers to something that is an interior conquest or self-mastery; the debased use of the term virtually telescopes it back into the bare notion of human persons as possessing a capacity to choose and then exalting the right to choose as exercised by all persons like so many gods, with no restriction but that of not disturbing the freedom of their neighbors.

But this way of conceiving personal liberty quickly shows severe limitations in the social sphere. As Maritain explains:

> Concerned mainly with abstract man, this political philosophy fails to recognize all the hard and severe constraints which weigh on the real man: actually, a few may enjoy the freedom so conceived only through the oppression of all the others. The social primacy of justice and the common good are eclipsed. And the inevitable tragedy of free will taken as an end in itself unfolds: the absolute right of each party to realize his choices tends of itself to the complete anarchical dissolution of the whole, and makes any realization of freedom, any work of autonomy, impossible in the order of, and by means of, the common life.[16]

Since this state of things is intolerable, it gives rise to a remedy diametrically opposed to it that exalts collective life and all but submerges the individual in social projects.

A better resolution exists in the old notion of society as personalist and communitarian. It is difficult for many people in the developed world to understand this vision of common life in pursuit of the common good, precisely because liberal conceptions of the individual have led us to overlook the numerous ways in which the person is from his earliest days always bound to a community for nurturing, protection, and education. In a similar fashion, we find it difficult to conceive of a common good that respects what is individual because we have inherited concepts of collective bodies that mirror materialistic images: a whole is merely an aggregate of subordinate parts. But persons and the communities they create cannot be properly understood in this perspective. A person is always more than himself, so to speak, even at a natural level. No one teaches himself to speak, for example, and our entry into the human community of speech, meaning, and purpose proceeds by way of

---

[16] Jacques Maritain, *Some Reflections on Culture and Liberty* (Chicago: University of Chicago Press, 1933), p. 16.

inter-personal relationships, since all persons are interpersonal without becoming solely products of the collective. Maritain and others, responding to the crises of liberalism and collectivism, asserted these truths three-quarters of a century ago. They still await a proper reception into our common ways of speech and thought.

Terminal freedom, however, rises even higher than these social considerations, crucial as they are to human existence, to a properly spiritual level. Being made as we are, we have a natural appetite for the divine, and where that proper appetite is frustrated by some inner or outer obstacle, we tend to make ourselves or some lesser thing into gods. That was the sin in the Garden of Eden, and it continues in some subtle and not-so-subtle forms today. It is no accident that Nietzsche, who rejected every notion of God, was led to proclaim the advent of the Superman. In various combinations and permutations—among them the new Soviet Man, the Nazi Teutonic master race, the radically autonomous individual in liberal Western democracies—these lesser gods are descendants of this same need to divinize ourselves in the absence of God. Perhaps when these substitutes fail, as they must (sometimes in spectacular evils), we can begin to see more clearly how the way to the divinization of man must be a certain holiness and wisdom under God that may lead to participation in the only true Divinity. Again, Maritain puts this splendidly:

> Finite and unhappy in his being, man can only escape his limits by adhering with his intelligence and love to a better object. God being at the summit of personality, and man also being a person in however precarious a way, the mystery of the conquest of freedom consists in the relation between these two persons.[17]

God and man are not competitors in this view, as if what has to be given up or accepted on man's part were somehow a diminishing of his autonomy. That has been the error of many in the past three centuries or so. Rather, it is the right and full appreciation of what autonomy would mean—perfect union with the Divine—that resolves what appears to be a conflict of wills by moving to a higher level where human freedom coincides with God's.

---

[17] Ibid., p. 24.

This is the truth that the world needs to hear so desperately today because it is the one and only truth that sets us free. This truth roots freedom in love, and in God's infinite love our limited being finds not competition or oppression but authentic liberation. The Gospel names this love, but human reason reflecting on its own capacities prepares love's reception and tells us why we long for it.

Francis Cardinal George, O.M.I.

Addendum

The following pages were omitted from the chapter **Maritain and Newman: Theology, Intellectual Freedom and Human Transcendence in University Education.** *They should be added to page 1 of the book after the title and before the section* ***Maritain*: Theology**

Jacques Maritain and John Henry Newman devoted significant attention to the subjects of university education and theology in the formation of the human person. Of Maritain, Gerald McCool maintains that his "influence on Catholic social thought and educational theory was as significant as his influence on Catholic speculative philosophy and theology."[1] Newman once famously remarked, "from first to last, education . . . has been my line."[2] Though an educational theorist, Newman never saw university teaching as independent of theology. In *The Idea of a University*, he maintains, "I have insisted on the important influence, which Theology in matter of fact does and must exercise over a great variety of sciences.... [I]t cannot be omitted without great prejudice to the teaching of the rest."[3] Newman may have agreed with Maritain's observation over fifty years ago about undergraduate theological formation: "It is a pity to see so many young people bewildered by highly developed and specialized, but chaotic, instruction about anything whatever in the field of particular sciences and miserably ignorant of everything that concerns God and the deepest realities in man and the world."[4]

Echoes of Maritain's concern expressed in 1962 can be heard in comments made in 1998 by Catholic theologian Thomas Rausch.

---

[1] Gerald A. McCool, S.J., *From Unity to Pluralism: The Internal Evolution of Thomism* (New York: Fordham University Press, 1989), p. 114.

[2] John Henry Newman, *Autobiographical Writings* (New York: Sheed and Ward, 1957), p. 259.

[3] John Henry Newman, *The Idea of a University* (Oxford: Clarendon Press, 1976), p. 92 (cited hereafter as "*Idea*").

[4] Jacques Maritain, *The Education of Man* (New York: Doubleday, 1962), p. 55.

to the student's philosophical reach extends further into a certain appreciation of the metaphysical and the beautiful. The two aspects that emerge within this process – goodness and beauty – are not sequential stages. Students do not first encounter something as "good" and then move on to think about it as beautiful or vice-versa. Perceptions of goodness and beauty are moments whose conscious realization remains particular to the apprehending intellect. "All that is good," Newman maintains, "all that is true, all that is beautiful, all that is beneficent, be it great or small, be it perfect or fragmentary, natural as well as supernatural, moral as well as material, comes from him [God]."[15] As the liberally trained mind learns to see knowledge philosophically, the mind can then perceive a matrix of relationships as good and beautiful in their formal integrity.

For Newman, theology assists in the education of students' minds toward a type of contemplation. Minds so shaped by liberal learning overcome constraints of pragmatic and utilitarian views. The way knowledge is seen in university education actually purifies the philosophical habits of students to discern and appreciate a richness and beauty unrestricted to specific subject-matters of science. Theology as contemplation helps them see a relation to the divine source to which they refer. At the same time, theology as contemplation also helps to bring about an intellectual transformation. It is this 'simple knowledge,' knowledge as both power and object, that relates to and assists in the intellectual apprehension of deeper questions and issues of religious, spiritual significance. The type of transcendence that Newman holds as constitutive of and ordered by university teaching concerns viewing liberal knowledge and theology together as assisting the human mind's contemplation of knowledge as both a metaphysical and an aesthetic experience.

---

[15] Ibid., p. 68. This idea is not unique to Newman. See *Philippians* 4: 8-10.

The Human Person
and
a Culture of Freedom

Maritain and Newman: Theology, Intellectual Freedom and Human Transcendence in University Education

Brian Hughes

Maritain: Theology

Maritain maintains a classic, Thomistic understanding of theology. It is "knowledge in the state of science—a knowledge which is both rooted in revealed data and rationally developed, logically and systematically articulated."[1] "Rooted in faith," theology is also the "highest wisdom that man can acquire as adapted to the procedures of human reason."[2] Theology engages subjects that are universal because it is, as Thomas tells us, more speculative than practical.[3] Its speculative and logical features describe a scientific discipline carried out by a believing intellect. But theology is also something more. It is, as Maritain holds, "a *habitus* of wisdom rooted in faith."[4] For Maritain, *habitus* means an intellectual habit or a virtue, a way of thinking and seeing that can be taught and learned.

It is important to recognize that this last description is different from discrete specialty fields such as patristic pneumatology or medical bioethics or orthodox religious iconography. When Maritain comments on the genre, the classification of Christian theology, which falls within higher education, he does not divide it into what Edward Farley calls he "four-fold" paradigm of theological education: systematic or dogmatic theology, ethics, church history and scripture.[5] Rather, Maritain characterizes theology as a single whole with different aspects,

---

[1] Maritain, *The Education of Man*, eds. Donald and Idella Gallagher (South Bend, Indiana: University of Notre Dame Press, 1976), p. 78 (cited hereafter as "EM").

[2] Jacques Maritain, *Education at the Crossroads* (New Haven and London: Yale University Press, 1943), p. 82 (cited hereafter as "*EC*").

[3] *EM*, p. 78; *EC*, p. 78.

[4] Jacques Maritain, *Science and Wisdom*, translated by Bernard Wall (London: Geofrey Bles, 1940), p. 113.

[5] Edward Farley, *Theologia: The Fragmentation and Unity of Theological Education* (Philadelphia: Fortress Press, 1983), chapter 4 ff.

speculative and practical being the most evident. Theology as a *habitus* develops with the assistance of grace, but builds upon the innate potencies or natural capacities of human intelligence—here, that of the undergraduate student.

Theology does play a crucial role, for Maritain, in undergraduate education. He maintains, for example, that theology is a "keystone of the edifice of learning in a Christian college."[6] But what does this mean? In part, it means that theology will not be taught as a practical or a professional field of specialization, as something akin to ministerial training. Maritain states, quite ahead of his time, that the teaching of theology be given in a quite different way from that appropriate to religious seminaries and be adapted to the intellectual needs of laymen; its aim should not be to form a priest, a minister, or a rabbi, but to enlighten students of secular matters about the great doctrines and perspectives of theological wisdom. Such teaching would not be concerned with the detailed apparatus of historical authorities, but it would rather lay stress on the intrinsic rational consistency of doctrines and the basic insights on which they depend. It would be free from any preoccupation with merely technical questions or dead quarrels and closely connected with the problems of contemporary science and culture. Studies in comparative religion would be included in it.[7]

Indeed, in terms of theological methodology, Maritain seems to describe an incipient correlational method, dialectically relating doctrines of faith to aspects of human culture. Yet, this is not an exclusively professional or graduate level undertaking. One can practice theological reflection and enter into theological discourse on the basis of "common sense and natural intelligence, sharpened by the infused virtue of faith . . . to understand . . . theology intelligently taught."[8] This description needs to be read carefully. It is not a description of theology as catechesis, if by that term one means religious instruction. Maritain acknowledges the importance of this in

---

[6] *EM*, p. 139.

[7] *EM*, p. 80.

[8] *EM*, p. 139.

spiritual and especially moral life, but it is not what he means by the teaching of theology here.[9] There is a formative role for theology. It is one that is distinct and proper to a liberal arts education. A key purpose of theology—as a formative habit of wisdom concerned with relating the divine to the human—is its contribution to intellectual freedom.

Intellectual Freedom

An integral aspect of a liberal arts education is the relationship between theology and intellectual freedom. To draw out the connection between theology and intellectual freedom, let us first examine Maritain's understanding of "freedom." In describing the difference between his view of freedom and that of philosophers such as Kant, Maritain prefaces his treatment by noting "the freedom of independence and of exultation . . . the freedom of expansion of the human person."[10] This freedom of independence and exultation is not free will or a freedom of choosing between this or that. Freedom as free choice is real and presupposed by Maritain. Yet free choice and the entire realm of human action primarily belongs to the rational appetite, a significant but secondary focus of university instruction.[11] University education primarily involves human intelligence. The freedom Maritain considers here denotes a deeper, more mysterious aspect of the human being as intellectual. It is about the natural aspirations of spirit that pertain to the infinite striving of human intelligence towards being, towards reality and knowledge. He writes:

> The chief aspirations of a person are aspirations to freedom. . . . I mean that freedom which is spontaneity, expansion, or autonomy, and which we have to gain through constant effort and struggle. And what is the more profound and essential form of such a desire? It is the desire for inner and spiritual freedom. In this sense Greek philosophy, especially Aristotle, spoke of the

---

[9] *EC*, p. 75.

[10] *EM*, p. 159.

[11] *EM*, p. 159f.

independence which is granted to men by intellect and wisdom as the perfection of the human being.[12]

The process of liberal education and the *habitus* of theology are precisely ordered to the freeing of the human personality as distinct from one's individuality or material "ego." Maritain holds that "the prime goal of education is the conquest of internal and spiritual freedom to be achieved by the individual person, or, in other words, his liberation through knowledge and wisdom, good will, and love."[13] It is what Newman expresses another way as "the enlargement of mind." This is different from the drive of the ego, our individuality, which Maritain describes as "a narrowness... forever threatened and forever eager to *grasp for itself*."[14] True human personality, the "self," moves outwards, so to speak, while individuality or the ego draws everything inwards.

Maritain characterizes the drive or dynamism of the human mind when it engages in thinking as "a vital energy of spiritual intuition grasping things in their intelligible consistency and universal values."[15] Such vital energy is naturally spontaneous in that it moves of its own accord toward understanding of not simply discrete subjects, but also of what they are, of how they are, and of why things are by virtue of judging according to the evidence. This is growth in personhood. This principle, this movement of vital energy, applies across the spectrum of the humanities which includes, for Maritain, not simply the traditional "liberal arts," (philosophy, theology, history) but also the mechanical and the "hard sciences," such as technology, physics, chemistry, and so on.[16] All of these sciences and disciplines can be known and penetrated for their value as revealing degrees and levels of real things external to the mind. Maritain elaborates:

---

[12] *EC*, p. 10-11.

[13] *EC*, p. 11.

[14] Jacques Maritain, *The Person and the Common Good*, translated by John J. Fitzgerald (Notre Dame, Indiana: University of Notre Dame Press, 1985), p. 37 (cited hereafter as "*PCG*").

[15] *EM*, p. 47.

[16] *EM*, p. 69.

> The freeing of the intuitive power is achieved in the soul through the object grasped, the intelligible grasping toward which this power naturally tends. The germ of insight starts within a preconscious intellectual cloud, arising from experience, imagination, and a kind of spiritual feeling, but it is from the outset a tending toward an object to be grasped. And to the extent that this tendency is set free and the intellect becomes accustomed to grasping, seeing, expressing the objects toward which it tends, to that very extent its intuitive power is liberated and strengthened.[17]

The student, however, must possess the proper dispositions in order to free the personality by its contact with such fields and disciplines. Maritain articulates several: a love of truth, a love of goodness and justice, a simplicity and openness concerning existence, "the sense of a job well done" as the outcome of deliberation and responsibility, and finally, a disposition for social and political life.[18] Proper teaching can cultivate dispositions that enhance personal freedom. Although there is no single way to achieve this, Maritain clearly spells out what this type of teaching is not.

Two major threats confront the development of intellectual freedom in a liberal arts education. The first threat is something common, especially to Americans and those in the teaching profession. It is to view one's occupation and its associated tasks as the "supreme end."[19] For Maritain, this is simply a reversal of what the genuine human attitude and disposition should be towards interests, activities, and especially towards the subjects of study. Knowledge approached from a pragmatic or utilitarian view turns realities and our knowledge of them into quantifiable products for consumption. As such, history or philosophy or sociology is not taught and learned as something good to know in and of itself, as something that can occasion spontaneous discrimination and connections of meaning in young intellects. Rather, such discrete subject matters and branches of knowledge are

---

[17] *EC*, p. 44.

[18] *EC*, pp. 36-8.

[19] *EM*, p. 101.

approached as means to an end: a grade, a diploma, a particular honor, a job. Such an attitude turns subject matters into commodities and actually impedes the personality's liberation. For Maritain, what results from this utilitarian commoditization of knowledge is not education but a technical conditioning. This kind of formation is the assertion of the individual's power, the ego. Students are not taught to really think but are expected to absorb the results and procedures of a science at high, concentrated levels. There is, consequently, no understanding or movement towards integration with other disciplines, with other forms of knowledge. There is little space for a radical receptivity and openness to truth in this view of knowledge and learning. It is precisely such receptivity and openness that Maritain holds as essential. He writes that:

> the spiritual activities of the human being are intentional activities; they tend by nature toward an object, an objective aim, which will measure and rule them, not materially and by means of bondage, but spiritually and by means of liberty, for the object of knowledge or of love is internalized by the activity itself of the intelligence and the will, and becomes within them the very fire of their perfect spontaneity. Truth—which does not depend on us but on what is—truth is not a set of ready-made formulas to be passively recorded, so as to have the mind closed and enclosed by them. Truth is an infinite realm—as infinite as being—whose wholeness transcends infinitely our powers of perception, and each fragment of which must be grasped through vital and purified internal activity.[20]

There must exist, in other words, a radically purified intellectual wonder, a freshness, within those studying that does not prearrange results or fit the "truth" to serve lesser motives. The pragmatic commoditization of knowledge and its influence over the learning process erodes the transcendental movement of the mind toward intellectual freedom and truth.

[20] *EC*, p. 11-12.

The other threat to intellectual freedom related to the "absolute primacy of work" is "the disregard for the human value of leisure."[21] There is little integration in university pedagogy between the "useful activity" of work and the opportunities it affords for "the joy, expansion, and delight of the spirit."[22] Here, Maritain identifies not simply a correlate to a bad education but also a feature of American culture. It is interesting to note that Maritain's claims in the late 1950s find support in the research of Boston College sociologist Juliet Schor. In 1991, Schor found that:

> [Work] hours have risen across a wide spectrum of Americans and in all income categories—low, middle, and high. The increase is common to a variety of family patterns—people with and without children, those who are married, and those who are not. And it has been general across industries and, most probably, occupations.

Since the 1960's, men and women work an extra month more per year with less leisure than ever before.[23] This is what undergraduates will face upon graduation: greater pressures to earn a living, to maintain relationships and, save for the few, reduced opportunities for leisurely activities. Even when given such time, people today find true and genuine leisure harder to enjoy.

Ironically, though Maritain would agree with Schor's impressive study concerning the lack of time for leisure, he would argue that Schor's study lacks a coherent definition of "leisure," preferring instead to call it a "residual," meaning time distinct from "total working hours."[24] Maritain would find this vague and indeterminate reference to "leisure" as unpaid free time an impoverished view. He links leisure explicitly to university instruction and liberal education. "Only that leisure," he writes, "is suitable to what is most human in

---

[21] Jacques Maritain, *Reflections on America* (New York: Charles Scribner's Sons, 1958), p. 156 (cited hereafter as "*RA*").

[22] *EC*, p. 89.

[23] Juliet Schor, *The Overworked American: The Unexpected Decline of Leisure* (New York: Basic Books, 1991), p. 29.

[24] Schor, p. 13.

man, and is of greater worth than work itself, which consists of an expansion of our inner activities in enjoying the fruits of knowledge and beauty. Liberal education enables man to do so."[25]

Here Maritain offers a much more specific and rich understanding that gets to the heart of the liberal arts enterprise and, in so doing, makes explicit what in Newman is implicit. Maritain remarks:

> The question will be to have leisure time occupied in a manner really profitable to man, and not entirely taken up by the sort of stupefying passivity that is more often than not developed by movies or television. As long as a new cast of mind does not develop, involving a certain amount of spiritual Epicureanism, the quality of leisure in the modern world will not be on a level with the quality of work.[26]

Maritain is referring to that special delight or joy of human intelligence in extending its range and its power towards what is true, beautiful, and unified in an exercise not pragmatic or egotistical. This type of activity is a kind of rest. As Josef Pieper reminds us, "The Greek word for leisure (σκολη) is the origin of the Latin *scola*, German *Schule*, English *school*."[27] Enlargement of mind and leisure enjoy a long relationship. Indeed, Maritain maintains that "higher forms of leisure are no longer leisure but act come to completion. And the highest form is contemplative activity. *Be still and know that I am God.*"[28]

Human Transcendence

At the higher levels of reasoning and understanding, human intelligence and personal freedom reach out towards being for its own sake. This is because, as Maritain states, "knowledge is contemplative in nature, and that education, in its final and highest achievements, tends

---

[25] *EC*, p. 90.

[26] Maritain, *RA*, p. 157.

[27] Josef Pieper, *Leisure, the Basis of Culture* (South Bend, Indiana: St. Augustine's Press, 1998; 1948 reprint), pp. 3-4.

[28] *RA*, p. 158.

to develop the contemplative capacity of the human mind."[29] When theology assists the minds of undergraduates to grasp the known for its own sake, a form of human transcendence connected to wisdom occurs. Maritain puts this beautifully:

> [K]nowledge is a value in itself and an end in itself; and truth consists in the conformity of the mind with reality—with what is or exists independently of the mind. The intellect tends to grasp and conquer being. Its aim and its joy are essentially disinterested. And "perfect" or "grown-up" knowledge ("science" in the broad Aristotelian sense) reaches certainties which are valid in their pure objectivity—whatever the bents and interests of the individual or collective man may be—and are unshakably established through the intuition of first principles and logical necessity of the deductive or inductive process. Thus, that superior kind of knowledge which is wisdom, because it deals not only with mastering natural phenomena but with penetrating the primary and most universal raisons d'être and with enjoying, as a final fruition, the spiritual delight of truth and the sapidity of being, fulfills the supreme aspiration of the intellectual nature and its thirst for liberation.[30]

There is enjoyment, a delight in learning. Given the right dispositions of students, intellectual transcendence can occur when the mind engages the most important, broadest realities. Such an experience lifts up and liberates.

Newman and Maritain both presuppose a Christian theological anthropology about the drive of the intellect. The natural drive of human intelligence is towards being as true, good, united and beautiful. To know for the sake of knowing, for the sake of sheer enjoying, transforms the student's intelligence toward the realities of knowledge, the objects of study, their relationships, their drifts of meaning. Maritain specifically has in mind the influence of those disciplines that directly entail the human person in all its dimensions, perspectives, and ideals—the humanities. Maritain states:

---

[29] *EM*, p. 54.

[30] *EM*, p. 47.

> Such things [the humanities] bring to us, in one way or another, the impact of the transcendentals, and oblige us to think really, or at the level of universality.... Knowledge of these things [humanities] helps man to advance toward liberty, fosters in him civilized life, and is by nature in tune with the mind's natural aspiration toward wisdom.[31]

Universal human experiences and emotions and ideas like joy, pain, pleasure, happiness, despair, love, justice, equality, beauty, and goodness are more naturally present and evident within the humanities. The process of studying the human person through the humanities ignites this enlargement of mind. This intellectual experience is an advance towards knowledge that "penetrates and embraces things with the deepest, most universal, and most united insights."[32] To put this differently, one could say that when the intellect "delights" or takes "joy" in an object of knowledge, it is a moment of real transcendence. In part, this occurs because, according to Thomistic teaching, a lower wisdom aspires to a higher wisdom. The natural drive of the human intellect is from the particular, the specific, and the lesser to what is more abstract, more general, and of greater value.

This principle does not simply apply to bodies of knowledge. Consider, for example, what Maritain frames in terms of the relationship between metaphysics and theological knowledge:

> The more metaphysics knows being the more it wants to see the cause of being, and in expectancy to pass beyond language and logic, and even in the discursive order to keep to the summits of its spiritual domain (of which it knows the gods are envious), of definitive data and absolutely certain landmarks, points of crystallization in the intellectual order which are more incontestable and more suggestive than those furnished by the senses in physical science. Theology will supply them.[33]

---

[31] *EM*, p. 84.

[32] *EC*, p. 48.

[33] Maritain, *Science and Wisdom*, pp. 24-25.

If theological knowledge represents human inquiry into Christian revelation and the ability to relate the created human order to what is divine, and if human intelligence is not impeded in confronting theological insights, claims, doctrines, and so forth, then a real dynamic movement of wonder and desire is awakened. A mind hungry and awakened to the majesty, the goodness, the truth, and the beauty of the real, if properly formed, will desire to move beyond that knowledge, that domain of the known, to something higher.

Conclusion

In conclusion, Maritain expands Newman's more narrow view of natural theology as suitable for undergraduate instruction to something more inclusive of Christian doctrine and its relation to other aspects of culture. He also develops a more sophisticated view of enlargement of mind as the intellectual liberation of the human personality. Moreover, Maritain makes explicit Newman's implicit view of theology as assisting the mind toward a kind of contemplation. For Maritain, the integration of theology with other subject matters becomes a dynamic way of focusing the undergraduate's mind upon the transcendentals of truth, goodness, beauty, and unity, energizing mental powers to be lifted up in their desire for theological and religious meaning.

What I have just described captures something of the 'end' of knowing in a religious and metaphysical sense. Newman and Maritain also offer key insights for how to attain this through the teaching of theology in the university. The development of what Newman calls the "imperial intellect" really concerns more the power of intelligence—its skills, its analytic and synthetic abilities—that a theological *habitus* makes possible. It is, I think, theologically presumptuous to rule out a priori the assistance of grace for any seriously open student. The development of such a *habitus* should not be another kind of pragmatic work suited for ministry or for unleisurely activity, as something catechetical or commoditized as raw data or "historical information." Cultivation of such habits should be a deeper entry into the metaphysical and religious density of human experience. What such a general theological *habitus* can do, in relating the principles of theology to the expanse of human knowledge and culture, is give way to an attentiveness that becomes intellectual prayer in joyfully reaching out towards created being as true, as an integrated whole, and as something eminently desirable to know for its own sake.

In a culture that does not value leisure highly, this is not an insignificant challenge. Intellectual instruction should, in some sense, move the person to find a joy that is transcendental. Such an approach sees the objects of knowledge and human capacities as oriented beyond the useful toward goodness, beauty, unity, and truth. In the end, both Newman and Maritain would have agreed with Simone Weil, who writes:

> The intelligence can only be led by desire. For there to be desire, there must be pleasure and joy in the work. The intelligence only grows and bears fruit in joy. The joy of learning is as indispensable in study as breathing is in running. Where it is lacking there are no real students, but only poor caricatures of apprentices who, at the end of their apprenticeship, will not even have a trade. It is the part played by joy in our studies that makes of them a preparation for spiritual life, for desire directed toward God is the only power capable of raising the soul. Or rather, it is God alone who comes down and possesses the soul, but desire alone draws God down. He only comes to those who ask him to come; and he cannot refuse to come to those who implore him long, often, and ardently.[34]

---

[34] Simone Weil, *Waiting for God*, translated by Emma Craufurd (New York: Harper Collins, 2001; reprint 1951), p. 61.

Causal Entailment, Sufficient Reason, and Freedom

Steven Long

It is well known how highly the Church regards human reason, for it falls to reason to demonstrate with certainty the existence of God, personal and one; to prove beyond doubt from divine signs the very foundations of the Christian faith; to express properly the law which the Creator has imprinted in the hearts of men; and finally to attain to some notion, indeed a very fruitful notion, of mysteries. But reason can perform these functions safely and well only when properly trained, that is, when imbued with that sound philosophy which has long been, as it were, a patrimony handed down by earlier Christian ages, and which moreover possesses an authority of an even higher order, since the Teaching Authority of the Church, in the light of divine revelation itself, has weighed its fundamental tenets, which have been elaborated and defined little by little by men of great genius. For this philosophy, acknowledged and accepted by the Church, safeguards the genuine validity of human knowledge, the unshakable metaphysical principles of sufficient reason, causality, and finality, and finally the mind's ability to attain certain and unchangeable truth.[1]

Introduction

My proximate object here is to address the famed view of Elizabeth Anscombe in her lecture "Causality and Determination"[2] to the effect that it is intelligible that all the requisites may be present for causation to occur (that, in the language commonly deployed, the "sufficient conditions" for causing be present) while nonetheless no causing occurs—even in the absence of all deprivation, impediment, or defect. This proposition, I wish to argue, is frankly unintelligible. However, I would like to take rather a leisurely course to this object because the metaphysical stakes urged on us by means of this proposition—the proposition that everything needed for causing may be present and yet

[1] Pius XII, *Humani Generis*, #29.

[2] G.E.M. Anscombe,"Causality and Determination," in *Metaphysics and the Philosophy of Mind* (Minneapolis: University of Minnesota Press, 1981), pp. 133-147. (The essay was first published as *Causality and Determination: an inaugural lecture* (London: Cambridge University Press, 1971).

there be no causing—seem high indeed: so high that, were this position correct, far from buttressing or supporting an Aristotelian stance with respect to causality, it might rather be thought that the general dynamics both of the Aristotelian and the Thomistic arguments for the reality of God would be undercut at their fount.

Hence, I propose to do five things: first, to outline an argument against the Humean view that a thing could simply come into existence without any cause; second, to buttress this argument by expounding (in an abbreviated and preliminary way) an account of sufficient reason as an analogical principle; third, to point out that the view according to which all conditions may be sufficient for causation, and causation not occur, destroys the very notion of terrestrial causation, and is incompatible with an analogical principle of sufficient reason; fourthly, to explain how this conclusion is reconcilable with the theistic conviction that God—while infinitely sufficient to cause numberless worlds-is not under the least constraint of necessity to create any world whatsoever; fifth, and finally, I propose to complement the argument vindicating the compatibility of the divine liberty with the nature of causal entailment, with an exposition of St. Thomas's vindication of the compatibility of human liberty with the total dependence of finite being and operation on God.

I. The Humean Proposition That Something May Come from Nothing Without Being Caused

David Hume's famous thought experiment[3] is worthy of reflection because it points the way toward understanding the principle of sufficient reason whose rational warrant he was concerned to deny. One argument against the possibility of the state of affairs he hypothesizes is as follows: it is by the very nature of the case impossible to distinguish between a thing coming into being without having a cause, and a thing having a cause for its being of which we are simply ignorant. By the nature of the case, every negation presupposes a prior

[3] See David Hume, *An Inquiry Regarding Human Understanding*, "Why a Cause is Always Necessary," taken from David Hume's *The Treatise on Human Nature*, Bk. I, Part III, Section III, the first Appendix (New York: Macmillan, 1985), pp. 177-180.

affirmation. The negation—"this new being does not have a cause"—presupposes some positive knowledge that might provide rational warrant for it. By the nature of the case, the negative proposition, absent any positive evidence, is impossible to prove. It follows—since we could never distinguish there not being a cause from our merely suffering ignorance of the relevant cause—that we cannot have any real warrant for the claim that a new being (or even a new change with respect to a being) is without any cause.

But, it might be alleged that the pertinent claim for Hume's thought experiment is not that a new being (or a new change in a being) is definitely without cause, but only that it is *possible* for a new being, or a new change in a being, to be without cause. But *possible* here means either merely conceivable, or *really possible. Real* possibility depends upon positive real evidence and not merely upon conceivability. That a person may conceive "X" does not in itself show that "X" is really possible, that is, that it is a state of affairs which can obtain in the actually existing world. For example: I can conceive that I am in Las Vegas as I write these words, but in reality this is not possible *because I am here*, and it is repugnant to a substance to be in different places at the same instant. Conceivability may in certain special cases give us evidence of real possibility, especially where the nature of the possibility in question concerns thought. But in itself it seems insufficient to establish real possibility.

Someone might say: "I acknowledge that *in this world* not everything conceivable is possible, but is there not a *possible world* in which, at this time, you are in *Las Vegas*?" The counter-question here is, *possible* to whom? If the question is whether we can conceive it, the answer is "yes." If the question is whether its conceivability suffices to make it a real possibility, the answer might seem to be: if there is an infinite, omnipotent God Whose power is limited only by the principle of non-contradiction, then to such a God it *might* really be possible to create such a world. If there is no such God, then the idea that because one can think something it must be realizable in the world seems to be a ludicrous illustration of wish-fulfillment posing as thought.

But even on the theistic hypothesis, real possibility is defined in relation to the divine power. This is to say that that to which the divine omnipotence extends is "possible" insofar as God "could" cause it. But what is really possible thus must take into account the divine wisdom, goodness, and will—for strictly speaking, by reason of the divine simplicity, nothing is possible with respect to the divine power which does not conform to the divine wisdom, goodness, and will, which is to say: any conceivable things contrary to divine wisdom and goodness are only possible in a Pickwickian sense, since divine power cannot be separated from divine wisdom and goodness. God cannot, as it were, maliciously torture a cat: not because God is not omnipotent, but because divine power is subject to divine wisdom and goodness, and defect, error, and evil are simply outside the proper object of God's power (God does not cause defect, error, and evil; indeed, these have no *per se* cause whatsoever, although they are a function of the defectibility of the creature). Thus, if someone wishes to say that with respect to the divine power some things may be possible in precision from the divine goodness or wisdom, this odd way of speaking should still acknowledge that such conceivables are not, absolutely speaking, *really possible* because the omnipotent God *will under no circumstances cause them*. Indeed, God cannot do so, because evil is further removed from the proper object of the divine will than is sound to the proper object of sight. Of course, this does not mean that God must cause "the best of all possible worlds," since any finite world is still infinitely removed from the divine perfection, and could be improved indefinitely by degrees; i.e., there is no best of all possible worlds. In any case, the divine simplicity in itself renders the use of "possible worlds" logic to be ontologically ambiguous and dubious, and indeed significantly *indeterminate* (for natural knowledge about the divine will appears to be extremely limited and incomplete). Of course—need it be said?-someone who takes himself to have no reason to affirm an omnipotent God has no warrant whatsoever to project any conceivable whimsy into an ontologically *real* possibility, in the absence of real evidence that can sustain such a claim.

The argument above does not completely rule out the use of imaginative thought experiments, because while there is no guarantee of real possibility for every conception, some may prove to be warranted or at least helpful in some respect. However, this is just the point: if a thought experiment is such that it cannot under any circumstances find warrant in real evidence, then—in the absence of any reason to hold that mere conceivability equates with real possibility- the content of such a thought experiment is something that we cannot have a reason to hold. This appears to be the case with

Hume's experiment. Every negation presupposes a prior affirmation. But since we cannot distinguish between there not being a cause of a new being, or a new change in a being, and there being a cause that we don't know, it follows that in principle we cannot have real evidence for holding it to be really possible that something can come from nothing without a cause. By disjunctive syllogism, either we can have reason for holding change in being to occur without a cause, or we cannot. But the former is ruled out because it is intrinsically devoid of rational warrant: ergo, the latter remains.

But supposing that God revealed it were possible, what then? This is a self-contradictory idea because what we mean by God is the first cause of all finite things. Ergo for God to reveal that there is a being He did not cause would be for Him to reveal He isn't God: which is to say, whatever else may be the case, God cannot reveal such a thing.

But all-these reflections on Hume are really a circumlocutory way of referring, by negative argument, to what is positively, more directly, and more clearly disclosed by the principle of sufficient reason.

II. The (Analogical) Principle of Sufficient Reason

Of course, this principle in itself could easily be the subject of an essay. And in a sense that is what this entire essay is in fact about, for the denial of the "nomologicality" or "rule-governedness" of causality as it pertains to terrestrial causes, is a frontal assault at least on certain versions of the principle of sufficient reason. What is at issue, however, is the principle of sufficient reason in its Thomistic rather than in its Enlightenment formulations: a principle stating that every being or reality is intelligible either simply by virtue of itself or through another. For Aquinas, this principle was a function of his teaching of the convertibility of *being* and *true*—i.e., the true is being (real or possible) in relation to some intellect.[4] And the *ratio* or ground for the being—and accordingly for the intelligibility—of anything is hence either purely intrinsic or through another. Hence, the words of St. Thomas regarding God: "that which has no cause is first and immediate,

[4] Regarding this teaching of the convertibility of being and true see, for example, his *Disputed Questions on Truth*, I, 1, 2, ad 1.

wherefore it is necessary that it be through itself and by virtue of what it is."[5]

Hence that which is most fully has its reason for being through itself—is *a se* and in no causal dependence for its being, truth, and good upon any other being—whereas, that which is caused has its being through that which is other than itself (through the divine causality). For Thomas, this is an analogical conception insofar as there are different orders of causality—material, formal, efficient, and final—and also different types of being. All being is intelligible through itself, or through another. While beings in the latter category (comprising things that exist through another) are not devoid of intrinsic causal principles (for example, those which pertain to matter and form), these intrinsic principles nonetheless are *caused* by something other than the subject characterized by them.

Because this account of Thomas's is founded on the convertibility of being and true, its metaphysical provenance is clear. This Thomistic version of the principle of sufficient reason affirms that being is intelligible, that its *ratio* is to be found in different types of causes and different types of beings, and that in every case either a being is simply intelligible through itself (God) or else its intelligibility is through another (such that the other on which it depends causes it to have the intrinsic principles that it has). No matter what order of causality we delineate or what degree or type of being we specify, the principle of sufficient reason will proportionately apply because being is intelligible in terms of being (nonbeing, and even deprivation, are not absolutely speaking *reasons*), and by the nature of the case such reason can only be internal or external. While many consider the phrase "sufficient reason" exclusively in its Leibnitzian sense (Etienne Gilson even accused Garrigou-Lagrange of rationalism because he affirmed that an analogical version of this principle is in all but name taught by Aquinas[6]), the texts indicate that Thomas offers a teaching which can

---

[5] *Summa Contra Gentiles*, II, 15: "...quod causam non habet, primum et immediatum est; unde necesse est ut sit per se et secundum quod ipsum."

[6] For one clear reference to this, see *Letters of Etienne Gilson, With Commentary by Henri de Lubac*, translated by Mary Emily Hamilton (San Francisco: Ignatius Press, 1986), note #3, p. 28, where de Lubac quotes and cites Gilson's *L'Etre et*

properly be denominated a metaphysical principle of sufficient reason. This principle of sufficient reason, like all metaphysical principles for Thomas, is analogical in that it pertains to different beings and to different types of causes in ways that are different and yet proportionately identical (analogy of proper proportionality).

Of course, in speaking at all of being, one runs the risk of violating the Russellian and Fregean embargo on "being" talk. But the datum that being is not an essential predicate does not suffice to show that it is no type of first order predicate whatsoever. Further, there is clearly a difference between the negation of any negation whatsoever, and negation in a real subject. To illustrate the latter: if one says that some person "does not *not* have a nose," this is not really different from saying that the person in question *does have a nose*—i.e., its meaning is ontologically positive. Whereas, if one says "were there no universe, no rational creatures would negate anything," *the lack of a real subject* in this proposition does not require that we affirm anything real whatsoever—there is no ontological positivity. So clearly there is a real difference between being and not-being.

Whenever one of two distinguishable items is real, the distinction is real, and clearly no one can deny the difference between real being and merely logical being (this last being the sort of being which pertains to the subjunctive phrase "were there *no universe, no rational creatures would negate* anything"—clearly "no universe" and "not negating" do not affirm some positive reality, because, in the absence of a universe, there is no real subject). That wherever one of the items distinguished

---

L'Essence (Vrin, 1948) to this effect. Gilson claims that the rational character of an analogical principle of sufficient reason is not Thomas's, but Leibnitz's or Wolff's doctrine. In the meantime, the proposition of St. Thomas that only that which has no cause must be first and immediate, exist through itself, and be necessary, is lost by Gilson in accidental comparison with the rationalists. One must observe here a complete failure on the part of Gilson to see beyond terminology to the doctrine expressly articulated by Garrigou-Lagrange —as though the rationalists owned the phrase itself, or as if Thomas's insistence that only a being *a se* could be by reason of itself does not logically imply an account of sufficient reason for being, a doctrine of that by virtue of which a thing is.

is real, the distinction is real, is evident in the fact that we cannot affirm that the first (the real item) really is the second (the unreal item). Further, there clearly is a difference between a nature conceived and the same nature "instantiated," a term which often is simply a circumlocution to avoid saying the taboo word "exists." And if the same nature that is "instantiated" is not conceived, then it would seem to follow as a necessary conclusion that we cannot know it. But since all negations presuppose prior affirmations, we have good reason to *set aside* negative judgments which imply that nothing in the world is naturally knowable, for by the nature of the case nothing could provide evidence of the truth of such propositions. For these and other reasons, the Russellian/Fregean embargo seems an insupportable legacy of anti-metaphysical bias.

To return to our theme, however, while it may be true that we can never have any warrant for claiming that something can come from nothing, it might be wondered whether this is the same thing as having adequate metaphysical grounds for holding that all being is intelligible either through itself or by virtue of another. What is the positive basis for maintaining this? Here one must consider what it means to affirm that the real is intelligible. The intuitive force of the principle is its affirmation that *to be* is *to have a reason for being*. An argument has already been given above, in relation to Hume, for saying that the negation of sufficient reason—the proposition that there is a being which has no reason for being—is indistinguishable from an avowal of ignorance.

Another way of pointing to the intuitive character of the principle is to consider what it means to say that "being is intelligible through being." Among other things, this implies that *nothing* is not an explanation, and so for anything to be intelligible is for it to be explained by principles either intrinsic to it or extrinsic to it. If neither is held to obtain, then it is simply affirmed that the being is unintelligible, for these are the only options. But by the nature of the case there cannot be a warrant for the claim that being is unintelligible in this way (for the reason cited in relation to Hume: one cannot distinguish between there not being a reason, and there being a reason of which one is ignorant).

Perhaps more to the point: if these extrinsic and/or intrinsic principles explain the being, then it is not the case that they do *not* explain it. That is, not only must any new being or change in being be explained, but it is also the case that the very idea of causal explanation involves identifying a factor in virtue of which one thing brings about another. X is only said to be the cause of Y in virtue of some definitory causal attribute, and if this attribute is indeed defined in terms of causal action, then we cannot coherently suggest that (apart from defect or impediment) this attribute is consistent with the absence of causation. This need not be confined to efficient causality—the final cause, the formal cause, and the material cause likewise account for proper aspects of the being they explain. Sufficient reason is an analogical principle extending to all the causes. But for some terrestrial cause to be such as to be fully adequate to account for an effect is–in the absence of any defect or impeding cause—for the cause actually *to cause*. This is to affirm that the primitive meaning of causality is bound up with the doctrine of sufficient reason.

The intelligence discerns that real changes in being require real causes, and further that that by reason of which a cause is the cause it is, is that by reason of which it is said to cause. So that when it is present, the cause causes, and when it is absent, the cause does not cause. It clearly is not intelligible to say that the causality of X with respect to Y is explained by Z, but that when Z is present and there are no defects or impediments, that Y may or may not occur. For this would then appear to be saying simply that Z may, or may not, be adequate to account for the causality of X with respect to Y. And at this point we will wish to find that *in virtue of which* Z sometimes explains X causing Y and sometimes doesn't, i.e., some mysterious factor which, in addition to Z, is needed for real causal adequacy.

We are here at a primary point where intelligence encounters the mystery of the real. Even those who are most suspicious of this principle at the theoretic level in fact conduct their affairs in the world entirely in accord with it. If one's car is not in the lot where one parked it, one does not suppose that it randomly fell into limbo but asks *where it went, how it got there, and why*—and, it may occur to one to ask as to its *material condition* as well.

If a truck hooks up to a car, and there is no impediment either intrinsic (faulty equipment) or extrinsic (some obstacle), and the truck starts to move, we rightly expect the car *to be moved*. If there is no impediment or defect along the way, we expect it to go where the driver directs it; likewise, we don't expect, upon its arrival, that it will be not a car, but a horse; nor do we anticipate that it will be a car made of broccoli rather than one made of metal. Likewise, if a cake is made with flour, baking powder, butter, eggs, sugar, salt, and vanilla, we do not anticipate that when it comes out of the oven that what it is made of (the second matter of the cake) will be leather; or that it will be, not a cake, but an automobile; or that (in the absence of defect in the oven or some impediment) it will not bake; or that it will begin to bake but never finish baking. To suggest that any or all of these might occur *in the absence of either deficiency or impediment* seems not to be intelligible.

Of course, if either the Russelian and Fregean, or the Kantian, or Wittgensteinian, or any of the multitude of other essentially anti-metaphysical protocols could be sustained, then we might have reason to abandon this principle. But these protocols rejecting the very idea of being as a real predicate appear unfounded. And so we are in a position to state the chief problem with the idea that terrestrial causality is not rule-governed in a way that flows directly from an analogical principle of sufficient reason.

III. The Problem with the Idea that Sufficient Conditions for Causing may Obtain without any Causing Occurring & in the absence of all defect or impediment

From the vantage of an analogical principle of sufficient reason—proportionately verified in every order of causation, and in every being—the problem with the denial of the *nomologicality* or *rule-governedness* of terrestrial causality is clear. *The problem with this idea (that all the required conditions for terrestrial causation may be present without any causing occurring) is that it implies that there is no causal distinction between nothing and something.* For being is intelligible in terms of being and not in terms of nothing, which is to say that non-being is only relatively speaking an explanation. We may say that the two cars collided on the foggy night because one *lacked* working headlights, and so the other *did not see it*, but the lack or nonbeing of working headlights in one car is only an explanation in relation to the reality of the two cars, the road they are traversing, and the real fog. Only in relation to being can deprivation in any sense explain.

The intelligibility in question may be intrinsic (formal or material) or extrinsic (final and efficient), but always when a being is not intelligible simply by virtue of itself, its being and its intelligibility must derive from another. For example: for a classical theist, clearly the form and matter of a physical thing are insufficient to account for its being, and indeed these principles of form and matter in the thing are themselves brought about in the divine causation of the being.

When we say that any new being or change in being must have a sufficient reason (something does not come from nothing), this implies that there is a principle by virtue of which these come to be. Now, in any terrestrial cause, to say that A causes C by means of B, is to state that when A is such that B obtains - absent any defect or impeding factor - that C is caused. For just as we may not affirm a new or changed being without a *ratio* of the being and the change, so to affirm such a *ratio* is to define it in relation to the being and change brought about. And so, if A causes C by means of B, and A is such that B obtains, then part of the reason why we say that C is caused is that *the causing of C is part of our definition of what it means to say that A is such that B obtains.*

The central and decisive point may be articulated either in strictly Thomistic terms or in more ordinary language. But the point remains. *In Thomistic language, a given quantum of act is associated with a given causal terminus because it is teleologically defined in relation to this causal terminus.* Just as we can't define the efficiency of shoveling snow without mentioning the moving of snow (even if the wind should blow the snow right back where it came from), so we can't define what it means to say that a new being or change in being requires a causal explanation (in whatever order of causation we are speaking, whether final, efficient, formal, or material) without making reference to that which makes us say that the causal principle obtains, which is to say its proper terminus or the respect in which it is a cause. *While this is true in every order of causality, there is a special relevance of this analysis to terrestrial efficient causality. For efficient causality presupposes a teleological ordering of efficient cause to proper effect, without which the efficiency cannot be defined.*

Hence, to say that a terrestrial efficiency is in play is to identify something already as its effect, such that we are not then at liberty to affirm the contrary - in the absence of defect or impediment - without contradicting the very affirmation of efficiency itself. Something is not an efficient cause of something else by *not* causing it, but by causing it. For instance, to say that I am shoveling snow is to identify already the effect of physically removing snow as the effect that my act achieves in the absence of defect or impediment. If we say that the efficiency is present, but the effect is not, we are simply denying that the *ratio* of a being is truly a *ratio* at all – we are implying that the being in question is efficiently unintelligible. I cannot intelligibly and literally be said to be shoveling snow if I am not removing snow. I may be trying to do so and being impeded by wind, by snow, by weakness in my limbs, or by snow-blindness, but if I am shoveling snow, then I am moving snow. That is what it means. Nor is this simply a logical point but rather a point regarding the very nature of every cause analogically speaking and which is particularly clear with respect to the nature of efficient causation (which obviously is, and is defined, in relation to its proper terminus).

Hence to deny the rule-governedness of causation is also to destroy the intelligibility of the claim that a thing is only a cause as *such a thing*, that is, in virtue of some principle *whereby* it causes – because we are saying that that in virtue of which a thing causes may be present while the thing *does not cause*. And to say that that in virtue of which a thing causes may be present while the thing does not cause is like saying that that in virtue of which fire is hot is *coldness*, or better, is a *mere capacity for heat*, as though this could explain *without a definite quantum of actual heat*, without a definite *ratio* of change, motion, and being. *If* one says that the operation of shoveling snow which moves the snow, and in virtue of which one affirms that snow removal is occurring, is present, *but one also says* that without defect or impediment no snow removal is occurring (even if the snow that is removed is blown back, it may still first be removed), *then* it is not clear that one is saying anything at all.

So that by virtue of which we identify sufficient reason in terrestrial things normally and naturally requires *entailment*. But note why efficiency (in particular) requires entailment: because efficiency is defined in relation to natural finality and so is not truly separable from it. This is in a sense analogically verified of all four causes, there is a "that for the sake of which" of matter, form, and efficiency, and the finality itself is only denominated as finality because it is actually related to these other causes in the way that it is.

So, terrestrial causality involves entailment for the same reason that change and new being require explanation, namely, that there must be *that in virtue of which* change and new being are intelligible, and if *that in virtue of which* change and new being are intelligible is present, then this naturally implies change and new being in the absence of defect or impediment. To say that A is such as to bring about B because of C does not permit us to waffle on whether C is the element whereby A brings about B. And it does not permit us to say that C sometimes does and sometimes does not enable A to bring about B, because that is to say either that the bringing about of B is without any *ratio*, or that C is not the *ratio* (which is a contradiction) or is only *part* of the *ratio* (if it were the whole, then B would be caused). And the reason for this is that we rightly and necessarily *define* the cause in relation to its proper terminus or effect.

Clearly, then, an efficient cause is defined by what it is ordered to bring about (teleology in the strict sense), and the other causes too are defined by the proper termini of their causing (a broad sense of the *teloi* of causes as such or that in respect to which they function as causes: for example, the end is defined as cause in respect of being that for the sake of which a thing is or acts; the agent or efficient cause is defined as cause in respect of being productive of motion or change; matter is defined as cause in respect of a thing's potential for substantial form, individuation, and change. . .).

But this affirmation that an analogical principle of sufficient reason requires us to affirm that a terrestrial cause - in the absence of defect or impediment - *entails* its effect, leads to a problem. The problem is this: does not the analogical principle of sufficient reason, thus articulated, require us to say that when the cause is present the effect must follow? But, *if* this is what the principle articulates, *then* it appears that it must be inconsistent with classical theism: because classical theism affirms that God is eternally existent and yet that God *does not need* to cause any world whatsoever, not even the least finite existent. Does this not then overturn the principle of sufficient reason? The remainder of this essay will attempt to address why this need not keep us from affirming a strong analogical principle of sufficient reason.

IV. The Problem of the Non-Necessity of Creation: The Divine Liberty

The true proposition that the cause, God, is eternally posited, while the effect (the world) is in no way necessitated inasmuch as God *does not need to create*, might appear to contradict the principle of sufficient reason. Doubtless there are variants of this principle other than the

Thomistic version which are contradicted by the lack of any real relation of God to finite effects and by the absolute freedom of God with respect to creation. But the Thomistic variant of this principle, which is essentially analogous, need not fear this counter-example.

The reason for the immunity of the analogous principle of sufficient reason from this difficulty is as follows: terrestrial causes *entail* their effects *because they are teleologically defined in relation thereto. In other words, terrestrial causes are naturally ordered to ends, and their action is defined by these ends.*

Hence, the question arises: what is the "natural end" of God? Insofar as God is being *a se*, perfect and unlimited, and in no way dependent upon any other being for any perfection whatsoever — just insofar as this is true — it appears that the *natural end* of God is the delectation of the divine being, goodness, and truth, and this end is infinitely fulfilled within God Himself. And so, by contrast with terrestrial causes— which entail their effects because these causes are teleologically defined in relation thereto as in relation to their natural ends— *God's action is only teleologically defined in relation to God Himself.* The only necessary entailment here is that God know and love Himself. Also, this means that creation is, in relation to God's natural end of knowing and loving Himself, utterly *ad extra* (with the advent of creation, there are more beings, but not more perfection of being: what changes is that there is a creature and not that the perfection of God is in any fashion altered or enhanced).

All this is to say that creation is utterly gratuitous in a way that is impossible for any instance of natural causality. For creation in no way augments, advances, or is necessary in the least for God to achieve the end of knowing and loving Himself. Whereas terrestrial causes entail effects owing to their definitive teleological relation to that which they cause, God has no such definitive teleological relation to the effect of the world, for the creation of the world will in no way aid God in attaining God's natural end, which is the infinite embrace of the divine perfection. Hence, creation of any world is an act for which there is no proper parallel in the natural world. For not only does creation (unlike natural causing) not presuppose some natural substrate in which it introduces a change (for creation is the *bringing about* of that which can be changed, not the mere introduction of change); but, even more importantly for our present purposes, creation *is not in any way* an act needed by God in order for God to achieve the divine natural end, for God already possesses the divine good perfectly. *Creation is utterly gratuitous, an act which while consistent with and conformable to the divine good, is so through the ordering of other, radically gratuitous beings toward the divine felicity.* What is teleologically ordered through creation is not God to Himself, but the creation to God – a creation, to say it again, which God simply does not need.

Hence, only in the case of God – in whom the sufficient condition is always to be found for any possible universe – is it true that when the sufficient condition truly is present that causality may not occur. The reason for the universal extension of this principle to finite being is the convertibility of being and true. Every causality represents a certain influx or surplus of *act*. For there to be such an influx or surplus of act is for causality to occur. For there not to be such where it is due, is for there to be impediment or defect. If causality is metaphysically intelligible in terms of the *quanta* of act – as Thomas clearly holds – then for the right quantum of act to occur is for causing to occur. The "sufficient condition" is neither more nor less than the quantum of actuality required, normally defined in terms of essential limits – that when C is present in A, A will, absent defect or impediment, cause B.

Created means are not necessary for God to attain the end of knowing and loving Himself; further, they do not even augment or aid Him to do this in the least. God's efficient causality of finite things, while it is conformed to His wisdom, is absolutely free. Finite things are ordered to God, but God does not need this order, and hence there is no necessity in God's willing creation. By contrast, creaturely causality is defined in relation to natural ends. Thus, for all creatures there is a certain generic necessity with respect to the ordering of means toward the end. Whereas, since God necessarily knows and loves Himself, there is a necessity with respect to the natural end, but no need of motion toward it (it is already infinitely possessed) and no need for means outside of God as requisite for attaining it.

Given the right *quantum* of act, causal motion toward the end on the part of a finite cause will occur because the end is *that for the sake of which* the motion, the quantum of act involved in its causation, and the substance actually causing the motion, exist. Further, and perhaps more importantly, *the motion, the substance actually causing the motion, and the quantum of act involved in causation, are all defined by their ordering to the end*. And as has been noted above, analogically speaking, this is verified of all the causes, which are defined by their proper termini. For this definition to obtain, it must be the case that where the cause is, there is actual ordering toward the natural terminus, which is to say, it must be the case that there is actual causing (absent defect or impediment). This natural ordering is, curiously enough, also the reason why Thomas affirms that there is remorse in Hell: because although the natural motion to the end is weakened by vice and evil, it cannot be utterly removed, and so even the souls in Hell are defined by their *motio* (however weakened, permanently frustrated, and deprived of its proper completion in perfect act) toward God.[7] This is to say that even the efficiency of the wills of those in Hell is defined in relation to their natural and supernatural good.

There is much more to be said regarding this idea that all the conditions for a finite thing to perform a causal act can be present with no internal defect or external impediment, and that consequently there still may fail to be any causing. But in essence this idea seems to involve a contradiction in terms: because for all the conditions to obtain means (for terrestrial causes) for that quantum of actuality that defines causality to be present. Nor is this merely an analytic point about the definition of the term; rather, it is a point about the nature of the reality so defined. For it makes no sense to say that everything necessary for burning to occur occurs, and that no burning happens (unless we refer to defect or impediment); indeed, this would be to misunderstand what "necessary" means, or alternately, it would imply that we are simply wrong about what is necessary for burning to occur.

This same point – that causality is associated metaphysically with a definite quantum of act or perfection – explains the classical view that *there is more in cause than in effect*. For, even when the cause is of like species with the effect (as for instance father, as partial cause, to son), the added actuality or perfection of causing pertains to the one but not to the other, and so in this relation the one with the added perfection of actuality is greater (this added actuality or perfection of *causing* can

---

[7] See *Summa theologiae* I.85.2.ad 3.

only accrue because something pertains to the cause as cause that does not pertain to the effect).

In relation to this entire argument and to the conclusions derived, some might wish to object that the discoveries of quantum physics deprive these of any general effect. For if those interpreters of quantum physics are correct who claim that determinate causality does not obtain with respect to quantum changes, then what has been said about an analogical principle of sufficient reason would seem to be inconsistent with the empirical evidence. But here the conclusions drawn from the encounter with the Humean thought experiment become relevant. First, it must be repeated that there is no way in principle to determine – even with respect to the Heisenberg Uncertainty Principle – that this does not pertain chiefly to our current capacity to measure subatomic events as opposed to reflecting the very nature of these events themselves (and even were our capacity to measure permanently impeded owing to natural limits, this would not necessarily imply the absence of real determination, any more than my incapacity to know what was in my brother's mind today indicates that today he was mindless). The mere absence of knowledge in itself never equates with an argument for the lack of sufficient reason (although, again, this is an analogical principle which is verified proportionately in differing causal orders). Second, even where we know that it is more or less permanently impossible – at least for the duration of this life – to discover the determinate characteristics of some event, we are not necessarily unreasonable in holding there to be such determinate characteristics. For example, one may not fully know what passed through the mind of one's beloved father during his last agonies. But clearly, he may have had thoughts, some of which he did not communicate to anyone. And such thoughts, undiscoverable though they now be, are reasonable to posit. Likewise, one may surmise that Napoleon did not communicate every single thought he ever had, even in the absence of any capacity for proof. Thirdly, one ought not be timid about insisting that causal reasoning in physics be intelligible, and where it is not, but involves a variety of murky or even contradictory ideas, this should be taken to expose deficiencies of present theory rather than a *lacuna* of intelligibility in the real itself. A pure delight in the whimsical aspects of *Gedanken* experiments, as helpful as this may be within hypothetico-deductive physics, must yield to the requisites of intelligible theory.

Of course, it is a clear metaphysical inference from all these considerations that it can't be the case that God gives us a causal nudge that might or might not eventuate in action: for this is to conceive of God as a creature. While how this may be true and reconcilable with created terrestrial liberty is a question requiring a larger canvas, nonetheless we may summarily identify three salient points reconciling divine liberty with an intellectualist, rather than libertarian, conception of freedom. To this summary purpose the final consideration below is directed, holding in mind the degree to which St. Thomas's teaching on these points is *terra incognita* for so much of modernity and postmodernity.

V. Divine Causality and Human Liberty

It is *infra dig* for many contemporary philosophers to imagine a serious metaphysical issue being solved by anyone, much less being solved by a Saint from the 13th Century. Nonetheless, Thomas did solve this problem, and he solved it moreover in the only manner in which it is susceptible of being solved without either treating God merely as a finite cause, on the one hand, or denying the rational liberty of man, on the other.

Thomas' position is well articulated in three discrete points. The first is clearly the salient along which the entire issue must be considered. To introduce this consideration, one begins with the issue Molina so well identified when he unwittingly unleashed the firestorm *De auxiliis* controversy: within a libertarian conception of freedom, *the will is free only when, all requirements being retained, the will can indeed act otherwise.*[8] Yet, this conception is clearly incompatible with divine omnipotence and with the affirmation that all being and operation depend upon God as First Cause. Especially is it incompatible with the proposition defended by St. Thomas that in each thing that operates, God is the cause of its operating (cf. the *Summa contra gentiles*.IIIa.67). It is ruled out by the divine simplicity alone – because the only difference between God simply willing "x" and God not simply willing "x" is not any change in God – for God has no real relation to or dependence upon creatures, but indeed the reverse is the case. Rather, the only

---

[8] Cf. Molina's *Concordia*, q. 14, a. 13, disp. II.

difference between the hypothetical and immutable divine simple willing of "x" and not-willing of "x" is that insofar as God wills "x", then *x exists.* It follows that if the divine will is considered a "requirement" or "condition," then it is impossible that when all requirements or conditions are retained that the thing be otherwise. For this will be a contradiction in terms: the contradiction of God actually bringing "x" about and – at the same time and in precisely the same respect – not bringing it about.

The root problem here is the insistence upon defining human liberty *in relation to God.* For the simple divine will is being treated as a "requirement" or "condition" where all such requirements and conditions are retained and the human will can do otherwise – do otherwise *even on the supposition that God by His simple will wills the contrary. On this decisive point of whether liberty should be distinguished in relation to God, St. Thomas is very clear: the answer is a resounding "no." And this "no" is the first of the salient points that define the issue and contribute decisively to its solution.* As St. Thomas argues:

> And in regard to knowledge this is clear from what was said above (in the Reply to 14): for just as divine knowledge is in relation to future contingent events, so our eye is in relation to contingent things that occur here and now, as was said (in the Response); hence just as we most certainly see Socrates sitting while he is sitting, but nonetheless it does not follow from this that his sitting is absolutely necessary, so also from the fact that God sees in themselves all the things that take place, the contingency of things is not done away with. And as regards the will we must take into account that the divine will is universally the cause of being and universally of all the things that follow on this, hence even of necessity and contingency; but His will itself is above the order of the necessary or contingent just as it is above all created being. And therefore necessity and contingency in things are distinguished not in relation to the divine will, which is a universal cause, but in relation to created causes which the divine will has ordered proportionately to the effects,

namely, in such a way that the causes of necessary effects are unchangeable, and of contingent effects changeable.[9]

Consider the concluding words of the quotation above: "Necessity and contingency in things are distinguished not in relation to the divine will, which is a universal cause, but in relation to created causes which the divine will has ordered proportionately to the effects, namely, in such a way that the cause of necessary effects are unchangeable, and of contingent effects changeable." As is clear in this quotation from *De malo* and elsewhere, Thomas teaches that God is the cause of universal being and that necessity and contingency are modes of being. Hence, the divine causality not only embraces all that is and that operates, but even embraces the *manner* in which it is and operates. If it were otherwise, necessary causes would be denominated as contingent because dependent upon God; and contingent causes, because actually caused by God, would be denominated as necessary. But necessity and contingency are determined "in relation to created causes" such that the cause of necessary effects are unchangeable, and of contingent effects, changeable.

That is, necessity and contingency are determined in relation *not* to the First Cause, but to the *proximate cause.* Contingent causes are contingent because they do not metronomically always bring about

---

[9] Leonine ed., *De malo*.16.7.ad15: "Et hoc quidem quantum ad scientiam patet ex his que supra dicta sunt: sic enim se habet diuina scientia ad futura contingentia sicut se habet oculus noster ad contingentia aue in presenti sunt, ut dictum est; unde sicut certissime uidemus Sortem sedere dumsedet, nec tamen proper hoc sit simpliciter necessarium, ita etiam ex hoc quod Deus uidet omnia que eueniunt in se ipsis, non tollitur contingentia rerum. Ex parte autem uoluntatis considerandum est quod uoluntas diuina est uniuersaliter causa entis et uniuersaliter omnium que consequntur <ipsum>, unde et necessitatis et contingentie; ipsa autem est supra ordinem necessarii et contingentis sicut est supra totum esse creatum. Et ideo necessitas et contingentia in rebus distinguitur non per habitudinem ad uoluntatem diuinam que est causa communis, set per comparationem ad causas creatas, quas proportionaliter diuina uoluntas ad effectus ordinauit, ut scilicet necessariorum effectuum sint cause intransmutabiles, contingentium autem transmutabiles."

merely one thing, or even one limited type of things. Whereas some causes are contingent by way of defect – as an engine is defective when sometimes it starts when the ignition is turned on and there is gas in the tank, and sometimes it doesn't – the human will is a contingent cause not by way of defect but by reason of the nobler mode of rational being *vis a vis* merely physical things. (Although, the noblest will of all would be immutably committed to and harbored in Perfect Good, it is indeed a natural limitation of our willing that its freedom renders acts that should be immutably sustained yet to be susceptible in this life of divagation: indeed, this is a reason why man stands in need of grace so as to be immutably sustained in good, as St. Thomas argues in *Summa contra gentiles*.3b.155, titled "*Quod homo indiget auxilio gratiae ad perseverandum in bono.*")

This leads us to the second point essential to the affirmation of human freedom within divine causality: namely, that the human will is said to be free because its proper object is one consequent upon intellect, namely the good in general, universal good. Unlike causes whose contingency is partial and is a function of defect or breakdown, the contingency of the human will derives from the nobility of the intellective form whereby it is specified. Because of this, the will enjoys a commanding indifference with respect to any finite good, for the finite good *is not* universal, and so *cannot* simply determine or necessitate the will.

As Thomas teaches (*Quaestiones quodlibet* 6, q. 2, a. 2), the motion of the will is an inclination following intellective form – "*motus voluntatis est inclinatio sequens formam intellectam*" – it is desire following and specified by reason. But no finite good is so good that it is universally good – every finite good is in some respect lacking, even though that finite good be here and now what is best for one. It may here and now be best for me that I cease writing and rest, but I can find the notion of rest, howsoever good for me, inferior to writing. Or, the converse may be true: it may be best for me here and now to write, but I may find the good of writing inferior to the good of rest. No finite good is so universally good as to command the will: even at the moment of choice in which one embraces some good, the intellect presents the good chosen as a *limited* good, and so as in some respect not-good, inferior to universal good.[10] Hence the will enjoys a dominating indifference to the object of choice *even at the moment of choice*, inasmuch as clearly no such object of choice is such as to be able to command the will.

It follows that freedom of the will is rooted in the nobility of intellective form, whereby no finite good can command the will, leaving the will free. Were the will ever to embrace good that is genuinely and perfectly universal good – the subsistent universal good Who is God – then the will would not be free to turn away, because it would have reached perfect repose and complete actuation in the Good. The end, whether natural or supernatural, is not among the things of which the human will is master. To the contrary, the will is ordered toward the Good, and while man may fall short of this ordering, he cannot replace it with another but merely falls into futility.

This leads to the third point. Although the will is free with respect to all finite goods because it is ordered to them under the *ratio* of its proper object, which is the good in general or universal good, nonetheless, the will is the second rather than the First Cause of its own acts. Here the famed words of St. Thomas from *De malo* q. 3, a. 2 ad 4 are clear: "When anything moves itself, this does not exclude its being moved by another, from which it has even this that it moves itself. Thus, it is not repugnant to liberty that God is the cause of the free act of the will."[11]

---

[10] For this teaching of St. Thomas that the rational will is not subjected to or of necessity moved by finite goods because the power of the will exceeds the individual good inasmuch as its capacity regards the universal and perfect good, see *Sth*.I.82.2.ad 2.

[11] "Similiter cum aliquid mouet se ipsum, non excluditur quin ab alio moueatur a quo habet hoc ipsum quo se ipsum mouet. Et sic non repugnat libertati quod Deus est causa actus liberi arbitrii." The antecedent text of this response to the fourth objection is also very much to the purpose: "Ad quartum dicendum quod cum dicitur aliquid mourere se ipsum, ponitur idem esse mouens et motum; cum autem dicitur quod aliquid mouetur ab altero, ponitur aliud esse mouens et aliud motum. Manifestum est autem quod cum aliquid mouet alterum, non ex hoc ipso quod est mouens ponitur quod est primum mouens: unde non excluditur quin ab altero moueatur et ab altero habeat hoc ipsum quod mouet." -- "To the forth it should be said that when it

Thus the will receives from God a motion whereby it freely determines itself to act ("being moved by another, from which it has even this that it moves itself"). "Free" here is not distinguished in relation to God, because no liberty of indifference to divine causality can exist within a created universe. Yet, this is not a mythical freedom – the will is not constrained by any terrestrial object of choice. Nor is it forced by God, since the very act of freedom is precisely what is caused by God: free self-determination is a natural effect of divine causality. Only the author of the natural motion of a thing may, without violence, apply this natural motion to act. The divine motion is not a violent motion contrary to the nature of that which is moved. Hence, the following words of St. Thomas:

> Free will is the cause of its own movement, because by his free-will man moves himself to act. But it does not of necessity belong to liberty that what is free should be the first cause of itself, as neither for one thing to be cause of another need it be the first cause. God, therefore, is the first cause, Who moves causes both natural and voluntary. And just as by moving natural causes He does not prevent their acts being natural, so by moving voluntary causes He does not deprive their actions of being voluntary, but rather is He the cause of this very thing in them, for He operates in each thing according to its own nature.[12]

---

is said that something moves itself, that the same thing is mover and moved. But when it is said that something is moved by another, the moved is taken to be one thing and the mover another. But it is clear that when something moves another, from this it is not taken to follow that it is the first mover: wherefore it is not excluded that from another it is itself moved and from this other it has even this, that it moves." Thence the lines follow that "when something moves itself, this does not exclude that it is moved by another from which it has even this, that it moves itself. And thus it is not repugnant to liberty that God is the cause of the free act of the will."

[12] *Sth*.I.83.1.ad 3: "Dicendum quod liberum arbitrium est causa sui motus; quia homo per liberum arbitrium seipsum movet ad agendum. Non tamen hoc est de necessitate libertatis, quod sit prima causa sui id quod liberum est; sicut nec ad hoc quod aliquid sit causa alterius, requiritur quod sit prima causa eius. Deus igitur est prima causa movens et naturales causas et voluntarias. Et sicut naturalibus causis, movendo eas, non aufert quin actus earum sint

It is of the nature of the free will that it freely determines itself, and this requires that it receive that motion which is given by God whereby it freely determines itself. For nothing can move itself absolutely from potency to act unless it first be moved to act, and the human will is no exception to this maxim. While the vindication of the ontological universality of act and potency as intelligible principles of being exceeds the scope of this treatment, it is without doubt the case that St. Thomas did not consider the human will an exception to this distinction. (Furthermore, denial of the universality of these principles will in short order lead to Parmenidean implications such as the impossibility of change: for in every order potency needs to be distinguished from act, and if there is no genuine potency but only lowest common denominator acts, then change appears impossible – for then nothing is such that it has the potency or power to be otherwise.) This teaching obviously places the activation of the power of the free will within the divine causality, retaining the freedom of the will precisely owing to the nature of the proximate cause and its relation to finite objects while affirming the objective universality of divine providence.

But does this not mean that the will moves of necessity? After all, when God moves me freely to determine myself to choose to eat French fries, I will do so. But how can I be free if I do not have the power to do otherwise?

Two points are pertinent here. The first point is that the fact that I will act in a certain manner if I am freely moved to do so, does not make the action other than free. Freedom is distinguished by the nature of proximate causes in relation to their objects, not by a mythical liberty of indeterminacy with respect to divine causality that erroneously confuses the universal causality of God with the finite causality of a creature. That an act will necessarily occur (necessity of consequence) does not mean that it will occur by means of necessity (necessity of consequent); to the contrary, the act may occur freely. This is manifest with respect to past action: it is necessary with the

naturales; ita movendo causas voluntarias, non aufert quin actiones earum sint voluntariae, sed potius hoc in eis facit; operatur enim in unoquoque secundum eius proprietatem."

necessity of consequence that I chose to swim yesterday (for this actually was my choice); but it is not necessary with consequent necessity, which is to say by means of necessity, because my choice was free.

The human will is not a mere sensible power ordered to a limited set of objects, inasmuch as its proper object is the universal good. Hence rational creatures are moved by God to their ends in an essentially higher fashion than are non-rational creatures. Nor will it be sufficient to say that even animals, because they are not mere mechanisms, are not subject to a prefixed operative power determined to one. For non-rational animals, while possessed of some spontaneity and exceeding merely mechanical limits, nonetheless are constrained within sensibly delineated boundaries of attraction and repugnance. There is simply no credible evidence that non-rational animals possess a capacity for conceptual as opposed to merely sensible abstraction. Hence they are limited to the sensible order, and as such they lack dominating indifference to sensible attractions and repulsions.

Secondly, even at the very moment when I am freely moved to do "X," I retain the power to do otherwise. But, it may be said, I do not have the power to do otherwise when God freely moves me to do something unless I can actually resist the divine will. Further, did not even the Council of Trent say that the will does not receive grace like something lifeless, and that the will can resist grace? To respond, one should proceed one step at a time. First, power and act are distinct. When it is said that I can act differently than I am freely moved to act by God, what does this mean? It cannot mean that I can simultaneously and in the same respect both act and not-act. Freedom cannot mean liberty from the law of non-contradiction. Hence, by virtue of the possession of rational will, at the very moment that one is freely moved to do "X" one's will nonetheless retains a dominating indifference to "X" inasmuch as the intellect presents "X" to the will as a finite good. Further, the will as a rational power always retains this indifference, even at the moment of choice.

Yet, when I am freely moved to act, I cannot at the same time and in the same respect freely be not-acting. So, in the divided sense - the sense in which one can sit while retaining the power to stand - one "can do other" than one is moved to do. But in the composite sense - the sense in which one clearly cannot sit and stand simultaneously -

one cannot do otherwise, inasmuch as one does not possess the power to act and not-act at the same time.

But what of the teaching of Trent? It helps to know whereof one speaks. To cite the fourth of the canons on justification from the Council of Trent:

> If anyone shall say that man's free will moved and aroused by God does not co-operate by assenting to God who rouses and calls, whereby it disposes and prepares itself to obtain the grace of justification, and that it cannot dissent, if it wishes, but that like someone inanimate it does nothing at all and is merely in a passive state: let him be anathema.[13]

One notes of this teaching, first of all, that it affirms that the free will is "moved" by God whose call is that whereby the will "disposes and prepares itself to obtain the grace of justification." So this is prima facie incompatible with any view which denies that God moves the will, unless it be said that the definition applies to nothing because predicated on a condition putatively contrary to fact, which is a ludicrous reading of a *de fide* pronouncement.

Further, Trent condemns the view that man's will "moved and aroused by God" does not co-operate "by assenting to God." But indeed, on St. Thomas's teaching, the very effect of the divine motion in the natural order, and of God's simple will to bestow grace in the supernatural order, is that the will operate with God: literally that it co-operate. Indeed, the canon of Trent is very clear: it is of the will moved and roused by God that we speak; it is such a will that actually and spontaneously co-operates. But of course: this is how co-operation occurs! It is a gift of God, suavely and without violence actuating the

---

[13] Henry Denzinger's *Enchiridion Symbolorum, The Sources of Catholic Dogma*, translated by Roy J. Deferrari (Fitzwilliam, New Hampshire: Loreto Publications, 1955), canon 4 of the Canons on Justification, p. 258, #814. (hereinafter cited as *Denzinger).*

freedom of the will. The authors of Trent, preponderantly sympathetic to St. Thomas's teaching, hardly wished to anathematize his doctrine.[14]

Further, the canon condemns the view that the will moved by God cannot dissent if it wishes. But this, of course, is perfectly consistent with the "can" of the divided sense; i.e., the will retains the power to dissent, but insofar as it is being moved and roused and insofar as it is cooperating with God, it certainly is not not being moved, roused, and cooperating and certainly is not actually dissenting. Thus the phrase "if it wishes." Moreover, the canon makes clear just what sort of denial of the free creature's power of dissent is sufficient to invoke the anathema of the canon, namely, any type that says that the free creature receives grace "like someone inanimate" that "does nothing at all" and is "in a merely passive state." But the will, on St. Thomas's account, is not inanimate, nor does it under the divine motion do nothing at all. Rather, it freely acts nor is it moved violently but according to its nature (God moves natural causes naturally and voluntary causes voluntarily) so the created will certainly is not "in a merely passive state." Indeed, the whole point of Thomas's doctrine is well articulated in Bañez's terminology of *praemotionis physicae* or physical premotion. "Physical" because real; "pre" because prior by nature – although not prior in time, since insofar as God communicates the divine motion the will freely determines itself; "motion" because a transition from

[14] Indeed, those inclined quickly to reject this teaching should reflect that while the Church does indeed grant liberty to its sons and daughters to expound this matter in different ways, it has indeed, in the words of Benedict the XIV, found that "The Thomists are proclaimed destroyers of human liberty and as followers, not to say of Jansenism but even of Calvinism; but, since they meet the charges with eminent satisfaction, and since their opinion has never been condemned by the Holy See, the Thomists carry on with impunity in this matter...". Of course, he likewise points out that "the followers of Molina and Suarez" can "continue" in defense of their teaching while noting that "the Roman Pontiffs thus far have not passed judgment on this system of Molina." So this pontiff (and this is of course *after* the controversy *de auxillis*) holds that the Thomist position has been adjudicated as meeting the charges with eminent satisfaction and so not condemned by the Holy See, whereas the Molinist position is literally unadjudicated. Cf. *Denzinger,* note #3, pp. 314-315, under text number 1090.

potency to act. Indeed, it is a contradiction in terms for the will to be willing and not to be willing at the same time. Insofar as God moves the will to its own free act of willing, it makes no sense to say that the will is not freely willing.

It is clear that in a very specific sense the will is "passive" in receiving grace: it is not the origin of grace, nor does it cause by itself what grace causes in it. But this is far from the "passivity" of inanimate being that is anathematized at Trent; indeed, there are potencies of living things and of spiritual things. Moreover, those at Trent knew well the Thomistic account, and if they had wished to deny the central teaching of Thomas that act and potency divide being, then they could have done so. That the *Summa theologiae* was instead an inspiration of their work, and is said to have been placed open at the altar near the Bible, is well-known.[15]

On St. Thomas's account, what is imparted to the will is that whereby it freely determines itself to act, so that insofar as the divine motion is received, the will freely determines itself through this motion. It is a capital error to conceive this motion like a violent and extrinsic motion, for it is precisely the perfection of the natural motion of the will in its further application to act that is caused by God. That is to say, what this motion bestows is that which is natural to the actuation of the will. Hence, St. Thomas (*Sth*.I.9.6 resp.) argues that only that which causes a thing's nature can cause a natural movement in it, and that God is the cause of the natural motion of the will to the universal good. And he further argues that:

---

[15] If this is a myth, its point becomes all the more perspicuous as manifesting the degree to which regard for the teaching of St. Thomas may be understood to have permeated the deliberations of the eminences at Trent. This is a widely held account – as the old 1914 *Catholic Encyclopedia* puts it as part of its listing for Aquinas, "But the chief and special glory of Thomas, one which he has shared with none of the Catholic Doctors, is that the Fathers of Trent made it part of the order of the conclave to lay upon the altar, together with the code of Sacred Scripture and the decrees of the Supreme Pontiffs, the *Summa* of Thomas Aquinas, whence to seek counsel, reason, and inspiration. Greater influence than this no man could have."

> But it is clear that just as all corporeal movements are reduced to the motion of the body of the heavens as to the first corporeal mover, so all movements, both corporeal and spiritual, are reduced to the absolutely First Mover, Who is God. And hence no matter how perfect a corporeal or spiritual nature is supposed to be, it cannot proceed to its act unless it be moved by God. Now this motion is according to the plan of His providence, and not by a necessity of nature, as the motion of the body of the heavens. But not only is every motion from God as from the First Mover, but all formal perfection is from Him as from the First Act. Hence the action of the intellect, or of any created being whatsoever, depends upon God in two ways: first, inasmuch as it is from Him that it has the form whereby it acts; secondly, inasmuch as it is moved by Him to act.[16]

God does not simply by Himself cause the free act – as though the will were not a genuine secondary cause, and the act of willing were bestowed to it like a cauliflower made by divine power to grow preternaturally out of a man's head. To the contrary, the free act is the act of the will itself; it is its own act, and the effect of the will is its own free determination in willing this or that. The distinctions in terms of act and potency preserve St. Thomas's teaching from what might otherwise be construed as some species of quasi-occasionalism. Thus what God provides (apart from the *esse* of everything in this process!) is that motion whereby the human will freely determines itself in act so that the will freely acts – which is to say that the human will then as a

---

[16] *Sth.*I-II.109.resp.: "Manifestum est autem quod sicut motus omnes corporales reducuntur in motum caelestis corporis sicut in primum movens corporale; ita omnes motus tam corporales quam spirituales reducuntur in primum movens simpliciter, quod est Deus. Et ideo quantumcumque natura aliqua corporalis vel spiritualis ponatur perfecta, non potest in suum actum procedere nisi moveatur a Deo. Quae quidem motio est secundum suae providentiae rationem; non secundum necessitatem naturae, sicut motio corporis caelestis. Non solum autem a Deo est omnis motio sicut a primo movente, sed etiam ab ipso est omnis formalis perfectio sicut a primo actu. Sic igitur actio intellectus et cuiuscumque entis creati dependet a Deo inquantum ad duo: uno modo, inquantum ab ipso habet perfectionem sine formam per quam agit; alio modo, inquantum ab ipso movetur ad agendum."

proper secondary cause brings about its effect of willing. Thus, nothing could be more contrary to Thomas's teaching than the idea that the will receives either the divine motion in the natural order, or in the supernatural order (grace), like something lifeless or inanimate, purely passively. Because it is the very nature of the reception of the divine motion that *pari passu* with its reception, the will freely, inwardly, and spontaneously co-operates. God is not a mere finite created cause, but the first cause of the creature and of every perfection that pertains to the creature, while the creature is the genuine and valid secondary cause of its own actions.

Thus the will is not moved violently, like a stone being violently thrown, but rather in both the natural and supernatural orders receives from God that whereby it determines itself freely to act. And what is that? It is divine motion whether in the natural or in the supernatural order (where it is called grace).

Further, as chapter five of the Council of Trent (On the Necessity of Preparation for Justification of Adults, and Whence it Proceeds) makes clear, our free act is anticipated by the grace of God:

> It [the Synod] furthermore declares that in adults the beginning of that justification must be derived from the predisposing grace [can.3] of God through Jesus Christ, that is, from his vocation, whereby without any existing merits on their part they are called, so that they who by sin were turned away from God, through His stimulating and assisting grace are disposed to convert themselves to their own justification, by freely assenting to and cooperating with the same grace [can. 4 and 5], in such wise that, while God touches the heart of man through the illumination of the Holy Spirit, man himself receiving that inspiration does nothing at all inasmuch as he can indeed reject it, nor on the other hand can he [can. 3] of his own free will without the grace of God move himself to justice before Him. Hence, when it is said in the Sacred Writings: "turn ye to me, and I will turn to you" [Zach. 1:3], we are reminded of our liberty; when we reply: "convert us, O Lord, to thee, and we shall

be converted" [Lam. 5:21], we confess that we are anticipated by the grace of God.[17]

This teaching refers to grace objectively. That is, any particular created grace, treated as an object, may be resisted: say, the grace of going to Mass, which may be resisted by one who instead prefers to sleep. But this teaching that created grace as an object is not unresistible is certainly not instructing us that *the simple will of God* that one actively receive grace is resistible. For the simple will of God is of that which God actually and absolutely brings about in all its determinate singularity (and so it is distinguished from that which God might will as good only more generally and abstractly but not here and now). The only distinction between God simply willing something, and not simply willing something, is that insofar as God simply wills something *it occurs*. Trent clearly is not authoritatively holding that if the omnipotent God here and now actually wills to bring about "x" that this is compatible with "x" being frustrated. Trent's teaching does not promulgate the subtraction of freedom from the created order and from God's providential government of the created order; the will is not demiurgically independent of divine causality, creating *ex nihilo* its own acts and merits. Indeed, it is Trent (cf. Denzinger, #810, from Chapter 16 of the Decree on Justification) that formally refers to Our Lord "whose goodness towards all men is so great that He wishes the things which are His gifts to be their own merits."

So indeed, one may resist as an object any finite good, including created grace. But this is not to say that the omnipotent God cannot breathe life into one in the supernatural order; it is not to say that God cannot move and rouse the will to Good; and it is not to say that if God simply wills the creature's free act that the creature's free act can in the composite sense fail to occur, although at the very moment of its occurring the creature will retain the power whereby it is capable of acting differently (while yet within the divine motion it will not freely act differently; the will can resist "if it wishes" but insofar as it is freely being moved to operate it is not *not* being freely moved to operate: insofar as it is freely moved *it does not wish to resist*). The author of

---

[17] *Denzinger*, #797, p. 250.

created liberty perfects this liberty in giving it that whereby it freely determines itself to act.[18]

Conclusion

While this essay has covered a great deal of ground, it is but a preliminary reconnaissance of a vast domain of inquiry. Within this domain we find:

---

[18] Of course, an objector might also cite Canon 17 from the Council of Trent's *Canons on Justification*, rendered in Denzinger as: "If anyone shall say that the grace of justification is attained by those only who are predestined unto life, but that all others, who are called, are called indeed, but do not receive grace, as if they are by divine power predestined to evil: let him be anathema." But the careful reader will not fail to observe the essentially qualifying phrase "as if they are by divine power predestined to evil" – a phrase that targets *positive* reprobation or any putative *active divine ordering* to evil and perdition (for, of course, the power of God is active power: there is no potency in God). But this is as far from negative reprobation as is *doing* from *not doing*. Whereas negative reprobation involves the teaching that God may not in every case overcome with His grace defects which He is capable of overcoming, positive reprobation involves the claim that defect is a proper effect of God; the latter teaching is directly contrary to right reason and to Catholic faith, whereas the former seems required by the convertibility of being and good. And if this were not sufficient – as frankly, in historical context, one might think it should be – it may also be noted that the claim that all the baptized are *ipso facto* predestined to eternal life is contrary to the teachings of Trent in the immediately antecedent canons #15 and #16. The first (#15) anathematizes anyone who says "that a man who is born again and justified is bound by faith to believe that he is assuredly in the number of the predestined." The second anathematizes anyone who says that "he will for certain with an absolute and infallible certainty have that great gift of perseverance up to the end, unless he shall have learned this by a special revelation." In short, the point of this canon 17 of Trent is not to deny the divine predilection in grace, but, first, to deny that the grace of justification is bestowed only upon those who are predestined unto life – for one may fall from grace after baptism – and second, also to deny that divine power positively predestines to evil. Needless to say, neither of these points is involved in the Thomist account of grace, nor would they have been thought to be so involved by the Council Fathers, whose preponderantly Thomist tendencies are beyond historical cavil.

- the vindication of the principle of causality and of causal entailment over against Humean objection;
- the perception that St. Thomas does indeed articulate a non-rationalist and analogical principle of sufficient reason in declaring that only a being wholly *a se* and lacking any cause can be its own reason;
- the realization that to say all causal factors are activated and no causing occurs is – in the absence of defect, impediment, or miracle – unintelligible with respect to terrestrial causality;
- the insight that divine creation is utterly free, because only in the case of God's *ab extra* causing of something from nothing is there efficient causality wholly and definitorily extrinsic to the attainment and possession of the natural end by the agent efficient cause (for God does not attain the natural end of His infinite Good by causing me and indeed need not "do" anything to attain His Good, in which he reposes in perfect beatitude);
- the realizations that freedom is not defined and distinguished in relation to God, which would make a muddle of understanding contingency and necessity in finite things, but is defined and distinguished by relation to the proximate cause and its objects; that rational will enjoys sovereign indifference with respect to any finite reality (even, objectively speaking, to created grace); and the realization that the free act of the will must be fecundated by the divine motion in order that it have that whereby it moves itself to act, so that it is the secondary cause, and God the first cause, of its own free acts.

All of these considerations are testimonies, inadequately framed by the present author, to St. Thomas's profound theological and philosophic science and wisdom.[19]

---

[19] For a far more comprehensive treatment of the fifth and final section of this essay, and a full response to Jacques Maritain's widely shared novel dissent to the classically theocentric Thomistic formulation of the problem of evil, the interested reader might wish to examine my essay "*Providence, Liberte Et Loi Naturelle*" translated by Hyacinthe Defos du Rau, O.P., and Fr. Serge-Thomas Bonino, O.P., and published in *Revue thomiste*, Sommaire *du n° 3*, December of 2002, which considers all these issues on a broader canvas. But even in this marginal space, it behooves one to note that the position of Maritain, Journet, Most, and many others concerning the divine permission of evil exemplifies a critical fallacy whereby the negation of negation by a real subject is treated as something that is not positive. When authors say that "if the creature does not negate the divine gift, then...." one must immediately interpolate: negation of negation in a real subject is something positive, and everything positive is from God. Hence, such authors should say, "If God wills to uphold the creature in good, then...." These cautionary words are framed with the object of alerting English-speaking theologians and philosophers to the dangers of sentiment and linguistic illusion replacing theological *scientia* with a rhetoric pleasing but disutile.

A Free Culture:

Living the Primacy of the For-Itself

John Cuddeback

A culture might be called "free" in any of a number of senses of the term "free." One sense of the term, namely, "that which is for-itself," receives relatively little attention in the vast literature of freedom. This, it seems to me, is much to the impoverishment of this literature, as well as of contemporary discussions of freedom, even among thinkers working in the broad Thomistic tradition. Here I will suggest that this sense of freedom, at the heart of the Aristotelian and Thomistic understanding of freedom, gives us the critical measure of the freedom of a culture. Indeed, a culture is most truly called free if it is free in this sense: its structures bespeak the ordering of all things toward what is for-itself.

The plan for this paper is as follows. In the first section, I consider the notion of "*causa sui*" as at the heart of the notion of freedom. This allows us to look anew at the different senses of freedom and to conceptualize a "freedom of the for-itself." This freedom of the for-itself is most properly found in the contemplative life. In the second section, I argue that this understanding of freedom allows us to make judgments regarding what constitutes a "free culture." Here I suggest that the "status" of the contemplative life and of economics are two key litmus tests for the freedom of a culture. In the final section, I seek to dovetail my treatment with Pope John Paul II's notion of a culture of life, or death.

Freedom and the For-Itself

Aquinas seems to take as the main *ratio* of freedom what is *causa sui*, on account of itself. In numerous texts, Aquinas uses this phrase, taken from Aristotle's *Metaphysics,* to explain freedom.[1] Let us consider how it can be used to explain different senses of freedom.

---

[1] The *Metaphysics* text is 982b25ff. See, e.g., *Summa theologiae* I 83.1ad3 on free will (judgment), I 96.4 on servitude in the state of innocence, II-II 19.4 on

We are perhaps all familiar with Maritain's distinction between two basic kinds of freedom: freedom of choice and freedom of autonomy.[2] Freedom of choice implies an active indifference of the will toward particular goods, an indifference rooted in its natural determination to goodness as such.[3] This freedom has the *ratio* of freedom inasmuch as the will is said to move itself to action. It is not determined to this action by nature or by the object, but by its own judgment. Thus it acts "*causa sui*" – on account of itself.[4]

Freedom of autonomy is not a natural endowment of the person, but rather it must be achieved and, in its truest form, can be seen as the very goal of the moral life. This is the freedom of always acting from one's own desires. In explanation of this freedom in *Freedom in the Modern World*, Maritain quotes a key text from Book IV of the *Summa contra gentiles* where Aquinas explains how the Holy Spirit moves us toward God. Aquinas says:

> We must observe, however, that the sons of God are led by the Holy Ghost, not as though they were slaves, but as being free. For, since to be free is to be cause of one's own actions [*sit qui causa sui est*], we are said to do freely what we do of ourselves. Now this is what we do willingly: and what we do unwillingly, we do, not freely but under compulsion.[5]

Thus to act from "our own" will or desires is to be free. This is distinct from freedom of choice, for one can "freely" choose to do something that is against his own desires – as when one obeys a law

---

servile fear, and *Summa contra gentiles* IV.22, on how the Holy Spirit moves man.

[2] See the first chapter of *Freedom in the Modern World* (New York: Charles Scribner's Sons, 1936).

[3] On the natural determination of the will, see *Summa theologiae* I-II 10.1; on the indifference of a "super-determinate cause," see Yves Simon, *Philosophy of Democratic Government* (Notre Dame, 1993), p. 34.

[4] See *Summa theologiae* I 83.1ad3, where Aquinas says that the will is "causa sui motus."

[5] *Summa contra gentiles* IV.22. Maritain's translation from *Freedom in the Modern World*, p. 37.

simply out of fear of punishment. We see again the notion of *causa sui*: here the person acts *causa sui*, or as cause of his own actions not only in the sense of acting from his own judgment, but also in the sense of acting from desires which are "his own."[6]

Now there is another sense of freedom, mentioned by Maritain in *Freedom in the Modern World,* which receives significantly less attention than the aforementioned kinds of freedom. Maritain speaks of the adhesion of the intellect to the last end, and he calls this a "freedom of exultation."[7] I think that we can call this third freedom, the freedom of the for-itself. Here we see the aspect of *causa sui* in its highest expression. If to be free is to be *causa sui,* then we should distinguish between two orders of causality: final and efficient or agent causality. In the first two kinds of freedom, the focus is on agent causality. For instance, Aquinas says, "*liberum arbitrium* is *causa sui motus*, because through *liberum arbitrium* man moves himself to action."[8] But the term "free" is also applied to what is *causa sui* in the order of final causality. Indeed, the text in Aristotle's *Metaphysics* to which Aquinas often refers is the following: "...but as the man is free, we say, who exists for his own sake [*causa sui*] and not for another's, so we pursue [wisdom] as the only free science, for it alone exists for its own sake."[9] Thus, the phrase *causa sui* can mean "to be for one's own sake," as in either the case of the master or of the science of wisdom. To be *causa sui* in the order of final causality, the most noble of causes, is precisely to be "for oneself" as opposed to "for another."

In considering freedom, I think we too often focus exclusively on what is self-moved in the realm of agency. When Aristotle and Aquinas consider the nature of slavery, they focus not so much on the fact that

---

[6] Of course in freedom of choice too one always acts from a desire in some sense "one's own;" but in freedom of autonomy the desire is in some further sense "one's own" - where the agent can say, "I really am acting from my own desire, not something imposed by another."

[7] Maritain, p. 34.

[8] Summa theologiae I 83.1ad3.

[9] *Metaphysics* I.2 982b25-27. *The Basic Works of Aristotle,* ed. R. McKeon (New York: Random House, 1941). All subsequent translations of Aristotle are from McKeon.

the slave's actions do not spring from his own desires, as on the fact that he is not ruled for his own sake.[10] We might say that the good of the slave does not have that characteristic which Aristotle assigns to the ultimate or chief good: that it is "final." He says: "[W]e call that which is in itself worthy of pursuit more final than that which is worthy of pursuit for the sake of something else...."[11]

Now, having seen how the ratio of freedom, to be *causa sui*, applies differently to three senses of freedom, let us look more closely at the last two – the freedom of autonomy and the freedom of the for-itself. Grasping what is meant by each of these freedoms, we can ask what these freedoms look like in their highest forms. As regards the freedom of autonomy, we should return to the above quoted *Summa contra gentiles* text where we see that the truest sense of the freedom of autonomy is to act from one's own desires *when* one's own desires are in accord with what Aquinas calls the "natural order of the will." He explains that the Holy Spirit moves us as free persons precisely because He gives us a *love* of things in accord with the natural order of our own wills. Thus, as moved by the Holy Spirit, we always act from our own truest desires since we love what is truly good for us. In other words, our own personal desires correspond with our deepest (natural) desires as human persons.[12]

Now where can we find the highest freedom of the for-itself? We can connect this question to our understanding of freedom of autonomy by asking another question: What does a person who has the freedom of autonomy actually *do*? In other words, if we say that the end of freedom of choice is to come to a freedom of autonomy in which all of one's actions spring from one's own truest desires, then just what kind of action is most characteristic of the truly free person? While of course such a person performs many kinds of actions, Aquinas's answer

---

[10] See Aquinas on the slave in *Summa theologiae* I 96.4, and Aristotle's *Politics* I.6 1255b10, where he speaks of the slave as a "part" of the master.

[11] *Nicomachean Ethics*, I.7 1097a30-32.

[12] Thus, this freedom of autonomy is of course higher than a freedom of autonomy in which I always act from my own bad desires. These latter desires, Aquinas explains, are not most truly my own, from the viewpoint of "the natural order of the will."

to this question is clear. Freedom of autonomy is ultimately a freedom for contemplation. If with the true freedom of autonomy I act most truly from my own love, then the act that I most love to do because it is most for-itself is the act of contemplation.[13] Contemplation itself, or the contemplative life, then, has the freedom of the for-itself in its highest manifestation.[14]

Aquinas argues on numerous occasions that contemplation stands apart from all other human actions as the action most sought for its own sake.[15] But not only is contemplation most sought for its own sake, it is also the end of all other actions.[16] According to the "natural order of the will," to use again the phrase from the *Summa contra gentiles* text, what is not for its own sake is ordered to what is for its own sake. We might also say, then, that true freedom of autonomy implies acting according to a love that orders all things to contemplation.[17]

---

[13] Cf. *Veritatis Splendor*, #86: "Freedom then is rooted in the truth about man, and it is ultimately directed toward communion." We should note that the freedom of the for-itself and the freedom of autonomy are both present, in their truest forms, in the perfection of man. Maritain explains that the first refers to the essential attaining of the end by the intellect, and the second to the will in adhering to the end. Maritain, p. 34.

[14] Maritain has a beautiful treatment of contemplation at the end of *The Peasant of the Garonne.*

[15] See for instance, *Summa theologiae* I-II 3.5c and *Summa contra gentiles* III 37.

[16] See for instance *Summa contra gentiles* III.37: "Further, all other human operations seem to be ordered to this as to their end;" and In *NE* #2101: "This is contemplative happiness to which the whole of political life seems directed;" and *Summa theologiae* I-II 3.5ad2: "And if this good [contemplation of truth] be perfect, the whole man is perfected and made good thereby; such a good the practical intellect has not; but it directs man thereto;" and II-II 180.4c: "... because this contemplation is the end of the whole human life. Hence, Augustine says (De Trin. I.8) that 'the contemplation of God is promised us as being the goal of all our actions and the everlasting perfection of our joys.'"

[17] Those who live what Aquinas calls the "active life" immediately order their actions to "the requirements of the present life in accord with right reason;" (*Summa theologiae* II-II 179.2ad3) but these actions are more ultimately

It goes without saying that the distinction between freedom of choice, too often mistaken for an end in itself, and freedom of autonomy which is the *telos* of that freedom, is a key first principle in conceptualizing what a free culture should look like. But as the third sense of freedom is freedom in the highest sense of *causa sui* since it is free in the realm of final causality, it is central to conceptualizing a free culture.

A Free Culture

In his great work *Happiness and Contemplation,* Josef Pieper defends the Thomistic thesis that man's perfection and happiness consist essentially in an act of the speculative intellect: contemplation. Late in the book he addresses several objections, one of them being the "common sense" assertion that surely this view is undervaluing the genuine goodness of the practical or active life. Here Pieper uses a phrase that captures a principle of the first importance in Aquinas's worldview. The key to getting this matter straight, says Pieper, is "hierarchical thinking." He explains:

> The hierarchical point of view admits no doubt about difference in levels and their location; but it also never despises lower levels in the hierarchy. Thus the inherent dignity of practice (as opposed to *theoria*) is in no way denied. ... But practice does become meaningless the moment it sees itself as an end in itself. For this means converting what is by nature a servant into a master - with the inevitable result that it no longer serves any useful purpose.[18]

Let us take a moment to appreciate the role of hierarchical order, and thus of hierarchical thinking, in the thought of Aquinas. Few principles show up in Aquinas's work with the regularity of this principle: the end provides the *ratio* of what is *ad finem,* or for the sake

---

ordered to contemplation, as the active life itself is ordered to the contemplative life - see, e.g., II-II 181.1ad3.

[18] Pieper, *Happiness and Contemplation,* translated by Richard and Clara Winston (South Bend, Indiana: St. Augustine's Press, 1998), p. 95.

of the end.[19] Put otherwise, what is for the end receives its goodness (its dignity, importance, and meaning) from its relation to the end. Indeed, Aquinas speaks of final causality as exercised in a *per se* series of causality. In a *per se* series of causality, the very character of causing is precisely from this member's being caused by the prior member. Thus, as regards final causality, or having that desirability which is goodness, a thing's goodness is caused by what is prior in the series of final causality, and ultimately by what is first in that series.[20] When arguing that a person desires all that he desires on account of the ultimate end, Aquinas says: "Hence secondary desirable things move the appetite only as ordered to a primary desirable thing, which is the ultimate end."[21] He is not making here simply the psychological point that I find something desirable only to the extent that I desire it as ordered to my end. Also implied is that the real desirability of what is for the end comes from its relation to the end.[22]

The significance of this emphasis on hierarchical thinking in Aquinas is this: for Aquinas, to remove from its order to the end that which is naturally ordered to the end is to destroy the root of its goodness. As Pieper held above, to remove that which naturally serves some end and to treat it as a master is anything but to emancipate. It is to wreak havoc. Here we touch upon the key to understanding what I will call an "unfree culture," but let us consider first a few characteristics of a free culture.

A free culture is one in which, on the whole, the practical life is ordered to the contemplative life.[23] Many important aspects of such a

---

[19] See for instance, *Summa theologiae* I-II 1.prologue and 12.4, and II-II 44.2ad3 and ad4.

[20] See *Summa theologiae* I-II 1.4.

[21] *Summa theologiae* I-II 1.6. Translation from J. Oesterle, *Treatise on Happiness* (Notre Dame, 1983).

[22] Note that even the goodness of a created person is ultimately said in relation to the whole, of which he is a part, as an end to which he is ordered; although he is ordered to it, for his own sake, in the sense that he performs the principle action of the whole. See *Summa contra gentiles* III.112.

[23] See *Summa contra gentiles* III.37 where Aquinas says, "Ad hanc etiam omnes aliae humanae operationes ordinari videntur sicut ad finem." And "Ut sic, si

society will certainly escape our description here. For the sake of illustration, a brief reflection on two general characteristics will suffice: a) in this society the contemplative life itself has a certain status, and b) the social and economic structures of the society reflect the pre-eminence of the contemplative life. We begin with the status of the contemplative life.

In his commentary on the *Sentences*, Aquinas says the following: "It is requisite for the good of the human community that there should be persons who devote themselves to the life of contemplation."[24] Now why is this so? Surely society needs contemplatives to see the highest things and then to share with the rest of us what they see, things that otherwise we would never see. But there is more implied in this text. Contemplatives should have a place of pre-eminence in society; indeed, they should stand as a reminder to all the rest of us what the end of life is – the end of life in *this* life, as well as the next. It is not unreasonable to conclude that a critical test of the freedom of a culture or society is this: As a whole, how does this society look upon the activity of contemplation, and more specifically, upon those persons exclusively devoted to it? Is the contemplative life generally held to be the highest life? Indeed, is it held, at least in some general way, as something served by other ways of life? In the *Summa contra gentiles,* Aquinas makes an even stronger statement than the one above. He says: "[A]ll human occupations appear to serve those who contemplate the truth."[25]

This brings us to the second point mentioned above: that the social and economic structures reflect the primacy of the contemplative life.

---

recte considerentur, omnia humana officia servire videantur contemplantibus veritatem." In *The Peasant of the Garonne* (New York: Holt, Rinehart and Winston, 1968), p. 224, Maritain quotes from Pope Paul VI's discourse at the close of the Vatican Council: "[C]ontemplation is the most noble and the most perfect form of human activity, against which one measures, in the pyramid of human acts, the proper value of these acts, each according to its kind."

[24] 4d26, I, 2. Translation from Pieper, p. 96.

[25] *Summa contra gentiles* III.37. Translation from A. Pegis, *Introduction to St. Thomas Aquinas* (New York: The Modern Library, 1948).

Here I will restrict myself to a brief consideration of a representative issue – the status, as it were, of economics in society. In the great Western tradition, what today we call economics (the realm of wealth production and distribution) was fundamentally seen as a matter of providing for human needs in order that, and in such a way that, higher human goods could be pursued. Aristotle and Aquinas could not be clearer on this point. Allow me to quote at some length from Book III of Aristotle's *Politics*:

> Whence it may be inferred that virtue must be the care of a state which is truly so called, and not merely enjoys the name: for without this end the community becomes a mere alliance which differs only in place from alliances of which the members live apart; and law is only a convention, 'a surety to one another of justice,' as the sophist Lycophron says, and has no real power to make the citizens good and just.[26]
>
> It is clear then that a state is not a mere society, having a common place, established for the prevention of mutual crime and *for the sake of exchange*. These are *conditions* without which a state cannot exist; but all of them together do not constitute a state, which is a community of families and aggregations of families in well-being, *for the sake of* a *perfect and self-sufficing* life. ... The end of the state is the good life, and these are the means towards it. ...Our conclusion, then, is that political society exists for the sake of *noble actions*, and not of mere companionship.[27]

For Aristotle and Aquinas, economics ("wealth-getting" for them) is ordered *immediately* to providing for basic human needs and *ultimately* to the life of virtue and contemplation.[28] A key word here for Aristotle and Aquinas is "needs." The basic needs of the community need to be met in order that higher goods can be pursued.

Both Aristotle and Aquinas express serious concern about the form of wealth-getting that is not limited by human needs and has as its end

---

[26] III.9 1280b6-10.

[27] 1280b30-1281a3 [emphasis added].

[28] See Aquinas's *On Kingship*, I, 15 [114-115].

profit in the form of money. Whence the concern? At risk of oversimplifying a very complex issue, I think we can point to two fundamental concerns. First, when the fulfilling of human needs, and here "needs" is opposed to "desires," is not the explicit *telos* of economic activity, then in fact those needs will often not be fulfilled for the community as a whole. To defend this point requires a separate argument that cannot be given here. Second, without the natural limit of serving human needs, this other form of wealth-getting has a tendency to corrupt moral character.[29]

I know that here I raise issues as controversial as they are complex. I raise them, however, because I think that they should be considered and discussed precisely in the context of a consideration of the "freedom" of a culture. While "economic freedom" is an issue given much attention, very little attention is given to the question of whether economic structures properly serve that which is for-itself. Just how economic structures should serve virtue and contemplation is open to question, but *that* they should serve them is, for Aristotle and Aquinas, beyond question. Further, while economic structures serve what is higher through attending to human needs, they can and should also serve them through *the ways in which* human needs are met. In other words, apart from the question of how well economic structures fulfill the human needs they directly concern is the question of how they

---

[29] See *Summa theologiae* II-II 77.4ad3, where Aquinas argues that clerics should not engage in "trading," i.e., trading for the sake of "profit" as opposed to for the "necessities of life." He says that this trading is not evil in itself, but it is "open to so many vices, since 'a merchant is hardly free from sins of the lips' (Ecclus 26:28). There is also another reason, because trading engages the mind too much with worldly cares, and consequently withdraws it from spiritual cares." Aquinas makes similar arguments regarding the danger of "trade" in *On Kingship*, II, 3 [139]. Here he makes a remarkable statement concerning a society in which there is a preponderance of "tradesmen:" "The result is that everything in the city will become venal; good faith will be destroyed and the way opened to all kinds of trickery; each one will work only for his own profit, despising the public good; the cultivation of virtue will fail since honour, virtue's reward, will be bestowed upon the rich. Thus, in such a city, civic life will necessarily be corrupted." *On Kingship: To the King of Cyprus*, translated by Gerald Phelan (Toronto: PIMS, 1982), pp. 76-77.

dispose, or indispose, toward virtue and contemplation. The realm of economics is not only lower than, it is essentially *sub-ordinate to* the life of virtue and contemplation. As such, it should be judged in terms of how well it disposes toward it.

Culture of Death and Culture of Life

In his social encyclicals, Pope John Paul II developed a profound critique of contemporary culture. One major expression of this critique is through opposing the notions of "being" and "having." In *Evangelium Vitae*, in the context of describing what he calls the "culture of death," the Pope says:

> The values of being are replaced by those of having. The only goal which counts is the pursuit of one's own material well-being. The so-called 'quality of life' is interpreted primarily or exclusively as economic efficiency, inordinate consumerism, physical beauty and pleasure, to the neglect of more profound dimensions - interpersonal, spiritual and religious - of existence.[30]

How are we to interpret this distinction of being and having? I want to suggest that we would do well to see this distinction as corresponding to the distinction between what is for itself and what is for another, or, put otherwise, between the speculative and the practical.

When he introduces the notion of a culture of death, the Pope turns immediately to discover the root of this culture. He has this to say:

> We have to go to the heart of the tragedy being experienced by modern man: *the eclipse of the sense of God and of man*, typical of a social and cultural climate dominated by secularism, which, with its ubiquitous tentacles, succeeds at times in putting Christian communities themselves to the test.[31]

---

[30] *EV* #23.

[31] Ibid., #21; emphasis in the original.

He sounds here a theme that he sounded often, quoting Vatican II, "But when God is forgotten the creature itself grows unintelligible."[32] Or as he says also in the next section of *Evangelium Vitae*: "By living 'as if God did not exist,' man not only loses sight of the mystery of God, but also of the world and the mystery of his own being."[33]

But just what is it about human nature that is lost sight of here? In the next chapter of *Evangelium Vitae*, entitled "I came that They May Have Life," the Pope expounds the Christian notion of human life and its end. He says, "The life which God bestows upon man is much more than mere existence in time. It is a drive towards fullness of life...."[34] And what is the fullness of human life? It is the Eternal Life of God that He shares with us. I quote again:

> Here the Christian truth about life becomes most sublime. The dignity of this life is linked not only to its beginning, to the fact that it comes from God, but also to its final end, to its destiny of fellowship with God in knowledge and love of him. In the light of this truth Saint Irenaeus qualifies and completes his praise of man: 'the glory of God' is indeed, 'man, living man,' but 'the life of man consists in the vision of God.'[35]

The Pope is arguing, then, that man does not understand himself especially when he does not understand his end as the contemplation of God.

But how then does man live when he loses sight of who he is? Speaking of "life issues," the Pope says, "[Man] is concerned only with 'doing,' and, using all kinds of technology, he busies himself with programming, controlling and dominating birth and death." This is where the Pope says the values of being are replaced by those of having. This same point was presented in his earlier encyclical *Centesimus Annus*:

---

[32] He quotes this text from *Gaudium et Spes*, 36 in Ibid., #22.

[33] Ibid., #22.

[34] Ibid., #34.

[35] Ibid., #38.

> It is not wrong to want to live better; what is wrong is a style of life which is presumed to be better when it is directed toward 'having' rather than 'being' and which wants to have more not in order to be more, but in order to spend life in enjoyment as an end in itself.[36]

After making this statement about the disorder of seeking what is for the end as though it were the end, he proceeds immediately to make the following strong claim about the proper subordination of economics:

> It is therefore necessary to create lifestyles in which the quest for truth, beauty, goodness and communion with others for the sake of common growth are the factors which determine consumer choices, savings, and investments.

Striking here is the way in which the Pope presents the contemplative endeavor, "the quest for truth, beauty, goodness and communion with others," as providing principles for economic decisions. Near the end of *Evangelium Vitae*, he makes a similar statement:

In a word, we can say that the cultural change we are calling for demands from everyone the courage to *adopt a new life-style*, consisting in making practical choices – at the personal, family, social and international level – on the basis of a correct scale of values: *the primacy of being over having, of the person over things.*[37]

Conclusion

Beginning with the root Aristotelian notion of freedom – what is *causa sui* – *what* is "on account of itself," I have argued that to develop a proper notion of a "free culture," we should use the notion of free as that which is for-itself. A free culture is one that is ordered to contemplation. In the rich and complex "order to contemplation," other goods participate, in lower and higher degrees, in the for-

---

[36] *CA*, #36.

[37] EV, #98. Emphasis in the original. The statement "the primacy of being over having" is footnoted to *Gaudium et Spes*, 35, and Paul VI, *Populorum Progressio* (26 March 1967), 15: AAS 59 (1967), 265.

itselfness of the ultimate end. These other goods have their proper place and dignity precisely as serving that which is most truly for-itself. Again, the key here is "hierarchical thinking:" To be ordered to what is for-itself pertains to the proper goodness of all lower things in the order. An *unfree* culture is one in which what is for-itself does not provide the first principles of order in society, and what is for another, as for instance economics, is treated as though it is for-itself.

I have also argued that this point is implied in John Paul II's distinction between the culture of life and the culture of death. The culture of death has lost sight of who man is; it has lost sight of higher and lower, of what is for-itself and what is not. The Pope has issued a call for a cultural change: He says that we must have the courage to "adopt a new life style, consisting in making practical choices - at the personal, family, social and international level - on the basis of a correct scale of values: *the primacy of being over having.*" One pivotal area in which we must do this is economics. The realm of economics should be seen and lived as subordinated to the end of contemplation. How should this be done? Again, this is a very difficult question. But it will never be answered until we first have a shared conviction that it is *the right question to ask.* Indeed, as regards the culture of death, the devil is not really in the details; he is in the first principles. In calling for a cultural change, Pope John Paul II pointed to the only true foundation for a culture of life and freedom: living the primacy of the for-itself.

From Rivulets to the Fountain's Source: Image and Love in Aquinas' Christian Anthropology

Heather Erb

In his descriptions of the divine love which communicates its goodness through creation, infusing its presence through the range of all levels of life and sources of action (especially in the human faculties, acts, and virtues), Aquinas uses the Platonic and Neoplatonic metaphors of light and water to mark the self-diffusive, dynamic character of God's love for creatures. Aquinas typically uses the metaphysical language of "light" to describe grace, its radiance refracted through the theological virtues and gifts,[1] while using the language of "water" to explore the relation of the extension of divine goodness and the *reditus* of creatures back to God. In the *Summa Contra Gentiles,* Thomas speaks of rivers of goodness which God pours into natures and beings, streams drawn back towards the unity of their source,[2] while God is often described as a living fountain not diminished in spite of its continuous flow outwards.[3] In a gloss on *Sirach* 1.7, Thomas notes that the rivers are being, life, and intelligence, the natural goods with which God has filled his creation. The source of these rivers is the Incarnation, wherein all natural goods are reunited as they are united to a lesser degree in *man,* the horizon where corporeal and spiritual being meets.[4]

---

[1] Thomas O'Meara uses this analogy in his work *Thomas Aquinas: Theologian* (Notre Dame: University of Notre Dame Press, 1997), p.121.

[2] *C.G.* II.2: "...If, therefore, the goodness, beauty, and delightfulness of creatures are so alluring to the minds of men, the fountainhead of God's own goodness, compared with the rivulets of goodness found in creatures, will draw the enkindled minds of men wholly to Itself." Cf. *C.G.* II.21.

[3] *Super Evangelium Ioannis Lectura* I.4 (Turin, 1952), l. 3 p. 20; cf. *In 10 Ethic.* L. 13 on God as "fons omnium bonorum."

[4] The gloss on Sirach is found in *In III Sent.* Prol. Cf. *C.G.* IV, 55 (#3937).

The Dionysian[5] and Biblical motif underlies the context of the second part of the *Summa Theologiae*, whose Prologue speaks of the attraction which God exercises on the human person made in the image of God.[6] Aquinas' Christian anthropology thus flows from the twofold movement of *descent* from the divine plenitude into human reality and the movement of *ascent*, which is man's answer to that which he has received. The metaphysics of creation and participation in being form the natural side of the analogy, while its supernatural dimension culminates in the life of contemplation, where one draws from the well of divine friendship and is united to the fountainhead of goodness.[7]

We will examine the ontology of "image" and "love" as participations in divine life, explaining the link between the notions of "image," "contemplation," and love as *amor, amicitia* and *caritas* in Aquinas. We will track love as both passion (*amor)* and as virtue (*caritas*), as it propels the soul towards beatitude and conditions human liberty. Both the nature of love as gift and bond, ecstatic and natural, and some effects of love applicable to the spiritual life will be treated. A study of Aquinas' uses of *amor* through the lens of *amicitia* will reveal within Aquinas' works "an Aristotelianism of grace within human activities,"[8] but when love becomes *caritas,* Aquinas' development of and departure from the Aristotelian concept of friendship (*philia*)

---

[5] It is found originally in Pseudo-Dionysius' *De div. Nom.* c. 4 #2. Aquinas uses the motif in his discussions of creation and participation in being: *S.T.* I-II 2.8 ad 1; 3.3 ad 2; 4.7 ad 2; 5.4; *C.G.* I 93; II 3. For an ethical context, see *In 10 Ethic.* L. 13.

[6] *S.T.* I-II Prol.: "Since, as Damascene states (*De fide orthodoxa* ii.12), man is said to be made to God's image, insofar as the image implies an intelligent being endowed with free-will and self-movement: now that we have treated of the exemplar, i.e.., God, and of those things which came forth from the power of God in accordance with His will; it remains for us to treat of His image; i.e. man, inasmuch as he too is the principle of his actions, as having free-will and control of his actions."

[7] The reference to contemplation: "Ille autem est felicissimus qui maxime amatur a Deo qui est fons omnium bonorum" (*In 10 Ethic.* L. 13).

[8] Thomas O'Meara, *Thomas Aquinas: Theologian*, p. 112.

through Dionysius' influence becomes evident. These twin influences, I will show, rescue Aquinas from the charge that *caritas* is a sort of disinterested and impersonal form of love in relation to God and men which involves no basis in true love of self.

The "*Imago Dei*" Doctrine[9]

Taking its inspiration from Scripture[10] and from Augustine's *De Trinitate*, the context for Aquinas' doctrine of the human being as "*imago Dei*" is an examination of the powers and actions which relate the human to his ultimate *telos* of beatitude. The notion of "image" is a subdivision of that of "likeness" or similitude, with the addition that an image has the mimetic function of imitating that from which it is expressed.[11] In this way, the human soul on the level of nature, grace and glory exhibits formal similarity to the processions of divine persons in the Trinity. In addition to the mimetic function of 'image,' there is its 'participatory' function, through which the image is said to conform or enter into that on which it is modeled, viz. the divine life itself.[12] The metaphysical context for the doctrine of "image" is threefold: (a) the network of causes (and distinction of effects) involved in the procession and return of creatures to their source (the *exitus/reditus* theme that governs the *Summa*), (b) the distinction between "univocal" and "analogous" images, and (c) the levels within

---

[9] This section was originally published as part of an article: Heather McAdam Erb, "Metaphysical Aspects of Aquinas' Doctrine of the Spiritual Life," in: "Atti del Congresso Internationale su L'umanesimo Cristiano nel III Millennio: La Prospettiva di Tommaso d'Aquino, 21-25 Settembre 2003" (Vatican City: Pontificia Academia Sancti Thomae Aquinatis, 2005), Vol. II pp. 409-412.

[10] The main text here is Genesis 1.26: "ad imaginem et similitudinem faciamus."

[11] *S.T.* I 93.1: An image must be a thing that is "expressed from another, for it is called an 'image' because it is made for the imitation of the other thing."

[12] The distinction between the "mimetic" and "participatory" functions of "image" has been suggested by Denys Turner, in his book *The Darkness of God: Negativity in Christian Mysticism* (Cambridge: Cambridge University Press, 1995), pp. 95-100.

the rational creature by which "image" participates in the divine model, culminating in the transformation of the person through glory.

Turning to the first consideration (a), the network of causes and effects involved in the motif of circulation, Aquinas establishes both the origin and return of creatures to God from the diffusive character of the divine goodness,[13] since creation flows from love. Through His wisdom and love God pours forth goodness into things[14] and directs everything towards its goal of gaining a similarity to His divine goodness.[15] This Neoplatonic doctrine of "circulation" is characterized by the identity of beginning and end, dovetailing formal into final causes, in that every effect is directed to its cause, as desiring its natural good.[16] Goodness is thus both origin and end, for it is the source of being and order, and the goal towards which all things strive.

If the teleology of nature involves the perfection, goodness and fulfillment of a thing's form,[17] then what does this say about the doctrine of "image" as applied to human persons? To answer this

---

[13] The self-diffusive character of goodness (*bonum est diffusivum sui esse)* is a theme he borrowed and adapted from Pseudo-Dionysius to include every being, and Aquinas understands this self-communication of goodness in terms of a final cause (*S.T.* I 5.4 ad 2; 44.4; *In 1 Sent.* 43.2.1 ad 4; *De Ver.* 21.1 ad 4).

[14] *S.T.* I 20.2.

[15] *C.G.* III 97; *In 1 Sent.* 14.2.2: "In the outpouring of creatures coming forth from their first principle, there is a sort of rotation or circulation from the fact that all beings moving toward their ultimate goal return to the source from which they came forth.... [T]he production of creatures has as its final purpose the movement of persons back into divine Life...."

[16] *In de div. Nomin.* c.1 l.3 #94: "...every effect reverts upon the cause whence it came forth, as the Platonists say. The reason for this is that every thing reverts upon its good by desiring it. Now, the good of the effect derives from its cause. Therefore every effect reverts upon its cause by desiring it. Therefore Dionysius, having said that all is deduced from the Godhead, goes on to add that all things revert upon Him through desire."

[17] Formal and final causality coincide inasmuch as the form's actuality and perfect operation represent a thing's end, and as such, is desirable (*C.G.* III 20; *S.T.* I 19.1).

query, Aquinas distinguishes 'imaging' and 'non-imaging' resemblances. 'Image' is a subset of 'likeness' or similitude, but it adds the note of "being copied" from an original. Something is called an "image" because it is produced as an imitation of another thing, approximating the perfection of the model.[18] Thus, within the hierarchy of beings that exist, live and have understanding,[19] there exist many beings which resemble God without properly 'imaging' His perfection. The distinction between "imaging" and "non-imaging" resemblances is expressed through an analysis of rational versus non-rational forms: Even irrational and inanimate creatures possess a natural desire or love for God, [20] in that they are intrinsically directed towards the realization of their forms.[21] "Natural" love does not imply a conscious, positive desire for an object here, but only the tendency towards the good of a thing's complete actuality (the tree grows, the flower blooms, etc.). Although a *rational* creature's desire for the fulfillment of its capacities is *also* the tendency towards self-perfection, it is better characterized as a kind of love for a completely satisfying good,[22] an openness to an infinite and perfect goodness through the rational indeterminacy of the mind and will.[23] Natural bodies are called "*vestiges*" in that they bear a likeness from causality with respect to God, without being true images or representations.[24] *Vestiges* fail to represent the *form* of their cause, but merely point to it, as in the case

---

[18] *S.T.* I 93.1.

[19] *S.T.* I 93.2.

[20] *S.T.* I 6.1; I-II 26.2; 109.3.

[21] Aquinas' favorite image here is that of the arrow which is directed by the archer to its target: *S.T.* I 103.1 ad 3, 8. Thus, God is said to direct all creatures to their proper ends (*S.T.* I 22.2; 103.1; I-II 93.5).

[22] *S.T.* I-II 5.7; 2.8.

[23] *S.T.* I-II 5.1; cf. I 93.4. Whereas the desires and acts of irrational creatures are determined to particular objects (*S.T.* I-II 13.2), the proper object of the will is the universal good, not any finite object, since no particular good is good without qualification (*S.T.* I-II 10.2; I-II 13.6). The will is, however, directed necessarily to the final end of happiness (*S.T.* I 82.1; I-II 1.7).

[24] The distinction between "image" and "vestige" is treated in *S.T.* I 93.6, *In 1 Sent.* 3.2.2 and *De Pot.* 9.9.

of footprints of an animal or smoke from fire.[25] Only *rational* beings represent God as Trinity by way of *image*, however, because it is only through the rational powers of intellect and will that the mimetic and participatory functions of "image" come into play,[26] as from our mind proceed wisdom and love in an imperfect way.[27]

The second notion involved in the ontology of "image" (b) is Aquinas' distinction between "univocal" and "analogous" images, which signals the imperfect mode of human resemblance to God. A *univocal* image shares the same species as the model (as a king's image appears in his son); whereas, an *analogous* image differs in nature or species (as the image of a king appears on a coin).[28] In this way, Christ is the perfect and univocal image of the Father; whereas, man is an imperfect, analogous image tending towards the perfection of the divine model. This is why he is not the image of God *simpliciter*, but rather made *to the image (ad imaginem),* a being capable of its final actualization but still a pilgrim and always a creature.

The partial and gradual ascent of "image" towards the perfection of the model characterizes the third element in Aquinas' doctrine of "image," namely, (c) the human journey through the three levels of "image" – nature, grace and glory.[29] For Aquinas, the relation between formal and final causes with respect to the notion of "image" means that human nature fulfils its destiny of becoming like God through the dual path of nature and grace. On the level of nature – called the image of creation– all people possess the natural power of knowing and loving God by virtue of possessing a spiritual soul. Although this presence of God in man surpasses the more "common" mode of divine presence through creative causality, it lies *below* the "special" presence of God to rational creatures through *grace*, by which people know and love God

---

[25] *S.T.* I 93.6. But even nonrational creatures represent the Trinity in their vestigial mode, in that they have a beginning, a form and an order to other realities (*S.T.* I 45.7).

[26] *S.T.* I 3.1 ad 2; 93.2, 6.

[27] *S.T.* I 93.6.

[28] *S.T.* I 35.2 ad 3; 93.6 ad 1.

[29] *S.T.* I 93.4 is a text summarizing this doctrine.

"actually or habitually." In *S.T.* I, 43.3, God is said to be present to rational creatures not merely through extrinsic causality and conservation (through His "essence, presence and power"), but also through a mutual indwelling of knowledge and love, to live in him as in His temple. Through the grace flowing from the Trinitarian missions, our powers of reaching God in thought and desire are spurred into action, and our souls are instructed in the savory, affective wisdom of the things of God.[30] The third and highest level of the image surpasses this second image - of the *new creation* - and occurs in the transformation of the human at the level of *glory*, whereby man is said to love God "actually and perfectly" and to enjoy the possession of Him without intermediary[31] - the image of *resemblance.* Man is qualified as an "image of God," therefore, first in the possession, second, in the dynamic actualization, and finally, in the perfection of his powers as directed towards the highest object, viz., God.[32] The three images of nature, grace and glory thus represent three stages of conformity towards perfect resemblance and divine indwelling, and exhibit the

---

[30] *S.T.* I 93.7; 43.5 ad 2. In the former text, the Trinitarian missions of the Son and Spirit are likened to the human intellect's knowledge of God and consequent love proceeding from that inner word; in the latter text, the Word that "breathes forth Love" (*Verbum spirans Amorem*) grounds the experiential wisdom that is the gift of the Spirit in the graced soul .

[31] *S.T.* I 93.8 and ad 1 on the "image in glory." Here, the transitional, evolutionary character of "image" is revealed as complete only in conformity to glory, where image reaches the level of "representation."

[32] *S.T.* I 93.8 establishes the restricted character of object sufficient to establish the image of the Trinity in man's soul (namely, God): "...[T]he divine image is noted in man according to the word conceived from the knowledge of God and the love springing forth from it." In his magisterial study of the issue, J. Merriell traces the evolution in Aquinas' thought: "In the *Scriptum* Thomas stressed the permanence of the image of God in the natural faculties of man's mind, while in the *De Veritate* he takes greater notice of the assimilation to God that is necessary for the actualisation of the image." (J. Merriell, *To the Image of the Trinity: A Study in the Development of Aquinas' Teaching* (Toronto: Pontifical Institute of Mediaeval Studies, 1990), pp. 132-33. Merriell follows de Beaurecueil's thesis that Thomas adds the "participatory" aspect of "image" (man's conforming to God through a participation in God's knowledge and love) in the *Summa Theologiae* (Merriell, p. 221).

motif of *exitus* and *reditus* in the creature. As J.P. Torrell summarizes the issue:

> ... [T]he image of creation, is the term of the 'going out'... . [T]he image of re-creation or according to grace, is that [term] by which the 'return' begins, inaugurating the movement that will be completed in heaven along with ... the image of glory, that is finally perfect resemblance...."[33]

The familiar paradox emerges then, that on his own man is not fitted for a supernatural destiny,[34] but nonetheless has a soul created in the image of God as *capax Dei,*[35] open to fulfillment through participation in the life of God.

Contemplation as *Reditus*

The contemplation proper to the interior life is not a metaphysical meditation on the first cause of being, but rather the connatural knowledge of God penetrated by love that is experienced in the context of the infused virtues, the gifts and fruits of the Holy Spirit.[36] It is the "contemplation of God under the impetus of divine love" that makes

---

[33] J.P. Torrell, *Saint Thomas Aquinas: Vol. 2: Spiritual Master,* translated by Robert Royal (Washington, D.C.: Catholic University of America Press, 2003), p. 90.

[34] *S.T.* I-II 114.2: "... [M]an cannot merit eternal life without grace, by his purely natural endowments.... [E]verlasting life is a good exceeding the proportion created nature...."

[35] C. O'Neill notes that Thomas' terminology in this regard denotes the finalization or actualization of man's nature. Aquinas' more frequent terms to describe this state of things is *capax summum boni; capax perfecti boni; capax visionis divinae essentiae; capax vitae aeternae,* etc. For references, see: C. O'Neill, "L'homme ouvert à Dieu (*capax Dei*)" in *L'anthropologie de saint Thomas,* ed. N. Luyten (Fribourg: Editions Universitaires, 1969), pp. 70; 74.

[36] For an examination of the different senses of "contemplation" in Aquinas and a detailed study of his notion of mystical contemplation, see: Heather M. Erb, "*Pati Divina*: Mystical Union in Aquinas," in A. Ramos, M. George, eds., *Faith, Scholarship and Culture in the 21st Century* (Washington, D.C.: Catholic University of America Press, 2002).

this sort of wisdom surpass every human activity in perfection and delight, Aquinas says,[37] and which constitutes our ultimate happiness.[38]

There are at least *four* central characteristics of the contemplation proper to Christian beatitude for Aquinas. *First*, wisdom in its perfect form is neither philosophy nor even theology, but Christ Himself.[39] *Second*, consonant with the plan of the Trinitarian missions, this contemplation reflects the "Word breathing forth Love" (*Verbum Spirans Amore*[40]) in its own "knowledge from which love springs," a contemplation rooted in what Thomas calls the human *intellect*'s "desire and love of the knowledge of divine things, as well as delight in it."[41] From our natural acts of knowledge and love to our grace-infused acts and habits, then, our rationality is stamped with a mimetic and participatory likeness of Trinitarian life. The *third* quality of contemplation proper to Christian beatitude for Thomas is that it is both *act*, as the full realization and immanent perfection of the agent, [42]

---

[37] *S.T.* II-II 180.7: "The contemplative life consists principally in the contemplation of God under the impetus of divine love; hence there is a delight in the contemplative life by reason of the act of contemplating and by reason of that divine love. In both respects the delight of contemplation surpasses every human delight."

[38] *C.G.* III 37.

[39] *In 1 Sent.* Prologue: "Inter multas sententias quae a diversis prodierunt, quid scilicet esset vera sapientia, unam singulariter firmam et veram Apostolus protulit dicens Christum Dei virtutem et Dei sapientiam, qui etiam factus est nobis sapientia a Deo." (The reference to St. Paul: *I Corinthians* I.26; 30). This is the Patristic and Pauline idea of truth.

[40] *S.T.* I 43.5 ad 2: "Now the Son is the Word – not any word of any kind, but the Word breathing forth Love (*Verbum spirans Amore)*: hence Augustine says... 'The Word we mean to speak of is Knowledge with Love.' Therefore the Son is not sent [to us] in any and every kind of knowledge we acquire but [only] in that kind of intellectual instruction whereby we burst forth with affections of love, as is said...in Ps. 38 (39).4: 'In my meditation a fire is enkindled'."

[41] *C.G.* III 25.

[42] *S.T.* I-II 3.2: "Insofar as man's beatitude is something created which has existence in himself, it must necessarily be said that man's beatitude is an

and divine communication or *gift*, as both a prelude to eternal life and as an emission of God's love generating within us a love resembling His own.[43] *Fourth,* this contemplation is born of wonder and ends in both *amazement* (due to the soul's inability to grasp the "whole" within its gaze[44]) and in the *peaceful repose* proper to the intellect's mode of possession or presence.

From these characteristics we can see that Aquinas' notion of contemplation dovetails into the notions of "image" and "love" in the following way: As the desire for God is the principle of all movement and activity in the cosmos (cf. Aristotle[45]), our noblest activity, the love of wisdom or contemplation[46] images and participates in the divine life to the *highest* degree.[47] Aristotle's "natural desire" inscribed in man's nature, however, now finds its culmination not only in knowledge but also in love, for which knowledge, whether it be "faith" or "vision," now proposes the object.

A central paradox involved in the spiritual life as Thomas conceived of it revolves around the issue of contemplation. Thomas' concept of beatitude combines Aristotle's emphasis on the application of our highest power on the most intelligible object, with Augustine's emphasis on affectivity and *caritas* in the soul's search for immutability.[48] Beatitude is for him ultimately an *intellectual* operation, but for the wayfarer *love* is more perfect than knowledge of God. Given these two seemingly opposed facts, how is man to anticipate his destiny

---

activity." (Cf. *De Ver.* 29.1 on the necessity that God's being is also active, in knowing and loving.)

43 *S.T.* II-II 26.3. Cf. *In de Div. Nom.* IV, xi, #444.

44 *S.T.* II-II 180.3 ad 3. Cf. *C.G.* IV.33. On this point, see: Josef Pieper, *Happiness and Contemplation,* p. 75.

45 *Meta.* 5.7 #1072b3-16.

46 *In 3 Sent.* D. 23, q. 1 a.4; *S.T.* I-II 57.1c. Gilson considers these arguments in his lecture *Wisdom and Love,* pp. 42-44 #3.

47 In 7 Ethic. L. 13.

48 These two influences on Aquinas' thought on beatitude are presented in the study by Marie-Anne Vannier, "Du bonheur à la béatitude d'après S. Augustin et S. Thomas" *La vie spirituelle* 698 (1992), 45-58.

of supernatural beatitude in this life? In this life we can more perfectly love God than know Him, because in *knowing* a good higher than itself, the mind assimilates an object to its own less noble state; whereas, a good that is higher than the soul draws the will towards it and opens the dynamism of love towards the horizon of spiritual realities.[49] Thus, the *viator's* existential perfection lies in being an entity "open to God" (*capax Dei*).[50] Man attains the summit of his perfection only through the practice of contemplation, through that type which is enflamed by the exercise of charity and its accompanying Gift of wisdom, a manner of judging all things in their relationship to God by way of inclination.[51] Thus is Aquinas' Aristotelian psychology of virtues, powers, and activities animated and directed by the motions of grace, which both deepen and elevate the operations of human nature.

Love and Charity in Aquinas' Spiritual Doctrine

A review of Aquinas' notion of "love" in its significations as *amor, amicitia* and *caritas* reveals both his dependence upon and departure from Aristotle's theory of friendship. Scrutiny of some key *effects* of love will show Aquinas' debt to Dionysius as both deliberate and fortuitous. Aquinas' understanding of the "love of friendship" (vs. the "love of concupiscence") precludes him, it will be shown, from identifying *caritas* with extreme altruism, a love lauded as pure, disinterested or "holy" by later spiritual writers, such as Fénelon.[52] In this regard, three issues will be treated. First, "love" as a virtue will be

---

[49] The situation is reversed in the case of a good known or loved that is *lower* than the human soul: here, it is better to know than to love it. *S.T* I 82.3; II-II 23.6 ad 1.

[50] Cf. J.-P. Torrell, Thomas *Aquinas: Vol. 2: Spiritual Master,* p. 86: "Man is fully himself only when he is under cultivation; similarly, the image of God in him will be fully itself only in the perfected stage of its spiritual activity."

[51] *S.T.* I-II 3.2 ad 4; II-II 180; 182.

[52] The critical edition of Fénelon's work: *Explication des maxims des saints sur la vie interieure,*Edition critique publiée d'après des documents inédits par Albert Cherel (Paris: Bloud et Cle, 1911). R. Merrihew Adams' treatment of Fénelon's views is found in: R. Merrihew Adams, "Pure Love;" in R. Merrihew Adams, *The Virtue of Faith and Other Essays in Philosophical Theology* (Oxford: Oxford University Press, 1987), pp.174-92.

distinguished from "love" as a passion through distinguishing *amor, amicitia,* and *caritas.* Second, some effects of love, such as "mutual indwelling," "melting," "joy" and "ecstasy" will be noted and applied to the graced personality. Third, I will analyze and evaluate Robert Merrihew Adams' rejection of Fénelon's identification of *caritas* with the notion of "pure, altruistic love" and offer Aquinas' solution to the problem of the relation of *agape* (connoted by the "love of friendship") and *eros* (connoted by the "love of desire or concupiscence").

a) Amor, Amicitia and Caritas

Turning to the first issue, we have seen that it is the effusive and gratuitous character of divine love that grounds the return of creatures to God, the "living fountain" which pours rivers of goodness into the variety of beings.[53] Grace is the new life principle which gives the soul a share in the divine nature and enables persons to be secondary causes in the supernatural order,[54] and so the divine initiative is the source of human virtues and loves. A cluster of terms surrounds the notion of "love" for Aquinas, including *amor, amicitia,* and *caritas.* An analysis of these terms reveals that love as passion (*amor)* is related to love as virtue (*caritas)* through the mediation of *amicitia* (friendship), and that in transposing Aristotelian elements of friendship into his theory of charity, Aquinas replaced the Stagirite's concept of friendship as an aristocratic exchange among equals with the Christian concept of self-gift and communion, based on the gratuity of creation, or superabundant outpouring of the goodness of God.[55]

---

[53] *C.G.* II.2. *In Super Evangelium Ioannis Lectura*, ch.1, 3. "God is a living fountain that is not diminished in spite of its continuous flow outwards."

[54] *S.T.* I-II 112.1, e.g. In *De Ver.* 27.1 ad 3, he says that "God, without any mediating agent, bestows upon us a gratuitous spiritual being, but nevertheless there is the mediation of a created form which is grace." As O'Meara notes ("Virtues in the Theology of Thomas Aquinas," *Theological Studies* 58 [1997], p. 263): "This 'spiritual being' is not the transitory actual graces of the later Baroque but a source of life."

[55] I am indebted to the insights of J. McEvoy ("Amitié, attirance et amour chez S. Thomas d'Aquin", *Révue philosophique de Louvain* 91 [1993]: 383-408) for drawing the connection between *amor* and *caritas* through the virtue of friendship. In his article "Thomas's Authority for Identifying Charity as

The analogous term *amor* is described by Thomas as a weighting of the will's tendency towards an apprehended good.[56] As the "first movement" of the will that is the change in the appetite produced by the appetible object, *amor* precedes the movement of the will towards the object, which is called "desire," and the repose of the will in its possession, which is called "joy."[57] The primary affection of both the sensory and rational powers, he notes, is love (*amor*), denoting the suitability or proportion of a being to that which constitutes its good;[58] indeed, "every agent, whatever it may be, carries out its action from some love."[59] As a passion, love is a motion resulting in a "complacency" whereby the beloved is said to be "rooted" in the lover's heart, causing either pleasure in its presence or longing in its

---

Friendship: Aristotle or *John* 15?" (*Thomist* 62 [1998]: 581-601), A. Keaty argues against certain modern interpreters that Aquinas is using Aristotelian categories of 'friendship' but is stressing the Gospel's notion of *caritas* in his development of the theme of union with God. In this emphasis on the Biblical origins of Aquinas' theory of friendship, Keaty is arguing against L. Gregory Jones ("The Theological Transformation of Aristotelian friendship in the Thought of St. Thomas Aquinas" [*New Scholasticism* 61 (1987): 373-99]) and Paul Wadell (*Friends of God: Virtues and Gifts in Aquinas* [New York: Peter Lang, 1991]), who argue for an exclusively Aristotelian basis of Aquinas' theory of friendship. Keaty's view is in accord with the more recent emphasis on Thomas as a biblical commentator.

[56] In *S.T.* I-II 28.1 ad 2, Aquinas differentiates between three kinds or stages of union involved in love, as found in man's second act of will, which is voluntary and explicitly rational: 1) the union that gives rise to love (consisting in *knowledge* of the beloved, making it attractive to the will; 2) the union that love desires ("caused by love effectively, since it moves the lover to desire and see the presence of the beloved as fitting and pertaining to himself"), and 3) the union of desiring love itself ("caused by love *formally*, since love itself *is* such a union or connection"). Cf. #67 below on the analogous senses of the term "love" (*amor*).

[57] *S.T.* I-II 26.2. Desire and joy are thus two secondary affections in the appetite: desire (*desiderium*), when the loved good is as yet not possessed; joy (*delectatio/gaudium*), if the good is possessed. All appetitive motions proceed from desire, which in turn derives from love (see *S.T.* I-II 25.1-2).

[58] *S.T.* I-II 26.2.

[59] *S.T.* I-II 25.2; ad 2;cf. *S.T.* I 20.1.

absence.[60] The love exhibited by natural or irrational appetite found in animals and inanimate creatures differs from human love in that it is directed unknowingly to its target through the principles proper to their own natures.[61] Because the human will adapts itself to its object as it exists in itself (versus the intellect, which assimilates it to its own mode),[62] the appetitive union also differs from the cognitive union: the will can love the total existent reality of the object in a perfect way, without that same object being perfectly known,[63] such that a higher object betters and perfects the will. *Amicitia* "friendship," denotes a fixed habit based on similarity and choice requiring mutual love, common knowledge about this love and free choice of each party.[64] Following Aristotle, Thomas says that only a certain type of love has the character of friendship, namely that which has three specific qualities: benevolence, mutuality, and a shared good.[65] Departing from Aristotle, he notes that the shared good that forms the basis of friendship with God is God's own beatitude, given gratuitously to men, making them "equals" not through merit but by *fiat*.[66] Whereas for

---

[60] *S.T.* I-II 28.2. Cf. I-II 27.2: "... But that kind of love which is in the intellective appetite also differs from goodwill, because it denotes a certain union of the lover's heart with the beloved, in as much as the lover deems the beloved as somehow one with him, or belonging to him, and so tends towards him...." The union which love is primarily occurs in the heart (*unio affectus/unio affectiva),* where a mutual presence of beloved and lover occur: "The beloved is contained in the lover insofar as he is impressed on the lover's heart by a kind of complacency" (*S.T.* I-II 28.2).

[61] The arrow/archer imagery is found in several places in Aquinas: *S.T.* I 103.1 ad 3, and I 103, 8. In *S.T.* I-II 26.1, he outlines the three levels of *amor,* as found in natural, sensitive and rational appetites ("... in each of these appetites, the name *love* [*amor*] is given to the principle of movement towards the end loved...").

[62] *S.T.* I 82.3.

[63] *S.T.* I-II 27.2 ad 2.

[64] *In 3 Sent.* 27.2.1.

[65] *S.T.* II-II 23.1.

[66] On the shared good of God's happiness, see *S.T.* II-II 23.1: "Accordingly, since there is a communication between man and God, insofar as He communicates His happiness to us, there must be some kind of friendship

Aristotle, friendship is an *instrumental means* for personal, earthly beatitude, in its best form, an aristocratic exchange between equals,[67] for Aquinas, friendship is now possible with God, whose unmerited love is displayed in the act of creation and in the redemption of sinners through the Incarnation. *Amor,* then, is related to *caritas* through *amicitia,* namely, through the higher type of friendship, now denoting the *perfection* of love valuing God as the highest good in and for itself,[68] and unlike the other virtues, flowing from an imperfectly possessed object (viz., God).[69] It is this interior end of already possessed union with God that acts as a principle in action and appetite, and orders the will towards beatitude.[70]

b) The Effects of Love and the Life of Grace

The second aspect of Aquinas' teachings on love concerns some key *effects* of love, namely, the "mutual indwelling" of lover and beloved, the "ecstasy" of the will, the "melting" of the heart in love, and the passion of "joy" that ensues on the possession of the beloved. In comparison to the love of concupiscence, which loves another for a

---

based on this same communication.... The love which is based on this communication is charity."

[67] As Eberhard Schockenhoff summarizes the Stagirite's teaching, "the Aristotelian ideal of friendship acknowledges no overcoming of distance and differences in rank; it is neither desire *(eros)* nor *agape,* but 'friendship' *(philia):* love of like for like and exchange among equal partners" (E. Schockenhoff, "The Theological Virtue of Charity [II-II qq. 23-46]" in: Stephen Pope, ed. *The Ethics of Aquinas* (Washington, D.C.: Georgetown University Press, 2002), p. 247. Aristotle's theory of friendship is found in his *Nicomachean Ethics,* Books 8-9.

[68] As such, charity is a form of the love of friendship, as opposed to the love of concupiscence, which loves the beloved for the sake of something other than itself (*S.T.* I-II 26.4).

[69] *S.T.* I-II 66.6. Here, he says that charity is the greatest virtue because "the love of charity is about that which is already possessed (i.e., God): for the beloved is in a certain way in the lover and the lover is also drawn through affection to union with the beloved...."

[70] *S.T.* II-II 26.1 and ad 1; II-II 25 on references for the term "*ex caritate*"; cf. II-II 23.3 ad 3; 27.4.

reason other than itself, the love of friendship aims primarily at *union* of the lover with the beloved.[71] Thus, the love of friendship consists in the bond of affection between the lover and beloved, which union is the love itself,[72] and carries the additional note of the mutual indwelling (*mutual inhaesio*) of these two.[73] This mutual interpenetration is perfected in the virtue of charity by which "we achieve a spiritual union with God, and are in a certain way transformed into our (supernatural) end (God)."[74] This characteristic of friendship, mutual indwelling, involves considering the beloved's good as one's own, and is described as ecstatic (self-forgetful), zealous, and the cause of all the lover does, feels and expresses.[75] As the result of the virtue of charity, mutual indwelling is an objective existential reality grounded in the Spirit of Love, whose first gift is Himself,[76] and is not merely a spontaneous passion. As·such, the effect of mutual indwelling is an extension of the loving affection by which the Father and Son love one another, in the act of subsisting love called the Holy Spirit.[77]

As Aquinas moves from a treatment of the *nature* and *causes* of love in the *Prima Secundae*, questions 26-27, to an analysis of the *effects* of love in question 28, the influence of Aristotle recedes and that of Dionysius becomes more evident. Love is conceived in Dionysian fashion as a "unitive force" which is the bond of affection leading to "real union" (28.1), whose effects include "ecstasy" and "zeal." In the former, the will is transported beyond itself in an act of generous benevolence, willing the good for another without a concern for the

---

[71] The distinction between these two types of love will be examined below in the analysis of the question of the possibility of the natural love of God above all else.

[72] *S.T.* I-II 28.1.

[73] *S.T.* I-II 28.2.

[74] *S.T.* I-II 62.3.

[75] *S.T.* I-II 28.3-6.

[76] *C.G.* IV.21.

[77] *S.T.* I 37.2 makes it clear that this is the love that extends itself to all creation. In *S.T.* I 37.1, the Spirit is called "the link (*nexus*) between the Father and the Son, insofar as He is Love."

self's own gain (28.3); whereas the latter causes one to oppose any force that could hinder the friend's good (28.4).

Another effect of love that finds its perfection in the virtue of charity as an image of the divine missions is that of the "melting" (*liquefactio*) of the heart. The heart or will "melts" under the influence of love when it shows itself to be ready for the entrance of the beloved, for the appetite is fitted to receive the good which is loved inasmuch as the object loved is in the lover.[78] In the context of charity, this "melting" occurs when one's heart is moved by the Holy Spirit to believe and love God and repent over one's sins,[79] so that the soul which was wrapped up in itself now tends to another.[80] Although a reflection of the divine mission of the Spirit that upholds our existence at each moment through love, "melting" is also a result of the Son being sent to us, enlightening our intellect through a knowledge bursting forth with love. Just as the Son is the Word breathing forth Love (*Verbum spirans Amorem*), so is the soul conformed to God through the imaging of the divine processions through the infused virtues and gifts.

A final effect of love that signals Aquinas' development of Aristotle's concept of *philia* is that of "joy" (*gaudium; laetitia*). Joy occurs as a result of the alteration in the appetite called "love" and the movement of the will towards the loved object, called "desire," and it is signaled by the will's rest in the possession of its object.[81] "Delight" (*laetitia*) expresses interior joy and "dilation," enlargement or exultation of the heart, Thomas says,[82] and is perfected in the virtue of charity. As the perfect exercise of a habit, a virtuous action well performed brings joy.[83]

---

[78] *S.T.* I-II 28.5.

[79] *S.T.* III 66.11.

[80] *In Ps. 21* [22]: 14. 14.221. This reference is found in W. Principe, "Affectivity and the Heart in Thomas Aquinas' Spirituality," in A. Callahan, ed., *Spiritualities of the Heart: Approaches to Personal Wholeness in Christian Tradition* (New York: Paulist Press, 1990), p. 47.

[81] *S.T.* I-II 26.2.

[82] *In Ps. 34*[35]: 27 14.276, in commenting on Psalm 118 (119): "You have enlarged my heart." This reference is found in W. Principe, "Affectivity and the Heart in Thomas Aquinas' Spirituality," p.46.

[83] *In 3 Sent.* 23.1.1 ad 4.

Although all virtuous actions must be performed with joy,[84] acts done out of charity are directed towards that perfect joy of selfless dissolution in Christ, which enjoyment is to be preferred even to the soul's union with the body.[85] Thus, joy is the lover rejoicing in being united to the beloved, or in the fact that the one we love is in secure possession of his own good,[86] and the necessary consequence of charity is joy since it involves abiding with God.[87] Far from being subjective, introverted psychological phenomena, the experiences of mutual indwelling, melting and joy signal the existential union through love by which one is co-natured with the beloved. Through the gift of wisdom, these effects are united in the mystical experience of the indwelling Persons of the Trinity.[88]

Through our analysis of love in its range of meanings and characteristics, we have discerned a theocentric and Trinitarian focus permeating Aquinas' spiritual doctrine, pointing to an existential union and fulfillment vitalized by grace. The movement of love towards its final achievement in charity is seen to involve the presence of God's activity at the root and centre of the interior life, as a principle and term of appetite, perfecting the effects of mutual indwelling, ecstasy, melting and joy, and drawing forth the core of our being as images of Himself.

---

[84] "Actions virtuously performed are naturally delightful.... We are neither good nor virtuous if we do not find joy in acting well": *In 1 Eth.* L. 13 (1099a17).

[85] *De caritate* 11 ad 8: "... [T]he Apostle clearly, unhesitatingly, and even boldly said, 'I desire to be dissolved and to be with Christ' (*Philippians* 1.23); this is perfect charity. It is from the necessity of charity that the soul prefers in any way, even imperceptibly, the enjoyment of God to the union with the body."

[86] Cf. *S.T.* II-II 28.2.

[87] *S.T.* I-II 70.3.

[88] *In 1 Sent.* 16.1.2c ("When the Holy Spirit is sent to us invisibly, grace pours into our minds from the fullness of divine love ; through this effect of grace we receive an experiential knowledge of that divine person ....") *S.T.* I 43.3 ad 1 links the gift of wisdom with the language of "fruition" or enjoyment of God.

c) The Problem of Pure Love

The third and final issue regarding love is the relation of self-love to *caritas* or *agape*, and how Aquinas' virtue of charity transcends the "egoism/altruism" opposition posited by later spiritual writers such as Fénelon, and theologians such as Anders Nygren, who juxtapose the natural drive for self-fulfillment in self-love with supernatural virtue.[89] In this regard, we will outline the position of Fénelon and analyze the solution of Robert Merrihew Adams. Then we will turn to Aquinas' position on the possibility of pure, disinterested love of God, and the relation of self-love to *caritas*.

Writing in the thirties of this past century, Anders Nygren echoed the sentiment of Fénelon, a seventeenth century spiritual writer, in proposing that the Catholic "*caritas* synthesis," that is, the marriage of the "incompatible notions" of *eros* and *agape,* reached its apex in the thought of Aquinas. According to Nygren, Aquinas reduced all of Christianity to a form of self-love through the mechanism of Aristotelian fulfillment of a form's potentialities.[90] In contrast, Fénelon opted for an altruism in which the pure state of charity is untainted by other motives, a state which Fénelon calls, following Francis de Sales, "holy indifference."[91] According to this theory, the will's "indifference" is its purity or singleness of motive in the act of loving God, an indifference which included the absolute or unconditional sacrifice of the soul's own self-interest for eternity.[92] This "neutralizing of the specialness of one's own self," as one commentator has called it,[93]

---

[89] Nygren, *Eros und Agape. Gestaltwandlungen der christlichen Liebe.* (Gutersloh, 1930, 1937), Vol. II, p. 110.

[90] Nygren, pp. 255; 465. A good treatment of Nygren's position can be found in Josef Pieper, *About Love,* tr. Richard and Clara Winston (Chicago: Franciscan Herald Press, 1974), pp. 60-66.

[91] Francois Fénelon, *Explication des maxims des saints sur la vie intérieure* (1697), as quoted in R. Merrihew Adams,"Pure Love, " p. 175. Fénelon's idea is echoed by Nygren's notion of the will's quality of "spontaneity" or "creative character" in agapeistic love, by being "indifferent" to predetermined values. On Nygren on this point, see Pieper, *About Love,* p. 61.

[92] Adams, p. 176.

[93] Adams, p. 177.

follows from Fénelon's fear that God will be loved by the soul with the inferior love of concupiscence, such that the love of God becomes an instrument of human happiness, and God is not loved in and for Himself.

In his treatment of Fénelon's concept of "pure love," Robert Merrihew Adams argues *against* the exclusion of self-love as an element in *caritas.* Fénelon's concern that one might love one's own *love for God* more than loving *God Himself* involved a disjunction between self-love, a type of *eros,* and pure love, or *agape/caritas.*[94] Adams makes the case that one's love of God can *never* be completely disinterested, for it entails at the very least the desire that *I* be the one loving God, which signifies a desire for relationship itself as a good.[95] Without this element of need-love or *eros,* he argues, the feature of "benevolence" in *agape* love would be impersonal and distant. Thus, Christian *caritas* must incorporate some positive aspects of *eros,* namely, the desire for personal relationship for its own sake.

---

[94]As Adams notes, Fénelon distinguishes three types of love for God, namely, "servile love" (which is love for the gifts of God, and not for God Himself); "concupiscential love" (whereby God is loved only as the only means and instrument of happiness) and "charity," or love of God for Himself ("Adams," p. 175). This last type of love for God is called "holy indifference" by Fénelon and involves the soul's indifference to all created goods, specifically her own good: "In sum, the good pleasure of God is the supreme object of the indifferent soul. Wherever she sees it she runs 'to the fragrance of 'its 'perfumes,' and always seeks the place where there is more of it, without consideration of any other thing.... [The indifferent person] would rather have hell with the will of God than Paradise without the will of God – yes indeed, he would prefer hell to Paradise if he knew that there were a little more of the divine good pleasure in the former than in the latter; so that if (to imagine something impossible) he knew that his damnation were a little more agreeable to God than his salvation, he would leave his salvation, and run to his damnation" (Fénelon, [*Explications...* 1697:56, as quoting Francis de Sales, in Adams, p. 176).

[95] Adams, p. 182: "But if part of what I am to desire for its own sake is not only that God's will be done, but also that *I* love and obey God, then it seems that my love for him is not to be completely disinterested: There is to be an element of self-concern in it. Thus Fénelon seems forced to admit an element of self-concern even in perfect love of God."

Having outlined the positions of Fénelon and Nygren, and having indicated Adams' objections, we turn to Aquinas' distinction between the "love of friendship" and the "love of concupiscence," as found in his treatments of love as a passion and as *caritas,* to determine his position on the possibility of a "pure" or "disinterested" love of God.[96] In his treatise on charity, Aquinas notes that, according to Aristotle, to love is to will the good for someone.[97] When the will's direction is towards the *person* who is loved, the "love of friendship" exists (*amor amicitiae),* and when the will is directed towards the *good willed for that person,* the "love of concupiscence" exists (*amor concupiscentiae).*[98] The two motions of the will coexist in the sense that in no case can one love a person without also wishing him a *good,* and in no case can one wish a good without extending that good to a *person.*[99] As well, the "love of friendship" is more basic than and inclusive of the "love of concupiscence," since wanting a good for a person involves some love for that person. Indeed, the love of persons (vs. things) constitutes the most basic direction of the human will,[100] whether this love is directed towards another or towards oneself.[101]

Many commentators on Aquinas, as well as spiritual writers, have juxtaposed these two movements of the will, seeing in them a distinction between a "disinterested love" and a "self-centered love," and framing their theories around the question of whether a non-egoistic love is possible.[102] Perhaps a better formulation of the issue[103] is

---

[96] His doctrine is found in several places, including: *S.T.* I 60.3; II-II 23.1; 25.2; *In de div. Nom.* Ch.4, L. 10 #405.

[97] *S.T.* II-II 23.1.

[98] By the 'love of friendship,' a *person* is loved as a good; by the 'love of concupiscence, ' some *thing* is loved as a good: *S.T.* I-II 26.4.

[99] (In this sense, Aquinas follows Aristotle's view that friendship exists between persons only.)

[100] *In de div. Nom.* Ch.4, L. 10 #404-405.

[101] *S.T.* I-II 26.4.

[102] This is certainly Rousselot's interpretation of the distinction (Pierre Rousselot, *Pour l'histoire du problème de l'amour au moyen âge, Beitrage zur Geschichte de Philosophie des Mittelalters* 6 [Munster, 1908]1-2; tr. Alan Vincelette, *The Problem of Love in the Middle Ages: A Historical Contribution*

expressed by Garrigou-Lagrange, who located the problem within Thomas' own more metaphysical perspective, asking whether the love of one's own proper good or the love of God is more primordial to our nature.[104] In Thomas' treatise on the passions,[105] the two motions of the will do *not* denote a distinction between selfish and disinterested love. Instead, they reveal an ordered relationship grounding all love in its primary form, viz., the love of friendship. In *S.T.* I-II 26.4, the love of friendship stands to the love of concupiscence as substance stands to accident, since the object loved with the love of friendship is loved simply and for itself (a person); whereas that which is loved with the love of concupiscence is loved not *simpliciter et per se,* but for the sake of something else (*alteri),* as good for something or someone else.[106] The well-wishing or benevolence that is extended to a person in the primary type of friendship need not conflict with concupiscent love,

---

(Milwaukee: Marquette University Press, 2002). Nygren's similar construct based on the *eros/agape* distinction (see #96 above); Descoqs (Institutiones Metaphysicae Generales [Paris, 1925]) offers a nonmetaphysical and strictly "moral" theory of pure love; d'Arcy (*The Mind and the Heart of Love* [New York, 1947) aligns *agape* or selfless, "ecstatic" love with the existential self (vs. the intellectualist 'essentialist' self). L-B. Gillon's view is similar to that of Rousselot (Gillon, "Génèse de la théorie thomiste de l'amour" [*Révue thomiste* 46 (1946) 322-29]). Cf. Paul Wadell's work (# 55 above).

[103] A.Keaty, "Thomas's Authority for Identifying #55 Charity as Friendship...," p. 587 #15. In that same article (p. 588 #16), Keaty discusses various interpretations of the two aspects of love, including the views of Simonin, Louis Geiger, Servais Pinckaers, and Albert Ilien.

[104] Garrigou-Lagrange, "Le problème de l'amour pur et la solution de saint Thomas" (*Angelicum* 6 [1929]: 83-124).

[105] *S.T.* I-II 26.4.

[106] The relation of the two aspects of love is compared to that between substance and accident since the substance possesses being simply, while the accident only possesses relative and dependent being: thus, the love of concupiscence depends on that of friendship for its being. This issue is treated again in terms of the object's degree of similitude to the person, in *S.T.* I-II 27.3. In the love of concupiscence, the will is directed to an accidental good desired as a perfection for a person; but in the love of friendship, the object has an actual, not merely a potential and accidental, similitude in relation to the person.

since in the latter the thing loved stands in an accidental relationship to the person loved.[107] The direction of natural inclinations to the common good, in combination with the fact that the divine good is greater than our share of good in enjoying that good, also establishes the fact that God ought to be loved chiefly and before all out of charity, in II-II 26.3. *Caritas* is a love in which the self is fulfilled and yet subordinated to its divine object.

From the above outline of Aquinas' position on the two aspects of love, we can conclude that the position of thinkers such as Fénelon (and Rousselot), which identifies the 'love of friendship' with a pure or disinterested love and the 'love of concupiscence' with a love motivated by personal gain (thus, a 'selfish' love), is ungrounded, as are the similar views of Nygren and other commentators.[108] We have seen that Aquinas' distinction between the two objects of the will does not involve a disjunction between the alternatives of egocentrism and altruism. On the contrary, the primary tendency of the will towards the love of friendship is foundational and inclusive of the love of concupiscence, although disordered, acquisitive love is possible.[109] Moreover, the love of self is included *within* "friendship love," since the primary direction of the will is towards persons, not things.

If the initial distinction between types of love is ungrounded, then it follows that Fénelon's, Nygren's and Rousselot's formulation of the problem of love is also in error. Thomas' analogy of the love of friendship and concupiscence with the relationship of substance and accident shows the impossibility of loving something with a love of concupiscence as an ultimate or final good, and since the love of friendship obtains in the natural state of self-love, the latter is not

---

[107] However, when the object (whether it be pleasurable or useful) is desired for oneself, then the case of a *disordered* type of concupiscence love exists.

[108] Descoqs, d'Arcy, Gillon, Wadell, etc.: see # 102 above.

[109] As A. Keaty puts it, "...the context of friendship love makes intelligible those instances when concupiscence love is disordered.... Concupiscence love in the pleasureful and useful friendship need not undermine these friendships as long as the love for the pleasurable or useful good is subservient to the well-wishing that characterizes love of friendship" (A. Keaty, "Thomas's Authority for Identifying Charity as Friendship... " p. 589).

egocentric. In addition, Aquinas' theories of "image" and "love" preclude the existence of a disinterested or "pure" love divorced from personal happiness. Inspired by both Aristotle and St. Paul, Aquinas knew that we love God for Himself alone precisely because He is the sum of that beatitude.[110] And involved in this natural search for fulfillment is the striving for one's own good, which means loving oneself - an impulse found even in the angels, according to Thomas.[111] Friendship is loving another as an *alter ipse,* "another self," on the basis of some shared good,[112] and takes self-love as its starting point standing to it as a copy to the original.[113]

Many of the threads of Aquinas' position are found in texts where he develops the discussion of charity within the Aristotelian framework of acts and habits. In II-II 23.2, Aquinas takes up the infamous thesis of Peter Lombard, which anticipates the views of Fénelon. Lombard could be interpreted as identifying the act of charity in the soul with the Holy Spirit itself. Like Fénelon, this view makes the soul a purely passive instrument in the bond of charity, a view Aquinas rejects because it denies creaturely freedom and the possibility of meritorious action. A created principle of action is necessary for the spontaneous and joyful exercise of acts of charity, and Augustine's stress of divine causality can lead to a distorted theory of "participation" in divine wisdom and love by the soul. Moreover, in Lombard and Fénelon we see the influence of Augustine's opposition of love and concupiscence (where the lack of charity is said to divert an action from its course towards the love of God, resulting in sinful self-love). Thomas rejects this tension by

---

[110] *S.T.*II-II 27.3: "....We do not love God because of anything else, but because of Himself alone. For, being himself the last end of all things, there is no other end to which he is subordinate, nor does he need any other form to make him good...." Here, the causal character of unparticipated goodness, viz. its unique ability to make all other things good, is at work. Cf. *C.G.* IV 92: "By nature the creature endowed with reason wishes to be happy and therefore cannot wish not to be happy."

[111] *S.T.* I 60.3: "Angels like men by nature strive for their own good and their own perfection; and this means loving themselves."

[112] *S.T.* II-II 26.7.

[113] *S.T.* II-II 26.4.

distinguishing the proper meaning of natural virtues from their ultimate perfection in charity: when ordered to a finite end, we may speak of virtue where there is no charity, providing the good in question is itself ordained to the final end (II-II 23.7). By grounding the natural movement of self-love in a metaphysical analysis of the levels of being, Aquinas preserves both the human integrity of natural virtue and its weight towards perfection in grace, thus avoiding the false dichotomy of the egoism/altruism distinction.

Aquinas interprets Aristotle's self-love of the virtuous man through the lens of St. Paul's distinction of the "inner" (vs. the "outer") man,[114] and, borrowing two classical images of friendship from Augustine,[115] describes the friend both in Aristotelian fashion as "another self" (*alter ipse)* and in Platonic fashion as "the other half of my soul" (*dimidium animae meae*[116]). Nonetheless, Aquinas says that we should love God *first* in the order of charity, for He is the fount of that good which forms the basis of all love.[117] This does not mean Fénelon's sense of loss of self or surrender of fulfillment, but rather the communication and fellowship or "communion" of divine beatitude to man, the divine life shared and made possible by divine immanence itself.[118] Thomas uses Dionysius' distinction between "unity" and "union" to illumine the role of self-love within charity: With regard to *himself*, man possesses substantial unity, which causes the instinct for self-preservation and fulfillment. When elevated by *caritas*, this self-love occurs out of a desire for *union* through friendship with God. As Thomas says, "among other things,

---

[114] Ibid.

[115] Augustine, *Conf.* IV, 6, 11.

[116] On this point, see: James McEvoy, "Amitié, attirance et amour chez S. Thomas d'Aquin" (*Révue philosophique de Louvain* 91 [1993]): 397: "S. Thomas a explicitement emprunté à S. Augustin les deux images classiques qui ont servi a présenter l'amitié depuis le début de la réflexion sur ce thème. La première image, qui remonte à Aristote (bien qu' elle fut sans aucun doute un proverbe qui etait en circulation bien avant lui) est celle de l'*alter ipse*, tandis que la seconde, qui est d'origine platonicienne, est celle de 'la moitié de mon âme', *dimidium animae meae.*"

[117] *S.T.* II-II 26.4.

[118] *S.T.* II-II 23.1.

which, as belonging to God, he loves out of charity, man also loves himself."[119]

In response to Adams' correction of Fénelon, one can clearly see that Aquinas does not envision the inclusion of *eros* in *agape* or *caritas* in the same way. Although Aquinas does admit that both the self and charity, not just God, ought to be loved out of charity,[120] this is not equivalent to Adams' setting up the ideal of "personal relationship" as an object of love to be included in *agape.* Far from positing a *tertium quid* between the lover and the object of his love, Aquinas is rather pointing to the self-reflexive character of rational acts. In the case of love, the will's object is the universal good, and since the act of loving oneself is a certain good, it too is an object of love. But since charity is *more* than mere love, the act of loving love itself is *not* equivalent to Adams' position. Instead of focusing the self on its own enjoyment (*frui)* of personal relationship, the love of friendship as expressed in *caritas* draws the person outside himself in affirming the objective good of the Other as an end in itself.[121] As one scholar has noted, it is the Biblical background of Thomas' texts on charity that provides this emphasis on grasping and appreciating the value of the end in itself. The words of Christ, "I will not now call you my servants but my friends" (*John* 15.15) cited in *S.T.* II-II 23.1 signal God's communication of His inner life, even

---

[119] *S.T.* II-II 25.4. Cf. *De caritate* 7 ad 11.

[120] *S.T.* II-II 25.2.

[121] *S.T.* I-II 28.2-3. Gallagher expresses this point well: "According to Thomas, it belongs essentially to the love of friendship to take as one's own good the good of the beloved. Thus, one's own good can be expanded, so to speak, when one has a love of friendship for another person.... If a person loves God with the love of friendship (*caritas*) then the good of God becomes his own good and his beatitude consists in possessing (by the *visio beatifica)* this good (II-II 180.1). The will's natural inclination to beatitude does not lock a person inside himself; rather, it draws him out of himself and into the possession of a larger good..." (David Gallagher, "The Will and Its Acts [I-II 99 6-17], in S. Pope," p. 85). L.B. Geiger has referred to the objective pole of willing as the "realism" of the will: Geiger, *Le Problème de l'amour chez Saint Thomas d'Aquin* "Conference Albert-le-Grand, 1952" (Montreal, 1952), pp. 70-73.

secrets, to the friend, who, unlike the servant, both grasps the end and appreciates the end for which the master acts.[122]

Thus far, our outline of the views of Aquinas on the love of friendship vs. love of concupiscence has revealed the following points. First, the two aspects of love are not juxtaposed (except in the case of a disordered concupiscential love); rather, the love of friendship is primary and foundational, ordering the love of concupiscence to itself, and inclusive of the love of self. Second, only the love of friendship can direct the will towards an ultimate or final good. Third, his Aristotelian theory of natural love and his Biblically inspired theory of 'image' combine to *preclude* the possibility of a 'pure' or disinterested love of God divorced from the pursuit of personal happiness. And fourth, although the act of loving *is* an object of love through the self-reflexive character of dilection, the supernatural nature of *caritas* elevates the self *beyond* the enjoyment of this natural, reflexive act and propels it towards an infinite, ungraspable objective good.

If Aquinas fails to incorporate the desire for "personal relationship" as an end in itself within *caritas,* how does he absolve himself from a charge similar to the one Adams levels at Fénelon, namely, the criticism that *agape* remains impersonal and unmeritorious if it lacks an element of personal desire within it, and is thus "unchristian" at the very least, if not contradictory? The answer to this question lies in a study of the three specific qualities of friendship (benevolence, mutuality, and a shared good[123]) against the background of the various effects of love.

In the effect of "union," as well as in those of "mutual indwelling" and "ecstasy," the intimacy of communion (*oikeosis:* fellowship)[124] is

---

[122] A. Keaty has studied this issue within the context of charity, in his article "Charity as Friendship..." While the servant is not entrusted with the master's secrets, and so is a mere instrument with respect to the end, the friend *is* so entrusted, and is a coagent with respect to realizing that end (*In Joan.,* c. 15, l. 3 #1).

[123] *S.T.* II-II 23.1.

[124] Communion with God is not only an aspect of friendship but its foundation, in that God, not self, is the principle and measure for all love, and it is God's gratuitous communication of His own beatitude which orders the human

based on the shared good of God's own divine life, which generates a concrete, intimate and profound exchange between God and man. Within the context of an Aristotelian natural drive for existential fulfillment, on the one hand, and the dynamic nature of the Dionysian good, on the other, we are far here from Fénelon's "trials of the indifferent soul."[125] No human compact can be compared with the intimacy of communication that proceeds from charity, since God opens the fullness of His triune life and raises humans' dignity to that of sons in offering Himself as their destiny.

The analysis of some key effects of love has thus *invalidated* the possible charge that Aquinas' notion of *caritas* is impersonal and unmeritorious. But the question still remains whether Aquinas' teaching on the will's natural inclination to beatitude is egotistical, since it involves obtaining a good for ourselves. For Thomas, the first act of the will is directed necessarily to the final end (beatitude; God), but determines itself only at the rational level of the second act of the will, choice.[126] The natural inclination of the will towards beatitude involves a love of friendship for oneself, with a love of concupiscence for the good that perfects us. While not the result of deliberate choice, this spontaneous inclination towards beatitude is nonetheless not

---

soul's towards goodness (*S.T.* II-II 26. 5; 12; 23.1). This communication which is the basis of supernatural friendship is also the basis of the notion of the "union of ends," such that the end of creation and the end of the creature's actions are the same - God's glory, through the community of life of God and His rational creatures. Thus it is that Aquinas gives a theological context and response to the problem of love. For a further analysis along these lines, cf. A. Wohlmann, "L'élaboration des éléments aristoteliciens dans la doctrine thomiste de l'amour" (*Révue thomiste* 82 [1982]: 261. On Aquinas' understanding of the Platonic and Stoic concept of "fellowship" (*oikeiosis*), cf. "Wohlmann," pp. 267-8.

[125] See Adams, p.180.

[126] On the necessity of willing beatitude: *S.T.* I 19.3; 41.2 ad 3; 60.2; *C.G.* I 80. Thus, the first act of the will towards the ultimate end is a determination which is a part of its nature, and Aquinas notes that even the sinner loves God in this way (*De malo* 16.3 ad 1; *In 2 Sent.* 5.1.2 ad 5). Aquinas refers to this act as *voluntas, simplex voluntas,* or simply *velle*: the act called "will" means simply, willing the end (I-II 8.2; cf. IIIa 18.4; 21.4; *De Ver.* 22.13-14).

merely a sensory movement, but rather opens the soul to universal good in a manner similar to the inclinations of the natural law, and to perfection within the context of another person - God.[127] The possibility of man's love of friendship for God, or the love of God in and for Himself, is grounded both in this natural inclination and in the *rational* character of the will, which directs it to the true order of goods, not fixing its gaze on any finite good, even the actualization of the self. In short, desire for the universal good in and for itself stems from the rational and immaterial character of the will,[128] which recognizes only an infinite end as maximally lovable. The object of our self-love, as finite, cannot be the resting place of the love of friendship. As a similitude of the creative goodness of God, the creature's love is primarily directed to un-participated goodness, the universal and total good of each creature.

While the natural inclination of the will to its ultimate end establishes the possibility of the natural love of God above self and recognizes the link between happiness and the love of God, this does *not* represent the love of friendship properly speaking between God and man, through *caritas.* Rather, its culmination is merely the wishing of God His own perfection and the referral of our perfection to this ultimate good. For a true, explicit friendship with God to occur, the presence of grace must be present, ensuring the common possession of the eternal beatitude proper to God. Only this supernatural elevation can guarantee the presence of the most proper cause of love, *similitude,* between the soul and God,[129] since the proper form shared in *caritas* is the very life of God. Moreover, just as the friendship of concupiscence derives from the love of friendship, so the love of friendship with respect to self participates in and is ordered to the love of friendship between the soul and God in *caritas.*

---

[127] The main outline of this description of the spontaneous inclinations can be found in Gallagher, p. 81.

[128] *In 12 Meta.* L. 7 (#2522); *C.G.* I 44; *S.T.* I-II 4.2 ad 2. In this respect, Fabro was correct in calling the will a certain "participation" in reason (C. Fabro, *La Nozione Metafisica di Partecipazione secondo S. Tommaso d'Aquino,* 2 ed. [Turin, 1950], pp. 291ff.). Cf. *In 3 Sent.* 35.1.1 sol. 4.

[129] *S.T.* I-II 27.3 identifies "similitude" as the most proper cause of love.

Our study of three topics within the general theory of love in Thomas' spiritual doctrine has yielded several conclusions. First, the convergence of Dionysian and Biblical influences on Thomas' thought resulted in his understanding of love as a passion (*amor)* and as a virtue (*caritas*) through the categories of Aristotelian *amicitia.* Second, a study of some key effects of love in the graced personality reinforced these twin influences in his theory of love, directing the natural inclination of love towards its fulfillment in *caritas.* Third, the question of the possibility of a pure, disinterested love of God was posed in the context of Fénelon's and Nygren's theory of *eros/agape* and Robert Adams' critique of the theory, and in light of Aquinas' own metaphysical formulation of the issue. Fénelon's and Nygren's portrait of disinterested, pure *agape* love proved a caricature both of Aquinas' natural, implicit love of God and of the inclusive, expansive character of Christian *caritas.* As the Greek and medieval philosophical heritage of love disappeared, so did the foundations and the heart of Thomas' theory of love. The union of the aspects of love, love's analogous meanings, similitude as the proper cause of love, and love's inseparability from the search for happiness, were forfeited by these thinkers in their suspicion both of nature and of the beneficent will of God.

Conclusion

Aquinas incorporated Biblical, Greek and Neoplatonic resources in his description of the *reditus* of creatures to their Creator through the notions of "image," "contemplation" and "love." The metaphor of a fountainhead infinite and undiminished in its source served well to describe the outpouring of the divine gift, the flowing of the twin streams of creation and grace throughout His works. Our treatment of the *reditus* theme accomplished three aims. First, the ontology of the *imago Dei* doctrine was seen to embed an Aristotelian psychology of natures and habits into the wider Christian context of the human as image of God participating in grace through the virtues and gifts of the Spirit. Through the possession, actualization and ultimate perfection of their powers, humans exhibit the images of nature, grace and glory as ascending stages of conformity towards perfect resemblance and divine indwelling. Second, the link of supernatural "contemplation" in the progression of the soul towards the image in glory was outlined, in terms of four characteristics, and the relation between "contemplation," "image" and "love" was illumined. Third, an analysis of the various meanings and effects of "love" revealed Thomas' transposition of Aristotle's theory of friendship into the theological virtue of charity partly through the influence of Dionysius, whose concept of the self-diffusive and gratuitous character of the good was grafted onto a Biblical and Patristic structure and provided him with a model for Christian communion in *caritas.* Finally, a study of the distinction between the "love of desire" and the "love of friendship" revealed the gulf between the later concept of pure, self-abandonment to the divine, which is depicted by Robert Adams as impersonal and deficient, and Aquinas' more robust concept of *caritas* or *agape* as a fulfillment of our existential perfection and as magnetized by a personal, effusive source of love.

For Thomas there is a mutual penetration of the realm of grace, which objectively grounds and illuminates the soul's ascent, and the realm of being in which activities flow from natures through the development of habits. The organic unity present in his thought between the theories of image, contemplation and love signals his rich and orderly use of the principles of emanation and return within a Christian anthropology and holds in balance the dynamism of human love with the "tranquility of order" that is wisdom.[130] In this way, he captures well for the minds of men the plenitude of perfection that is the fountain of God's goodness drawing rivulets of goodness towards itself.

---

[130] *S.T.* II-II 45.6: "Those persons are called peacemakers who bring about peace to a certain extent in themselves and in others. Both occur because those in whom peace is established can be reduced to right order. Peace consists, as Augustine says in Book XIX of *City of God*, precisely in a 'state of orderly rest' (*tranquilitas ordinis).* But this order, as the Philosopher indicated in the beginning of his *Metaphysics,* is the task of wisdom . In this manner, readiness for peace is adequately correlated with wisdom."

ANTON PEGIS'S THOMISTIC THEORY OF MAN AS AN INCARNATE SPIRIT

Desmond FitzGerald

Anton Charles Pegis (1905-1978) was a colleague of Étienne Gilson in their work of the revival of Thomism. His death some twenty-five years ago ended a collaboration that extended over some forty years, and while Gilson's baton has been taken up by others, it is fitting that Pegis' work be remembered on this quarter century anniversary of his death, ironically in the same year as his *cher maître* Gilson.

Pegis was born in Milwaukee to the parents of Greek descent who provided their son with an education in the Greek language thus, as Fr. Armand Maurer says in his obituary, "giving him an invaluable tool for his future studies in philosophy."[1]

Pegis received his B.A. from Marquette University in 1928 and his M.A. in 1929 while doing graduate work as well with the University of Chicago professors Paul Shorey on Plato and Aristotle, and Carl Buck on ancient Greek dialects. "These professors instilled in him a profound love of Greek literature and philosophy which remained throughout his life."[2]

In the fall of 1929 Pegis came to the newly founded Institute of Mediaeval Studies, Toronto, where he began his medieval research under the direction of Fr. Gerald B. Phelan and Etienne Gilson. He received his Ph. D. in 1931 from the University of Toronto and began teaching the same year at Marquette. His dissertation, *The Problem of the Soul in the Thirteenth Century,* was published in 1934 in the St. Michael's College series, *Mediaeval Studies.* In 1937, he joined the graduate faculty of Fordham University and in the mid-1940's he became a member of the staff of the now Pontifical Institute of Mediaeval Studies teaching alternative two week sessions at Toronto and New York. He developed a three-year cycle teaching in the first year the "Greek Background to

---

[1] Maurer, *Mediaeval Studies,* Vol. XLI (1979), p. xvi "Anton Charles Pegis, (1903-1978)," xvii-xix. For the biographical material on Pegis I am indebted to Fr. Armand Maurer, C.S.B.'s obituary.

[2] Ibid.

Mediaeval Philosophy," then "early Background to Mediaeval Philosophy" which went to the end of the 12th century, then finally "Later Mediaeval Philosophy" which started with his introduction of Aristotle into the Latin West and went on to William of Ockham in the 14th century.

In 1946, Pegis was elected President of the Pontifical Institute succeeding Msgr. Phelan, who went to Notre Dame to found a Mediaeval Institute at South Bend. That year also he served as President of the American Catholic Philosophical Association; later, in 1975, he was awarded the Association's Aquinas Medal.

In 1952, he resigned as President of the Institute and returned to New York to head the Catholic textbook Division of Doubleday and its popular Image paperback series. Incidentally, one of the important books in this series was *A Gilson Reader: Selections from the Writings of Étienne Gilson.*[3] In this collection, a number of papers and lectures scattered in various periodicals were brought together in one handy paperback.

When he retired from Toronto, Pegis undertook to help found an Institute for Thomistic Studies at the University of St. Thomas, Houston, until ill health led to Vernon Bourke of St. Louis University taking over. Bourke was also one of the early students of the Institute in the 1930's.

Perhaps, Pegis is best known as the editor of *The Basic Writings of Saint Thomas Aquinas,* [4] which made available to students the English version of the *Summa Theologiae*, Part I, and in the second volume the *Summa Contra Gentiles,* Book III, and selections from Part II of *Summa Theologiae.* A couple of years later, Random House published in their Modern Library series *An Introduction to St. Thomas Aquinas*[5] whose introductory essay by Pegis strikes me as one of the best essays on the

---

[3] Pegis, *A Gilson Reader: Selections from the Writings of Étienne Gilson*, (Garden City: Doubleday and Company, 1957).

[4] Pegis, *The Basic Writings of Saint Thomas Aquinas* (New York, New York: Random House, 1945).

[5] Pegis, *An Introduction to St. Thomas Aquinas* (New York, New York: Modern Library, 1947).

significance of Aquinas. In 1949, he edited *The Wisdom of Catholicism:*[6] a collection of significant Catholic writings ranging from Ignatius of Antioch to contemporary writers such as Jacques Maritain, G.K. Chesterton, Christopher Dawson and, of course, Étienne Gilson.

A *Festschrift* edited by Fr. J. Reginald O'Donnell C.S.B, *Essays in Honor of Anton Charles Pegis,*[7] contains a bibliography of the many essays, reviews, and books published by Pegis up to 1974.

In his dissertation,[8] Pegis examined the theories of St. Bonaventure, St. Albert the Great and St. Thomas. He noted that all were attempting to understand the human person in the context where the Augustinian theory of man as a soul sent to rule the body was being confronted with the recently acquired view of man as a composite of the soul and body. This Aristotelian man was complicated by being accompanied by the interpretations of Avicenna, Averroes and Alexander of Aphrodesia.

What was at stake was to achieve an interpretation of man as a unity, as our experience of ourselves indicates, and at the same time account for the immortality of the soul, which the Platonic/Augustinian theory of man as a soul, does very easily. The theory of man as a composite of matter and form accounts for the unity of the person, but there was one great difficulty: all the Aristotelian interpretations of composites of matter and form involved these forms as "material forms" ceasing to be when the composite corrupts or, in our case, the person dies.

What Pegis emphasizes is Aquinas' originality in proposing that the human soul is a subsistent form conferring the act of existing on the body which it informs. God created the soul, the lowest of the Intelligences, needing sensation in order to fulfill its nature as a knower, as the life-giving soul of the human body.

---

[6] *The Wisdom of Catholicism*, ed. A. Pegis, (New York, New York: Random House, 1949).

[7] *In Honor of Anton Charles Pegis,* ed.J. Reginald O'Donnell, C.S.B. (Toronto, Canada: Pontifical Institute of Mediaeval Studies, 1974).

[8] Pegis, *St. Thomas and the Problems of the Soul in the Thirteenth Century* (Toronto, Canada: Pontifical Institute of Mediaeval Studies, 1934).

In his thesis, Pegis used the early writings of St. Thomas, *The Scriptum Super Sententiae*, the commentary on Peter Lombard's sentences, but more especially he used Book II of the *Summa Contra Gentiles*, especially chapter 68: "How an Intellectual Substance can be the Form of the Body." As Aquinas says: "From the preceding arguments, then, we can conclude that an intellectual substance can be united to the body as its form."[9] Then, reviewing alternative theories which he rejects, St. Thomas says:

> It remains that the human soul is an intellectual substance united to the body as it form. This conclusion can be made evident as follows. The second requirement then follows from this, namely, that the form and the matter be joined together in the unity of one act of being ... the fact that an intellectual substance is subsistent does not stand in the way of its being the formal principle of the being of the matter, as communicating its own being to the matter. For it is not unfitting that the composite and its form should subsist in the same act of being, since the composite exists only by the form, and neither of them subsists apart from the other.[10]

St. Thomas returns to this theme later in his career when he comes to the *Disputed Questions on the Soul,* article one. Here he takes up the same question essentially when he asks: "Whether the Soul can be a Form and a Particular Thing?" The phrase "particular thing" is the translation of the Latin *hoc aliquid,* and as Aquinas says at the beginning of his response, "'A particular thing' properly speaking designates an individual in the genus of substance." Thus he is asking again whether or not the human soul can be the form of the body, and also be a subsistent being, a being having its own act of existing (*esse*) which it confers on the body when it informs the body:

---

[9] "How an Intellectual Substance Can Be the Form of the Body,"*Summa Contra Gentiles,* also known as *On the Truth of the Catholic Faith,* translation by James F. Anderson (Hanover House, Garden City, New York, 1956), Book Two, p. 203.

[10] Ibid. p. 204.

> ... it is obvious that the soul is a reality which gives life to the body. Moreover, vital activity (*vivere*) is the act of existing of the living things.[11]
>
> Consequently the soul is that which gives the human body its act of existing. Now a form is of this nature. Therefore the soul is the form of the body.[12]

Later Aquinas adds:

> For inasmuch as the human soul has an operation transcending the material order, its act of existing transcends the body and does not depend on the body ... consequently, if the human soul, ... has an act of existing which transcends the body and does not depend on it, obviously the soul is established on the boundary line dividing corporeal from separate substances.[13]

Here, Aquinas is breaking the new ground that Pegis extols as unique to the thirteenth-century discussion. He is affirming man is the lowest of the intellectual beings, a separate substance, an intelligence that requires a body in order to understand its proper object: the essences or natures of material things. This is the theme Pegis returns to in a series of articles and papers he authored throughout his teaching career.

After he became President and a professor at the Institute, he contributed an article, "Man as Nature and Spirit," to the Italian Dominican periodical *Doctor Communis* in which he put the Thomistic position as always in a historical context. He opened with this remark: "Three related Aristotelian doctrines have conspired to make the Thomistic notion of man the baffling novelty that it was in the 13th century and that it still is, seemingly in the 20th."[14] The three doctrines to which Pegis is referring are: that the rational soul must be the sole and unique substantial form, if man is to be one being; secondly, that

---

[11] *The Soul,* A translation of St. Thomas Aquinas *De Anima* by John Patrick Rowan (St. Louis, Missouri: B. Herder Book Company, 1949), p. 9.

[12] Ibid.

[13] Ibid.

[14] Pegis, "Man as Nature and Spirit," *Doctor Communis* Vol. IV (1951): 52.

substantial forms are the cause of the being of the individual man (against the Platonic teaching that man is a system of participations in the hierarchy of forms); and thirdly that man's nature is part of an economy of operation and dynamic finality. But while this is Aristotle, the problem is how can the Christian view of man fit into the rest of Aristotle's system where the world is an eternal self-existing world and the best that man can hope for is a momentary fulfillment of his nature through the contemplation of the highest things? (*Ethics*, X, 7) or, as Pegis says: "How, then, can St. Thomas bottle the Augustinian man in an Aristotelian nature? How, more explicitly, can he say with Aristotle that man is endowed with a nature possessing a proportional causality and end, and with St. Augustine that man is a mind made in the divine image and for a divine destiny."[15]

This combination of St. Augustine and Aristotle is the insight that Pegis returns to in his historical analysis of Thomistic theory of the human person. The special quality of Aquinas' answer to the problem of explaining human immortality and maintaining the unity of the human person as a hylomorphic composite is the achievement of Aquinas that Pegis is seeking to recognize and communicate, believing this aspect of Thomism has not been appreciated in our time.

With St. Thomas following Aristotle, we can see what man is in his nature; with St. Thomas following St. Augustine we can see what he is in his history. With St. Thomas, the common disciple of both Aristotle and St. Augustine, we may say that man is an incarnate spirit not in order to lose himself in the world of matter, but in order to become by means of matter wholly mind and spirit .... He is incarnate spirit, an intellectual creature whose sight is abstractive and via sensibility and whose intellectual life is a journey through the world of sensible things.[16]

Pegis prefers to use the expression "incarnate spirit" and not "angel" since the human intelligence needs the body with its sense powers to know the material things of this world; whereas the knowledge of an angel is innate, intuitive and independent of things, as

---

[15] Ibid., p. 53.

[16] Ibid., p. 58.

Maritain brought out so well in his essay on Descartes in *Three Reformers*.[17]

In 1955, Pegis contributed an essay, "St. Thomas and the Unity of Man," to a collection of papers organized to honor the Reverend Charles A. Hart, professor of philosophy at the Catholic University of America, who had served for a long time as the secretary of the American Catholic Philosophical Association. In his opening paragraph wherein he says his topic will be St. Thomas' doctrine of the unity of man, he adds:

> ... In its intention, this Thomistic doctrine is disarmingly simple and straightforward; so much so, that it is a puzzle to understand why the doctrine found so little acceptance in St. Thomas' own day and since that day. What is even more puzzling, the Thomistic doctrine on the unity of man, which its author presents as Aristotelian, is unknown within the history of Aristotelianism before St. Thomas. To complicate matters still further, the Thomistic doctrine on the unity of man's nature is intended by its author to be an answer to a classic Aristotelian dilemma voiced in the twelfth century by the great Averroes.[18]

Thus Pegis has set the scene for the thrust of his essay, which is devoted largely to an examination of Averroes' understanding of Aristotle's *De Anima*. Without trying to give a précis of the paper, let us just recall that Averroes understood Aristotle's *De Anima*, III, 5 as involving one separate intelligence whereby all humans understand. St. Thomas counters by affirming each person has an intellectual soul which has its own act of existing and which it confers on the composite. As Pegis says:

> ... The soul is, therefore not a substance and a form, but a substance as a form, a substance whose spiritual nature is essentially suited to informing matter. And it is in the soul that

---

[17] Maritain, *Three Reformers: Luther, Descartes, Rousseau* (London: Sheed & Ward, 1932), p. 57.

[18] Pegis, "St. Thomas and the Unity of Man,"in *Progress in Philosophy*, Philosophical Studies in Honor of Rev. Doctor Charles A. Hart (Milwaukee, Wisconsin: The Bruce Publishing Company, 1955), p. 153.

> the reason for this union is to be found; whatever the human body is, this it is for the sake of, and in view of, the human soul. It is in the soul, therefore, that we must find St. Thomas' answer to our question.[19]

Here, Pegis goes on to review St. Thomas' position that the soul is a spirit, the lowest of the intellectual substances, and this spirit is an intelligence which needs a body in order to carry out its purpose as a knower of sensible things. This is an understanding of man of which Averroes, and even Aristotle, never dreamed. Pegis adds:

> ... Extraordinary as this Thomistic notion of man is in itself and in the history of Aristotelianism, what is more extraordinary is its nearness to St. Augustine.... Seen in the perspective of St. Augustine's doctrine, the Thomistic notion of man is not so astonishing as it might seem. Man is an intellect, an incarnate intellect, and this by nature. He is an intellect needing a long existence-- the 'longer way'-- in the world of matter in order to complete his intellectual nature.[20]

In response to his election as a Fellow of the Royal Society of Canada in 1952, Pegis presented a paper entitled "Some Permanent Contributions of Medieval Philosophy to the Notion of Man." Against the background of crisis posed to the Augustinian tradition confronted with the introduction of Aristotle's writings in the early 13th century, Pegis returned to this theme of Aquinas integrating the Augustinian man as a mind with the Aristotelian man as a composite of soul and body.

> St. Thomas' acceptance of the Aristotelian definition of the human soul as part of the human composite did not involve an abandonment of the Augustinian notion of man as a soul using a body. On the contrary, St. Thomas undertook to show that the Aristotelian metaphysical psychology explained what man is, whereas the religious psychology of St. Augustine explained what man should become. Furthermore, these two notions so

---

[19] Ibid., p.168.

[20] Ibid., p.172.

> compliment one another that we begin to see in all its fullness the mystery of man's reality and life.[21]

Later, Pegis reiterates the essence of the Thomistic position when he says:

> What is man? If it be true that he is a composite with a spiritual existence, then the only way to put our finger on his oneness in nature is to say he is an incarnate spirit because by nature the soul needs the completion, the growth, and the development which incarnation can give.[22]

Later, Pegis continues: "The Thomistic man is an Aristotelian composite aiming to become an Augustinian mind; but in this becoming he aims not to divest himself of temporality, but by spiritualizing what is temporal in flesh and mortality, to save and eternalize time itself."[23]

On the occasion of Gilson's seventy-fifth birthday (1959), a number of his North American students presented his with a tribute in gratitude for what he had given them as their teacher. The volume contains an essay by Pegis entitled: "Some Reflections on *Summa Contra Gentiles,* II, 56."[24] The title of the article is "In What Way an Intellectual Substance can be united to the Body?" As Pegis proceeds in his essay, he seems to be little concerned with a step-by-step analysis or exposition of what Aquinas answered. In fact, Aquinas presents and rejects a number of ways others have tried to give an answer, reserving his own answer to *SCG II*, 68 "How an Intellectual Substance can be the Form of the Body," the article which Pegis has repeatedly shown to be one of the crucial statements of Aquinas' theory of man.

---

[21] Pegis, "Some Permnant Contributions of Medical Philosophy to The Notion of Man," translation of the Royal Society of Canada. Vol. XLVI, Series III (June, 1952), p. 71.

[22] Ibid., p. 73.

[23] Ibid., p. 75.

[24] *An Étienne Gilson Tribute, Presented by his North American Students with a Response by Étienne Gilson,* edited by Charles J. O'Neil (Milwaukee, Wisconsin: Marquette University Press, 1959), p.169.

What does Pegis do in his tribute to Gilson? While his article relates to his exposition of the Thomistic theory, this time he approaches it from a different direction. He is concerned to show how Alexander of Aphrodias and Averroes were attempting to grapple with the problems of the immateriality of the intellect and the unity of man. Again, this is not a reproduction of the content of the paper but an indication of how Pegis returned to this topic in what is for him a subject of central interest. In the course of this historical exposition it should be noted that Pegis brings in the contribution of Siger of Brabant and also the great sixteenth century Aristotelian, Pietro Pomponazzi (1462-1525) who knew his St. Thomas but could not get over the fact that, on immortality, Aquinas was not as Aristotelian as he Pomponazzi, was. Pegis would, in a sense agree; the Aristotelian man of St. Thomas was hardly someone Aristotle would recognize.

> ... St Thomas, having created the philosophical notions that express with perfect adequacy the reality of the human person clothed these notions in the language of Aristotle. The result, being a true creation in its own order, was as new to Christian ears as it was unknown to the Aristotelians.[25]

In 1962, Pegis was invited to Villanova University to give their annual St. Augustine lecture; this University, of course, was founded by members of the Order of St. Augustine and the purpose of the lecture series has been to keep alive the Augustinian tradition. It was a most appropriate invitation for Pegis, since it provided him with still another occasion to present his understanding of the Thomistic man as an incarnate spirit. Using as his title "At the Origins of the Thomistic Notion of Man," he once again reviewed the historical context of the crisis of the 13th century when the newly recovered writings of Aristotle challenged the Platonic view of man as developed by St. Augustine and those in the Augustinian tradition.

Here, again, Pegis brings out how St. Thomas used the hylomorphic theory of Aristotle to explain natural substance. "I refer to his unvarying teaching that the human's soul is joined to the body as substantial form to matter constituting a unitary being, with an essence

[25] Ibid., p.187.

that is as one in its integrity as the being whose essence it is one in its substantiality."[26] Then, having acknowledged Aquinas' debt to Aristotle's hylomorphic theory, Pegis proceeded to show how St. Thomas is still part of the Augustinian tradition by confirming man is a soul bringing its act of existing to be the act of existing of the composite.

> ... And this means that the soul is destined to be part of man, it also means that in the unity and concreteness of his being man is no more than the soul in the fullness of its nature—an incarnated spirit, whose unity is that he is wholly spirit but spirit involved in a discursive intellectual life on the horizon of matter, in rational motion within matter, and in a progressive approach to intellectual formation and spiritual unification.[27]

Again, Pegis has stressed that using the language and principles of Aristotle, St. Thomas created a theory of man Aristotle would not recognize— a spiritual substance that is a substantial form of the body it makes to be human and to be alive and which needs its body to know and to choose along with its passions. But he is a being with a spiritual destiny transcending this life.

> If St. Thomas made man a genuine composite it was not to bury the soul in the body, it was to express with deep loyalty and fuller adequacy, a notion dear to St. Augustine: the incarnate soul was a peculiar spirit that somehow needed to live in the world of matter and time in order to grow into its destiny.... To fill the Aristotelian bottle of matter and form with the life of the Augustinian wayfarer was certainly to create a new reality, the notions of man as an incarnated intelligence. This is a Thomistic creation which has no predecessor but which expresses in the language of metaphysics what St. Augustine has expressed in the language of history .... St. Augustine and St. Thomas are united at

---

[26] Pegis, *At The Origins of the Thomistic Notion of Man* (New York, New York: The Macmillan Company, 1963), p.22.

[27] Ibid., pp. 45-46.

this moment, and the Thomistic doctrine of man was born in this unity.[28]

In 1967, a couple of years after Vatican II, St. Michael's College celebrated the centenary of the British North America Act, which brought Canada as we know today into existence, by holding an international conference of theologians and philosophers on the *Theology of Renewal.* The speakers ranged from some of the stars of Vatican II, such as Karl Rahner, M.D. Chenu, and Yves Congar to noted philosophers such as Gilson and Pegis. Pegis chose as the title of his talk "*The Notion of Man in the Context of Renewal.*"[29]

In his remarks, Pegis returned to what he has said before about how original Aquinas was to analyze man as a subsistent soul which was the substantial form of the body. Then, commenting on the problem this innovation presented to Aristotelianism, Pegis said: "His defense is as well known as it is astonishing. Giving to Aristotle the benefit of his own metaphysics, St. Thomas created that most remarkable of philosophers, the Christian Aristotle, and unless you read him carefully you can easily conclude from him that Aristotle held the doctrine of an individual immortal soul informing the human body and constituting man himself by their unity. The Thomistic Aristotle evidently held such a doctrine, and it is also a fact that the doctrine exactly suited the nature of the Christian man as a being composed of an incorruptible soul and an organic body."[30]

Of course, Pegis continued stressing that the soul received an act of existence which it shared with the body; this act of existing the soul received from God at its creation. Pegis notes it can be argued that Aquinas' creation did not represent the Aristotle of history, but, at a particular time in history, St. Thomas gave his answer to a theological and philosophical problem involving personal immortality and the

---

[28] Ibid., p. 59.

[29] Pegis, "The Notion of Man in the Contest of Renewal," in *Renewal of Religious Thought*, Proceedings of the Congress on the Theology of Renewal of the Church Centenary of Canada, 1867-1967, edited by Laurence K. Shook, C.S.B. (Montreal, Canada: Palm Publishers, 1968).

[30] Ibid., pp.253-54.

unity of man (incidentally a problem Descartes was to face in the 17th century but failed to answer satisfactorily).[31]

At Cincinnati in 1975, Pegis was awarded the Aquinas Medal of the American Catholic Philosophical Association; he had been the president of the Association in 1946 and a leading participant in many of its meeting. In his response to the award, Pegis took the opportunity to reflect on his almost 50 years of studying St. Thomas and the status of Thomism at that time. He began by acknowledging some of his great friends and teachers. Amongst the former were Gerard Smith, S.J., of Marquette and Henry Veatch of Georgetown; among the latter were Fr. John F. McCormick, S.J., and Étienne Gilson. It was in Fr. McCormick's class in 1927 that he first encountered writing of St. Thomas and it was at Toronto's Institute in 1929 that he met Gilson, who was to be the greatest living influence on his intellectual life.

There was a hint of sadness in his remarks as he recognized that the evaluation of Gilson had changed in recent years; Gilson had been hailed for his great scholarship as a historian of philosophy, but, after he came to identify himself as a Thomist and to insist that St. Thomas was first and last a theologian, and to be critical of those who were cutting and pasting pieces of his writings to create a Thomistic philosophy, his popularity suffered. With respect to the suggestion that Thomists should catch up with Heidegger, Pegis said: "...he rather thinks that Heidegger—or at least the Heideggerians—should catch up with the metaphysics of St. Thomas."[32]

Pegis noted a falling off of enthusiasm for Aquinas even amongst his own graduate students, who, while appreciating St. Thomas, left the impression they should be working with contemporaries such as Husserl, Heidegger and Wittgenstein. He said he appreciated their concern but warned against attempts that have been made to

---

[31] Cf. Colin F. Fowler, O.P., *Descartes on the Human Soul, Philosophy and the Demands of the Christian Doctrines* (Dordrecht/Boston/London: Kluwer Academic Publishers, 1999).

[32] Pegis, "Medalist Address," *Philosophy and Civil Law. Proceedings of the American Catholic Philosophical Association.* Vol. XLIX, (Washington, D.C.: The Catholic University of America, 1975), pp. 228-237, p. 230.

"modernize" Aquinas as had been attempted before World War II in epistemology with Cartesian and Kantian forms of Thomistic epistemology. He granted that in recent years he, himself, had used Husserl along with Aquinas in the study of intentionality. He argued that if St. Thomas could not hold his own, it would be a dead Thomism. However, he concluded by affirming that the metaphysics of Aquinas was not dated, and indeed, was very much alive.

> I find him living and ready to teach one how to think about philosophical problems. He is not here to do my thinking for me and, in this sense, I must do it for myself—I must risk my own life in the world of philosophy. At this moment, sensible as I am of the present occasion, I should like to say that St. Thomas has made my intellectual life a precious adventure. This is all the more reason for me to thank the Association for the generous gift.[33]

And so one concludes that for Anton C. Pegis the Thomistic understanding of man as an "incarnate spirit" is a truth that transcends time.

---

[33] Ibid., p.237.

Strauss, Darwinism, and Natural Right[1]

Carson Holloway

> Social Science, as the study of things human, cannot be based on modern science, although it may judiciously use, in a strictly subordinate fashion, both methods and results of modern science. Social science must rather be taken to contribute to the true universal science into which modern science will have to be integrated eventually. — Leo Strauss, *Social Science and Humanism*

I. The Problem: The Crisis of Natural Right

Can the insights of evolutionary biology resolve some of the deepest problems of political philosophy? Some scholars think so. In recent years, a new Darwinian approach to political science has emerged, advocated by, among others, James Q. Wilson, Larry Arnhart, Roger Masters, Francis Fukuyama, and Robert McShea.[2] Drawing on contemporary ethology and sociobiology, these scholars point to a wealth of empirical evidence that moral inclinations such as care for kin, sympathy for others, and justice as reciprocity, arise not solely from variable cultural learning but from universal human biology. Moreover, they contend, the natural status of such moral proclivities makes sense in light of modern evolutionary theory: insofar as humans, like many other animals, require each other's assistance to secure their fundamental biological interests in survival and reproduction, it is predictable that natural selection would over time favor those with spontaneous inclinations toward cooperation and sociability.

The proponents of this Darwinian approach most concerned with its implications for political philosophy, Larry Arnhart and Roger Masters,

---

[1] I wish to express my thanks to the Earhart Foundation for generously supporting the research that led to the preparation of this essay.

[2] Consider Wilson's *The Moral Sense* (New York: The Free Press, 1993), Arnhart's *Darwinian Natural Right: The Biological Ethics of Human Nature* (Albany, New York: State University of New York Press, 1998), Masters's *The Nature of Politics* (New Haven: Yale University Press, 1989), Fukuyama's *The Great Disruption: Human Nature and the Reconstruction of Social Order* (New York: The Free Press, 1999), McShea's *Morality and Human Nature: A New Route to Ethical Theory* (Philadelphia: Temple University Press, 1990).

present it as the solution to what they, following Leo Strauss, regard as the key difficulty in contemporary political theory and indeed as the predominant moral and intellectual problem of our time: the crisis of natural right. Belief in natural standards of justice that transcend, and thus can guide, human willfulness and passion no longer seems credible. In the absence of natural right, we seem to lack any objective, rational basis on which to reject what strike us as immoral regimes and policies. Hence, Strauss's concern that the "contemporary rejection of natural right" amounts to "nihilism," according to which "everything a man" - or a government - "is willing to dare will be permissible."[3] Masters and Arnhart share Strauss's concerns. The former implies that in the absence of natural standards of right, we have no "objective" basis on which to prefer participatory constitutionalism to oppression.[4] Similarly, the latter argues that without a "natural standard," we have no ground on which to condemn cultural practices, like female circumcision, that harm women.[5]

While such reflections may stimulate a desire for a solution to the problem of natural right, the impediments to such a solution seem daunting, for the loss of natural right's intellectual credibility is, according to Strauss, due to no less an intellectual authority than modern natural science. Arnhart and Masters take as their point of departure Strauss's statement, in *Natural Right and History,* of the cause of the crisis of natural right: "Natural right in its classic form is connected with a teleological view of the universe," according to which man, like all "natural beings," has a "natural end" in light of which reason can discern his good operation; but this "teleological view of the universe, of which the teleological view of man forms a part, would seem to have been destroyed by modern natural science," which has

---

[3] Strauss, *Natural Right and History* (Chicago: The University of Chicago Press, 1953), pp. 4-5.

[4] Masters, *The Nature of Politics*, pp. xiv-xv.

[5] Arnhart, *The Darwinian Natural Right*, p. 124.

opted, with impressive success, to understand the phenomena under its study in light of a "nonteleological conception of the universe."[6]

II. The Solution: The Immanent Teleology of Darwinian Biology

Taking up the challenge implicit in Strauss's statement of the problem, Arnhart and Masters contend that Darwinian biology can restore natural right's credibility even while embracing modern natural science's denial of the teleological character of the universe. This Darwinian solution to the problem of natural right is possible on the basis of a distinction between, in Arnhart's words, *cosmic* teleology, which is no longer credible, and *immanent* teleology, which is. That is, Darwinism demonstrates how a purposeless cosmos can give rise to purposeful beings, beings with an internal teleology from which we can derive natural standards of right.

While Darwinism, like all modern natural science, rests upon a denial of cosmic teleology,[7] it nevertheless sustains the notion that living beings possess natural purposes. As Arnhart states, "[A]lthough the evolutionary process does not serve goals, the organisms emerging from that process do."[8] Without positing even so elementary a teleology as an orientation to survive and reproduce, Darwinism claims to explain the purposive behavior of living beings in all its complexity. It just happens, as a result of necessity, that currently surviving organisms are descended from those possessing inclinations and capacities useful with a view to reproduction of their genes in succeeding generations. Those without such inclinations and capacities of necessity died out. Moreover, these capacities and inclinations come to be experienced by animals as intrinsically good. They emerge and persist because they serve genetic fitness, but they are able to serve

---

[6] Strauss, *Natural Right and History*, pp. 7-8. Also see Arnhart, p. 3 and Masters, "Evolutionary Biology and Natural Right" in *The Crisis of Liberal Democracy: A Straussian Perspective*, ed. Kenneth Deutsch and Walter Soffer (Albany, New York: State University of New York Press, 1987), p. 49.

[7] Arnhart, p. 245; Masters, "Evolutionary Biology," p. 63.

[8] Arnhart, p. 245.

genetic fitness because the organism spontaneously pursues them. For example, as our kin share some of our genes, and as cooperation with non-kin is often mutually beneficial, we have natural desires to assist relatives and others generally.

Insofar as these biological capacities and passions are experienced as desirable for their own sake, however, they become natural *teloi,* ends or goals pursued by organisms. Consequently, biologists cannot understand animal behavior without inquiring into its purposes.[9] To be sure, such purposes are, from a cosmic standpoint, merely contingent and temporary; but from the standpoint of the individual, they are established and enduring natural facts.[10] Hence, we have Arnhart's assertion that "Darwin's biology" can affirm "the immanent teleology displayed in the striving of each living being to fulfill its specific ends."[11]

Finally, Arnhart and Masters contend that natural right can be derived from these immanent natural ends. The good, Arnhart contends, is that which satisfies our natural desires, including our moral and sociable desires. Thus we can judge as good those behaviors – such as conjugal bonding, parental care, and reciprocal cooperation – that respond to natural desires, and condemn as bad those – such as female circumcision, communal child-rearing, and slavery – that frustrate natural desires.[12] Similarly, Masters holds that humans have evolved a biologically-based repertoire of sociable behaviors – such as "voice" or the ability to exert some influence on the groups to which we belong – and therefore that efforts to deprive us of such behaviors "can clearly be described as 'contrary to nature'" and hence objectionable.[13] In sum, for Arnhart and Masters, we can establish natural right upon the teleology implicit in human nature, even in the absence of a teleology of the cosmos. Indeed, they suggest that

---

[9] Ibid., p. 243; see also Masters "Evolutionary Biology," p. 60.

[10] See Arnhart, pp. 232-36.

[11] Ibid., p. 245.

[12] Ibid.

[13] Masters, "Evolutionary Biology," p. 62; see also Masters, *The Nature of Politics*, pp. 213-223.

Darwinian biology, insofar as it establishes the natural status of the moral and sociable desires of human beings, offers a scientific restoration of *classic*, and especially Aristotelian, natural right.[14]

III. Strauss, Darwinism, and Classic Natural Right

Because Darwinian natural right is proposed as a solution to a problem identified by Strauss, we wonder whether Strauss would regard the proposed solution as successful. Would he recognize Darwinian natural right as a restoration of classical natural right? Indeed, would he view Darwinian biology as a satisfactory basis for natural right in any form?

There is good reason to doubt that Strauss would regard Darwinian ethical naturalism as a restoration of classical natural right, for the two teachings seem to differ considerably. Most obviously, classical natural right, as understood by Strauss, is guided by a concern with human excellence, a concern all but absent from Darwinian natural right. According to Strauss, "the classics viewed moral and political matters in light of man's perfection," and therefore their political teaching takes its bearings not only from the various legitimate regimes but ultimately from the best regime.[15] Classic natural right, it seems, proceeds on the basis of a distinction between ordinary goodness, on the one hand, and perfection or excellence, on the other, or between the just and the noble.[16]

Strauss recognizes the sober realism of the classics.[17] Nevertheless, as a result of its preoccupation with human perfection, classic natural right is characterized by a certain otherworldliness. While the best regime is according to nature, it is perhaps never realized in practice.[18]

---

[14] See Arnhart, *Darwinian Natural Right*, p. 17; and Arnhart, "The Darwinian Biology of Aristotle's Political Animals," *American Journal of Political Science* 38 (2), pp. 465-85, pp. 479-480; and Masters, *The Nature of Politics*, pp. xv, and 225.

[15] Strauss, *Natural Right and History*, pp. 134, 140 and *What is Political Philosophy?* (Chicago: The University of Chicago Press, 1959), p. 34.

[16] Strauss, *Natural Right and History*, p. 140.

[17] See Strauss, *What is Political Philosophy?*, p. 43.

[18] Strauss, *Natural Right and History*, p. 139.

Consequently, the notion of "transcendence" is "not a preserve of revealed religion" but is "in a very important sense implied in the original meaning of political philosophy as the quest for the natural or best political order." This "transcendent" aspect of classical political philosophy, moreover, alienates men - or the best men, those who most earnestly pursue perfection as classic natural right understands it - from their communities and from the world itself. Thus, natural right "tends to make" men "strangers", and even strangers on the earth."[19]

Darwinian natural right, however, is not guided by the lofty concerns of Strauss's classic natural right. Expressions such as "nobility," "excellence," and "perfection" form no part of Arnhart and Masters' moral vocabulary, and their political teaching is guided by no conception of the "best regime" as Plato and Aristotle would understand it. They are rather preoccupied with minimal standards of moral decency that are necessary to the ordinary flourishing of any society. Thus, in Arnhart's *Darwinian Natural Right*, most of the discussion of substantive moral principles concerns such things as justice as reciprocity, conjugal bonding, and parental care. Similarly, in *The Nature of Politics*, Roger Masters admits that his biological "standards of natural justice" are probably more "useful in identifying injustice" than in revealing the contours of a life that is in principle best for human beings as such.[20] Thus, Darwinian naturalism appears to be limited to establishing minimal principles of moral obligation.

Because of its concern with decency instead of perfection, Darwinian natural right appears rather earthbound, in contrast to the aforementioned transcendence of classic natural right which, on Strauss's account, culminates in a transcendence of not just this or that community, but of the human things themselves, because it culminates in philosophy. "On the basis of the classical hypothesis," Strauss writes, "philosophy requires radical detachment from human interests: man ought not to feel absolutely at home on earth, but ought to be a citizen of the whole."[21] It is true that Arnhart's contention that "nature" is our

---

[19] Ibid., pp. 14-15.

[20] Masters, *The Nature of Politics*, pp. xv, 225, 232.

[21] Strauss, *On Tyranny*. Revised and Expanded edition, editors Victor Gourevitch and Michael S. Roth (New York: The Free Press, 1991), p. 212.

"home" bears some similarity to Strauss's contention that the philosopher is a citizen of the whole.[22] Arnhart, however, means that we can and should be at home in nature and with our own nature, with the most powerful and common desires that all human beings share. In contrast, the classical philosopher, as Strauss presents him, becomes a citizen of the cosmos by being somewhat alienated from ordinary human nature. The things that animate most people most of the time are of little consequence to him.

These differences arise because the classical and Darwinian teachings derive their principles from radically different understandings of nature. Darwinian naturalism – denying, as we have seen, the existence of a cosmic teleology and hence a cosmic hierarchy of ends – takes its bearings from the biologically-rooted, naturally evolved desires of human beings. Given the variety of these natural desires, however, there is a need to prioritize among them if a coherent account of natural right is to emerge. In the absence of some principle outside of human nature in light of which to rank the various human desires in terms of their dignity or nobility, Darwinian natural right is guided by what it understands to be the most powerful desires. Thus Arnhart, for example, relies repeatedly on the observation that the moral desires are "deeper" or "more enduring" than their contraries.[23] Ultimately, then, Darwinian natural right is guided by a concern with the quantity of pleasure enjoyed in life: the moral life is finally justified because it results in more satisfaction than the alternative.

In contrast, the classics, on Strauss's account, take their bearings from a hierarchy of human capacities,[24] a hierarchy understood implicitly with reference to some principles external to human nature itself. In *Natural Right and History*'s discussion of the classical position, Strauss raises the possibility of something like the Darwinian position, that "moral distinctions" could be based on human nature alone, regardless of the possible moral indifference of the "cosmic order." To arrive at natural right, however, "we must distinguish between those

---

[22] Arnhart, "Evolutionary Biology," p. 275.

[23] Ibid.

[24] Strauss, *What is Political Philosophy?*, pp. 126-127, 162.

human desires and inclinations which are in accordance with human nature and therefore good for man, and those which are destructive of his nature or humanity and therefore bad. We are thus led to the notion of a life, a human life that is good because it is in accordance with nature."[25] But how are we to make this distinction? The approach adopted by Darwinian natural right is to regard as most "in accordance with human nature," and therefore "good for man," the naturally most powerful human desires.

This is not, however, how the classics distinguish the better from the worse. Strauss contends that the philosophic tradition associated with Plato and Aristotle holds that "the noble and the just are fundamentally distinguished from the pleasant and are by nature preferable to it."[26] Thus Strauss, in explicating classic natural right, denies that we can distinguish a good from a bad life in terms of the amount of pleasure they involve.

> We admire excellence without any regard to our pleasures or to our benefits. No one understands by a good man or man of excellence a man who leads a pleasant life. We distinguish between better and worse men. The difference between them is indeed reflected in the kinds of pleasure which they prefer. But one cannot understand this difference in the level of pleasures in terms of pleasure; for that level is determined not by pleasure but by the rank of human beings.[27]

For the classics, then, there "are things which are admirable, or noble, by nature, intrinsically," and whose nobility cannot be understood in terms of pleasure; thus, it "is characteristic of all or most of them that they contain no reference to one's selfish interests or that they imply a freedom from calculation."[28] Strauss elsewhere claims that for Xenophon "the rank of the various kinds of pleasure ultimately depends on the rank of the activities to which the pleasures are related. Neither the quantity nor the purity of the pleasures determines in the

---

[25] Strauss, *Natural Right and History*, pp. 94-95.

[26] Ibid., p. 167.

[27] Ibid., p. 128.

[28] Ibid.

last resort the rank of human activities."[29] To speak of the rank of various natural human capacities, however, implies the existence of a principle of judgment beyond the capacities themselves and the satisfactions accompanying their exercise. On the classical view, then, natural right is not simply derived from human nature.

Strauss does not leave this to mere implication. In "The Three Waves of Modernity," he suggests that the classical view is informed by the notion that man "has a definite place within the whole, a very exalted place."[30] This notion would seem to be essential to the classical view that "not the maximum of pleasures but the purest pleasures are desirable."[31] That is, man has a composite nature – not all of the elements of his nature are equally related to his lofty position in the cosmos – and it is better for him to prefer the parts that are better as judged in relation to some understanding of the order of the whole. It makes no sense, however, to speak of man's "exalted place" within the whole unless there is some hierarchical ordering of the whole. Strauss's account of the classical position thus indicates its reliance on an understanding of a cosmic order or hierarchy that is denied by Darwinian natural right.

For Strauss, it is precisely this reliance on a cosmic hierarchy that fundamentally distinguishes classical from modern political philosophy. "The first characteristic feature of modern thought," he contends, "is its anthropocentric character," which he contrasts "with the cosmocentric character of classical thought." The "underlying idea" of modern thought "is that all truths or all meaning, all order, all beauty, originate in the thinking subject, in human thought, in man." This represents a radical departure from the approach of the ancients, who "took it for granted that man is subject to something higher than

---

[29] Strauss, *On Tyrrany*, p. 204.

[30] Strauss, *An Introduction to Political Philosophy: Ten Essays by Leo Strauss,* editor Hilail Gilden (Detroit: Wayne State University Press, 1989), p. 85.

[31] Ibid., p. 86.

himself, e.g., the whole cosmic order, and that man is not the origin of all meaning."[32]

On Strauss's account, then, Darwinian natural right is clearly modern, despite its proponents' claims to have restored classic natural right. Arnhart expressly denies that nature has any value apart from human desires. "All judgments of value are 'anthropocentric' in the sense that whatever we believe to be good must ultimately be good *for human beings* as satisfying *human* desires."[33] Masters tries to avoid this conclusion. "Naturalism," he argues, "directly challenges" the view that meaning derives only from human thought by suggesting that the basis of meaning is present in other animals as well. "Individual self-consciousness, intentionality, laughter, deceit, pity, murder and warfare have now all been observed among chimpanzees. If these phenomena are at the root of meaning, then surely humans cannot pretend that meaning itself is absent from the animate world."[34] Strauss's account, however, implies that cosmic nature has a meaning that is discernible to reason, not merely that living nature has a meaning posited by the desires. In any case, Masters' example establishes not so much that animate nature has meaning, but that mammalian nature has meaning. That is, nature has meaning precisely to the extent to which it shares the qualities of human nature. Such a position seems hardly distinguishable from modern anthropocentrism.

One manifestation of modernity's derivation of all meaning from man himself is its derivation of morality from the human desires, or rather from the most powerful human desires. "Connected with" modernity's "anthropocentric character is a radical change of moral orientation:" "the emergence of the concept of rights," and more specifically the notion that "the basic right coincides with a passion."[35] According to Strauss, this modern understanding was first articulated

---

[32] Strauss, *Jewish Philosophy and the Crisis of Modernity: Essays and Lectures in Modern Jewish Thought by Leo Strauss*, editor Kenneth Hart Green (Albany: State University of New York Press, 1997), p. 102.

[33] Arnhart, *Darwinian Natural Right*, p. 237; emphasis in original.

[34] Masters, *The Nature of Politics*, p. 247.

[35] Strauss, *Jewish Philosophy and the Crisis of Modernity*, p. 103.

by Hobbes, who held that "the good is fundamentally identical with the pleasant" and that natural right must be based on the most powerful of human desires, the desire for self-preservation.[36]

This characteristically modern approach, however, is also as we have seen, the approach of Darwinian natural right. This is not to say that Darwinian natural right and modern natural right are identical. They differ in important ways. Most notably, Darwinism arguably offers a more complete account of the natural human desires than does modern, and especially Hobbesian, natural right. That is, while the former recognizes our natural sociable desires, Hobbes denies them. Thus, it is reasonable for Darwinian naturalists like Arnhart and Masters to present their account as in some sense refuting modern political philosophy and possessing some kinship with classical political philosophy, which also presents human beings as naturally sociable and moral.

Nevertheless, such considerations should not obscure the more fundamental kinship between modernity and Darwinian natural right, a kinship that sets both apart from classic natural right. Both Darwinian and modern natural right, denying the possibility of a cosmic hierarchy in light of which to evaluate the nobility of the natural desires, must seek to be guided by the most ordinary and powerful natural desires. Classic natural right, in contrast, recognizes the possibility of principles of right existing in cosmic nature itself, in the light of which it can seek to identify and be guided by the most dignified or lofty of human desires. Put another way, both Darwinism and modernity take their bearings from the aspirations of normal human beings, while classic natural right ultimately takes its bearings from the aspirations of the best human beings. Thus, Darwinian natural right participates in the lowering of the standard of political life characteristic of modernity.[37]

---

[36] Strauss, *Natural Right and History*, pp. 169, 181, 227.

[37] See Strauss, *An Introduction to Political Philosophy*, p. 84.

IV. Strauss, Modernity, and the Failure of Darwinian Natural Right

It seems, then, that Strauss would not regard Darwinian naturalism as a restoration of classic natural right. Nevertheless, while he might object to its inability to sustain a commitment to the highest human possibilities, he might at the same time appreciate its effort to establish a natural basis at least for common decency. We are thus led to our second question: Would Strauss regard Darwinian naturalism as an adequate basis for natural right of any kind, even a morally minimalistic, modern natural right?

The assertion that he would is met by immediate difficulties, for Strauss seems to have been aware in principle of the possibility of such a project and to have rejected it as unworkable. In *Natural Right and History*'s description of the contemporary crisis of natural right, Strauss notes that the "majority among the learned who still adhere to the principles of the Declaration of Independence interpret these principles not as expressions of natural right but as an ideal, if not as an ideology or a myth. Present day American social science, as far as it is not Roman Catholic social science, is dedicated to the proposition that all men are endowed by the evolutionary process or by a mysterious fate with many kinds of urges and aspirations, but certainly with no natural right."[38] Strauss was certainly not aware of sociobiology or the later efforts to derive an ethical theory from it. Nevertheless, this passage indicates that he was aware, in principle, of the possibility of such an undertaking, for Darwinian natural right is an effort to derive principles of right from the "urges and aspirations" by which "all men" are "endowed" by "the evolutionary process." Strauss, however, apparently regards such an undertaking as fundamentally different from "natural right," and in fact presents the embrace of the "evolutionary" alternative as related to the crisis of natural right. It would seem that the effort to derive moral principles from "aspirations" arising from an "evolutionary process" that can be viewed as a "mysterious fate" – that is, an evolutionary process governed by chance and necessity, which is how Darwinism views it – is

---

[38] Strauss, *Natural Right and History*, p. 2.

inadequate. Strauss exempts Catholic social science from this difficulty, presumably because it posits a cosmic hierarchy in light of which these various "urges and aspirations" can be evaluated and a cosmic teleology in light of which they can be seen as products of an evolutionary process guided by a benevolent cosmic intelligence. Darwinian naturalism, however, rejects such notions and is therefore left with only the (seemingly inadequate) fact of these various aspirations and their unintelligent origins.

Similarly, later in *Natural Right and History,* Strauss, this time more clearly speaking in his own name, again indicates his awareness and rejection of such a solution as Arnhart and Masters offer. One possible conclusion from the loss of the teleological conception of the universe, Strauss contends, is a "non-teleological conception of human life." This "'naturalistic' solution," however, "is exposed to grave difficulties: it seems to be impossible to give an adequate account of human ends by conceiving of them merely as posited by desires or impulses." Consequently, Strauss presents the crisis of classic natural right as a crisis of natural right simply. He suggests that the loss of the teleological conception of the universe is corrosive not only of classic natural right, but also of natural right in any form. For Strauss, "all modern men" - whether they are "liberals," on the one hand, or "disciples of Thomas Aquinas," on the other - are "in the grip of the same difficulty," which is the apparent refutation, by modern natural science, of the "teleological view of the universe" with which classic natural right is connected.[39]

Aware of these difficulties, Masters tries to surmount them by suggesting that Strauss engages in a kind of esotericism in the "Introduction" to *Natural Right and History.* On this view, Strauss does not really regard the teleological conception of the universe as essential to natural right. That is, he does not regard the rise of the mechanistic account of the universe, characteristic of modern natural science, as necessarily destructive of natural right, as his remarks appear to contend. According to Masters, for Strauss the real threat to natural right is not the mechanistic physics of such as Newton and Galileo but instead the chance-dominated physics of the 20th century.

---

[39] Ibid., pp. 7-8.

For Strauss, then, neither natural right generally, nor classic or Aristotelian natural right specifically, requires belief in the teleological conception of the universe, only belief in certain regularities of movement from which we can derive ends as posited by the passions.

Masters contends that the Aristotelian passages to which he refers in support of his analysis actually point to an understanding of the problem of natural right different from that sketched by Strauss on the surface of his account. Strauss argues that modern natural science has adopted a mechanistic or non-teleological account of the motion of the heavenly bodies, but that for Aristotle the manner in which this question is resolved is decisive for the issue between the "mechanical and the teleological conception of the universe" as a whole.[40] That is, a mechanistic (or non-teleological) conception of the heavens compels a mechanistic understanding of the cosmos, and this renders classic natural right, and any natural right, impossible. Strauss cites the *Physics,* 196a25 ff. and 1999a3-5, as evidence of Aristotle's view of the decisiveness of the account of the heavens. According to Masters, however, these passages deal not with the problem of a mechanistic and non-teleological account of the cosmos, but instead with the problem of regarding the cosmos as governed by "spontaneity" or "chance." Why, Masters asks, "does Strauss speak of a 'mechanical conception of the universe' (a phrase that brings to mind the physics of Galileo and Newton), while citing passages in Aristotle that refer to 'chance' or 'spontaneity' (phenomena that call to mind the physics of Bohr and Heisenberg)?" The answer, he suggests, is that Strauss "intended to direct our attention to quantum mechanics rather than to Newtonian mechanics." For "[d]espite appearances" that the crisis of natural right "is due to a non-teleological view of physics like that of the seventeenth century (laws of nature exist, but do not provide a natural ground for human purpose since they establish mere regularities of motion)," it is actually "caused by the twentieth century's non-teleological view of physics (laws of nature are man-made creations, imposed on a chaotic and meaningless process of chance and spontaneity)."[41]

---

[40] Ibid., p. 8.

[41] Masters, "Evolutionary Biology," pp. 51-52.

Indeed, Masters contends that Strauss's understanding of modern natural science's hostility to natural right is only intelligible if that science is understood as chance-based rather than merely mechanistic or non-teleological. "Without the challenge of twentieth century physics," Masters argues, "Strauss's characterization of the 'modern predicament' makes no sense. A non-teleological but mechanistic physics, like that of Galileo, *is* readily consistent with a modern conception of natural right like that in Hobbes, Locke, or Spinoza." Masters notes Strauss's aforementioned objection to this approach, his assertion of the seeming impossibility of adequately accounting for "human ends by conceiving them merely as posited by desires or impulses." Masters retorts, however, as follows: "*[H]ow* do we know that the political teaching of Hobbes, Locke, and Spinoza is not an 'adequate account'?" Aristotle's remarks on chance are "insufficient evidence" for rejecting the modern understanding, and neither Hobbes nor his followers "have admitted that it is 'impossible to give an adequate account of human ends by conceiving them merely as posited by desires or impulses.'"[42] If it makes no sense to present a mechanistic and non-teleological account of the universe as inconsistent with natural right, Strauss must be understood as referring to a more modern and more radical science that treats the cosmos as a chaos and therefore renders all so-called "laws" of nature utterly arbitrary human constructs.

Masters' attribution of such an esoteric intention to Strauss suffers from three problems. First, he does not even hint at the reasons Strauss might have had to veil his teaching. What possible incentive could Strauss have for shielding 20th century physics from the obvious charge that it is incompatible with natural right, while deceptively directing his criticism toward the earlier mechanistic conception of the universe? Second, Masters ignores Strauss' understanding of the classical account of the relationship between chance and a non-teleological or mechanistic physics. In *Thoughts on Machiavelli,* Strauss contends that from "the point of view of Aristotle, or of Plato, every doctrine which understands the world as the work of soulless bodies

---

[42] Ibid., p. 53; emphasis in original.

not tending toward ends in fact identifies nature and chance."[43] On Strauss's understanding of Aristotle, it is, contrary to Masters' argument, impossible to distinguish a mechanistic account of the whole from one that attributes everything to chance.

The third difficulty requires more elaboration. Masters doubts the earnestness of Strauss's claim that non-teleological natural science destroys the basis for natural right because such science *is* the ground of the modern natural right teachings of Hobbes and his successors, who claim to understand human ends as merely posited by the passions, and who have not admitted the inadequacy of their approach. It does not follow, however, that just because some thinkers have tried, on the basis of a non-teleological science, to derive ends from passions, and have not acknowledged their failure, that Strauss is not serious in his rejection of such an approach. Masters presents Strauss as ignoring, deliberately and for some esoteric purpose, modern natural right; but this presentation is only possible because Masters ignores, deliberately or not, Strauss's many remarks in his other writings indicating, without evident irony, the inadequacy of modern natural right. What Masters sees as an ironic overlooking of modern natural right is rather a subtle criticism of modern natural right. Masters is compelled to misread Strauss in this way because to read him properly – to take him seriously when he contends that a non-teleological natural science destroys natural right because one cannot give an adequate account of human ends by treating them as merely posited by desires – would be to admit that Strauss had, in principle if not in detail, foreseen and rejected Darwinian natural right, which Masters wants to present as a solution to the problem of natural right identified by Strauss.

Most instructive in this regard is the "Introduction" to *The City and Man*. There Strauss asserts that "the core of the contemporary crisis of the West" can be found in the fact that "modern political philosophy... has been replaced by ideology: what originally was a political philosophy has turned into an ideology." This seems to be another statement of the crisis of natural right described in the "Introduction" to *Natural Right and History*. What was once a political philosophy or

---

[43] Strauss, *Thoughts on Machiavelli* (Chicago: The University of Chicago Press, 1958), p. 222.

natural right, knowledge of right based upon nature, has turned into an ideology, the groundless assertion of certain ideals. Here in *The City and Man*, however, it is clear that modern political philosophy's transformation into mere ideology is related to its commitment to modern science's non-teleological understanding of the whole. "Modern political philosophy," Strauss writes, "presupposes Nature as understood by modern natural science and History as understood by the modern historical awareness. Eventually these presuppositions prove to be incompatible with modern political philosophy."[44] The modern natural science to which Strauss here refers must be understood, moreover, as the mechanistic and non-teleological account of the 17th century and not as the chance-dominated version of the 20th century, as Masters wishes to claim. For only the former, and not the latter, could be said to be a presupposition of modern political philosophy.

What, on Strauss's view, is the difficulty with modern natural right, and hence with Darwinian natural right - both of which present themselves as efforts to derive moral standards from human desires in the absence of a cosmic hierarchy in light of which to evaluate the various human desires? While the complete answer to this large question is beyond the scope of this paper, it is possible to suggest two possible beginnings to a full answer.

First, one cannot derive reliable standards of right from the natural human desires alone because those desires are various and contradictory. This understanding is implied by Strauss's initial statement of the crisis of natural right mentioned before:

> Present day American social science, as far as it is not Roman Catholic social science, is dedicated to the proposition that all men are endowed by the evolutionary process or by a mysterious fate with many kinds of urges and aspirations, but certainly with no natural right.[45]

---

[44] Strauss, *The City and Man* (Chicago: The University of Chicago Press, 1964), p. 1.

[45] Strauss, *Natural Right and History*, p. 2.

One cannot successfully derive natural right solely from the "urges and aspirations" of "all men" because those urges and aspirations are of "many kinds." Again, as Strauss' exception of Catholic social science suggests, the manifold character of human desire is not an impediment to natural right when one claims to possess knowledge of some cosmic hierarchy in light of which to evaluate the nobility of the various desires. In the absence of such knowledge, however, it seems impossible to reduce the variety of natural human desires to a reliable standard of natural right.

The difficulty posed by the variety of natural desires undermines Darwinian natural right, as the following example demonstrates. Arnhart devotes the longest chapter of *Darwinian Natural Right* to a moral critique of slavery. His argument necessarily takes the following form: slavery is contrary to natural right because it is contrary to certain natural desires. Arnhart's argument fails, however, because he cannot escape the contradictory nature of human desire, which points simultaneously to different moral conclusions.

Slavery, Arnhart points out, contradicts the natural desire of slaves to be free from exploitation and the natural desire of masters to engage in reciprocal cooperation.[46] Therefore, it is a violation of Darwinian natural right. This easy conclusion, however, quickly runs up against Arnhart's admission that, in addition to these natural desires that support freedom, there is also a natural desire to exploit others that points in the direction of slavery.[47] In the absence of some principle beyond the natural human passions, Arnhart cannot explain convincingly why the desires for freedom and reciprocity should take precedence over the desire to exploit. He can observe correctly that slavery is problematic because its contradiction of important desires makes it unstable,[48] but this alone does not explain why masters should not seek to overcome or at least manage that instability through force, especially in view of the great rewards slavery may offer for oneself and for one's kin. Put simply, slavery is not contrary to nature as

---

[46] Arnhart, *Darwinian Natural Right*, p. 162.

[47] Ibid., p. 160.

[48] Ibid., pp. 207-08.

Darwinism understands it, but is rather ambiguously natural. Thus, Darwinian natural right cannot offer a convincing condemnation of it.

As this example indicates, Darwinian natural right can give only ambiguous support to what we commonly understand as morality. Arnhart and Masters claim to have solved the problem of natural right by demonstrating that human beings have natural moral proclivities. While they do in fact succeed in demonstrating the natural status of our moral proclivities, that alone is not sufficient to show that human beings are naturally moral. Thus, Arnhart and Masters fail to provide us with natural right, when it is evident that human beings also possess other natural desires that are amoral or immoral. And Strauss was aware of this problem, as is clear from the following statement of Machiavelli's position: "Man is not by nature directed toward virtue. If he were, pangs of conscience would be the greatest evil for him; but in fact we find that the pangs of disappointment are at least as strong as the pangs of guilt."[49] That is, one cannot derive natural right from human nature alone when that nature includes not only moral desires but also opposed desires that are no less natural and just as strong as the moral desires.

On Strauss's view, then, Darwinian natural right, which is based on modern, non-teleological natural science, appears no more consistent than modern natural science itself. That science, Strauss contends, continues, due to the survival of certain utilitarian habits of thought, to take for granted certain decent aspirations like health, long life, and prosperity. On the non-teleological view of modern science, however, "these ends can no longer claim the evidence they once possessed" because "they appear now" only "to be posited by certain desires which are not 'objectively' superior to the opposite desires." As a result, modern science is "unable to justify the ends for which it seeks the means," and it consequently "is in practice compelled to satisfy the ends which are sought by its customers, by the society to which the individual scientist happens to belong."[50] That is, in the absence of

---

[49] Strauss, *What is Political Philosophy?*, p. 42.

[50] Strauss, *Liberalism, Ancient and Modern.* (New York: Basic Books, 1968), pp. 22-23.

teleological principles independent of, and not just derived from the natural desires, modern natural science is reduced to relativism. As the preceding discussion suggests, Strauss regarded this as a very real difficulty, and he therefore appears to be in earnest, Masters to the contrary notwithstanding, when he suggests, in the "Introduction" to *Natural Right and History,* that "it seems to be impossible to give an adequate account of human ends by conceiving of them merely as posited by desires or impulses."[51]

To this difficulty, the complexity of the natural human desires, Darwinian natural right adds a second: the impermanence of human nature itself. Even if the natural human desires, taken in the absence of any external principle, were sufficiently coherent to generate coherent standards, those standards would still prove illusory because Darwinism contends that human nature is subject to historical change. As Arnhart observes, Darwinism holds that "species are not eternally fixed since they have evolved into their present form and will continue to change in the future."[52] Standards derived from a changing nature are necessarily changeable standards, yet Strauss contends that "[i]t is granted on all sides that there cannot be natural right if the principles of right are not unchangeable."[53] The Darwinian account is essentially the same as that of Rousseau, who held, according to Strauss, that human nature is the product of a historical process "which is not teleological," or that our humanity is the product of accidental causation. On this account, however, human nature becomes radically problematic as a standard: now arguments "taken from man's nature" are "no longer of importance" because "what is called man's nature is merely the result of man's development hitherto."[54]

There are two possible solutions to the difficulty posed by the accidental and impermanent status of human nature. We might, like Kant, try to take our bearings from an abstract reason that somehow transcends human nature. The Darwinian naturalists, however,

---

[51] Strauss, *Natural Right and History,* p. 8.

[52] Arnhart, *Darwinian Natural Right,* p. 233.

[53] Strauss, *Natural Right and History,* p. 97.

[54] Strauss, *An Introduction to Political Philosophy,* pp. 90, 92.

forthrightly repudiate this as "dualistic." Alternatively, one might seek guidance from this historical process by positing its rationality.[55] This Hegelian solution is likewise unavailable to the Darwinians, who insist that evolution is not directed toward any particular outcome. Here Darwinian natural right resembles historicism, which, according to Strauss failed to find reliable standards in history because those standards turned out to have been merely "thrown up by" a "meaningless process" and therefore "could no longer claim to be hallowed by sacred powers behind that process."[56]

V. Conclusion

While Arnhart and Masters offer their Darwinian ethical naturalism as a solution to the crisis of natural right identified by Strauss, the preceding argument suggests that Strauss would have to regard that proposed solution as a failure. This conclusion, however, seems at first glance to render the crisis of natural right even more intractable than Strauss initially suggested. Strauss's own writings indicate the unworkability of the Darwinian effort to establish natural right in the absence of cosmic teleology, yet Strauss himself seems to speak as if modern natural science has destroyed the possibility of belief in cosmic teleology. Does the Straussian critique of Darwinian natural right then terminate in nihilism?

There is reason to think that for Strauss the situation is not in fact so grave. To begin with, Strauss would not concede that modern natural science has destroyed the possibility of belief in cosmic teleology. Although Strauss speaks often of the triumph of modern, non-teleological natural science, this seems to be more a victory in gaining public acceptance than an irrefutable philosophic advance. Strauss concedes that modern science "is the only authority in our age" that "enjoys universal recognition."[57] Nevertheless, he uses more cautious language when discussing modern science's substantive merits. For example, he states that the "proof" for the "untenable

---

[55] Ibid.

[56] Strauss, *Natural Right and History*, p. 17-18.

[57] Strauss, *Liberalism, Ancient and Modern*, p. 22.

character of teleological natural science. . . was supplied, *or was thought to be supplied*, by the new natural science of the 17th century."[58] Similarly, he elsewhere equates "modern natural science" with "what we *believe to know* of nature."[59] Thus, in *Natural Right and History,* Strauss is careful to frame the crisis of natural right as follows: "The teleological view of the universe, of which the teleological view of man forms a part, would *seem* to have been destroyed by modern natural science."[60]

Indeed, for Strauss modern natural science has not refuted, but merely turned away from investigating, the possibility of cosmic teleology. On his view, Socratic or Platonic political philosophy, which seeks knowledge of the whole despite its imperfect availability, "differs radically from a typically modern conclusion according to which the unavailability of knowledge of the whole demands that the question regarding the whole be abandoned and replaced by questions of another kind, for instance by questions characteristic of modern natural science."[61] Similarly, Strauss elsewhere suggests that "the questions raised by a Thomist, or an Aristotelian, physics" might "retain their full significance regardless of any progress that modern science has achieved by raising questions of an entirely different type."[62] For Strauss, then, modernity's rejection of the possibility of cosmic teleology is not obviously more reasonable than the classics' pursuit of it.

Moreover, while the particular cosmologies of the ancient philosophers may be discredited, Strauss contends that classical political philosophy depends not on any specific cosmological account but only on "the quest for cosmology."[63] And this openness to cosmic teleology remains eminently reasonable, according to Strauss's understanding. We are in fact compelled to such openness by the

---

[58] Strauss, *What is Political Philosophy?*, p. 47; my emphasis.

[59] Strauss, *The City and Man,* pp. 1-2; my emphasis.

[60] Strauss, *Natural Right and History,* pp. 7-8; my emphasis.

[61] Strauss, *The City and Man,* p. 20-21.

[62] Strauss, *What is Political Philosophy?*, p. 286.

[63] Ibid., p. 39.

evident inadequacy of the alternative accounts of the human situation that try to dispense with cosmic teleology. Strauss at one point speaks of the possibility of "humanism," that is, of knowledge of moral principles based solely on knowledge of our humanity, without reference to the "divine." Humanism holds out the hope that by growing in "awareness of what is common to all human beings. . . and of the goals toward which all human beings are directed by the fact that they are human beings," we may come to some understanding of "man's distinctive completeness, purpose, or duty." Strauss concludes, however, that "humanism is not enough," that man "cannot be understood in his own light." Thus, man must be understood in light of the whole to which he belongs, which is "either subhuman or superhuman."[64] Nevertheless, Strauss elsewhere concludes that in light of the subhuman "man as man is wholly unintelligible."[65]

The argument of the preceding sections of this paper indicates why such alternatives are insufficient. On the basis of human nature alone, man is unintelligible, or his completion and purpose are unclear, because human nature is made up of a variety of competing desires pulling him in different directions. Nor can these desires be prioritized, and man thus rendered intelligible, on the basis of knowledge of their subhuman – that is, unintelligent and immediate material and efficient – causes. The only remaining alternative is for man to seek guidance from the "superhuman," which requires an openness to the notion that man is not "an accidental product of a blind evolution" but the result of a "process leading to man, culminating in man," and "directed toward man."[66] Strauss, of course, suffers from no dogmatic delusions about the easy availability of knowledge of the teleology of the universe. He notes that philosophy, the quest for "knowledge of the whole," might "appear as Sisyphean or ugly, when one contrasts its achievement with its goal." Nevertheless, the pursuit of such knowledge appears not only as our only way to approach knowledge of our true end, but also as responsive to a natural and noble longing of the human soul. Thus,

---

[64] Strauss, *The Rebirth of Classical Political Rationalism,* selected and introduced by Thomas Pangle (Chicago: University of Chicago Press, 1989), p. 7.

[65] Strauss, *What is Political Philosophy?*, p. 38.

[66] Strauss, *An Introduction to Political Philosophy*, p. 7.

Strauss concludes that this quest is, despite its imperfect fulfillment, "necessarily accompanied, sustained, and elevated by *eros*. It is graced by nature's grace."[67]

Strauss is, then, both less sanguine and more hopeful than the proponents of Darwinian natural right. On the one hand, because of the failure of the Darwinian attempt to establish moral standards in the absence of cosmic teleology, for Strauss the problem of natural right remains. On the other hand, despite the Darwinian denial of cosmic teleology, for Strauss the full restoration of natural right based on cosmic teleology remains an open possibility.

---

[67] Strauss, *What is Political Philosophy?*, p. 40.

Aquinas and the Limits of Political Authority: Natural Lawyer or Virtue Politician?

Gavin Colvert

Politics and The Renaissance of the Virtues

One of the most significant developments in moral philosophy at the close of the 20th century was a renaissance in the study of the virtues. Thinkers such as Alasdair MacIntyre sparked renewed interest in ancient virtue theories, especially that of Aristotle. As any good student of the Stagirite knows, *moralis philosophia* is a genus that includes the study of the individual and political goods among its species. According to Aristotle, the legislator is the primary person who must engage in the careful examination of human excellence undertaken in the *Nicomachean Ethics*.[1] One should therefore expect a close connection between the revival of virtue ethics and the application of virtue theory to politics.

Interest in 'virtue politics,' however, has lagged behind that of virtue ethics until recently. A plausible explanation for this gap is the natural tendency of virtue theory toward substantive and even perfectionist accounts of the common good, which is difficult to square with the procedural minimalism dominating recent liberal political theory.[2] This substantive conception may well be regarded as a virtue rather than a vice in the theoretical standpoint of virtue theories. Communitarians have rightly pointed out that procedural liberalism is unable to sustain a suitably robust understanding of civic virtue and a shared conception of the human good, which are required for a healthy

---

[1] See e.g. *Nicomachean Ethics*, I.13, 1102a2ff.

[2] For a version of this thesis see Will Kymlicka, *Contemporary Political Philosophy: An Introduction* (New York: Oxford University Press, 1991). For the best example of the minimalist view see e.g. John Rawls, *A Theory of Justice*, (Cambridge: Harvard University Press/Belknap, 1972) and also *Political Liberalism* (New York: Columbia University Press, 1993). For an excellent critique of the view see Michael Sandel, *Liberalism and the Limits of Justice* (Cambridge: Cambridge University Press, 1982) and *Democracy's Discontent* (Cambridge: Harvard University Press/Belknap, 1996).

common political life.[3] On the other hand, we must acknowledge that the more substantive conception of the common good endorsed by many communitarians, if left unchecked, threatens to create an authoritarian state in the name of the production of civic virtue.[4]

Developing a satisfactory political theory thus requires one to seek a golden mean between the extremes of radical communitarianism and procedural liberalism. This mean must combine a revitalized focus upon the virtues with real limits upon the legitimate extent of political authority. It must therefore bring together concerns of virtue theory with those of political liberalism. It must provide a defensible conception of shared civic interests, rooted in an appropriate substantive account of the human good, at the same time as it articulates principled limits upon power. Here it will be argued that Aquinas' moral and political philosophy can provide the necessary golden mean.[5] This conclusion will be demonstrated through an examination of the recent debate concerning whether Aquinas is more properly described as a virtue theorist or as a natural lawyer. While that dispute has often been framed as a question about his ethics, it has obvious and immediate implications for his political theory.

Aquinas certainly had an abiding interest in the virtues on account of his thoroughgoing Aristotelianism. His mature treatise concerning

---

[3] See e.g. Sandel, *Liberalism and the Limits of Justice,* p. 179ff. See also, Alasdair MacIntyre, "The Privatization of the Good," in *Review of Politics* 52, Summer 1990, pp. 3ff.

[4] For a discussion of this concern, see e.g. Kymlicka.

[5] As will become clear in the course of this study, although I am not prepared to agree completely with John Finnis' claim that Aquinas proposes a purely instrumental conception of the political good, my account draws upon his presentation of the essential limitations of the role of government and law in Aquinas' political philosophy. See e.g., "Public Good: The Specifically Political Common Good in Aquinas," in Robert P. George, ed., *Natural Law and Moral Inquiry: Ethics, Metaphysics, and Politics in the Work of Germain Grisez* (Washington, DC: Georgetown University Press, 1998). A revised version of this article appears in Chapter VII of Finnis' recent book: *Aquinas: Moral, Political and Legal Theory*, in *Founders of Modern Political and Social Thought* (Oxford: Oxford University Press, 1998).

the practical dimensions of the moral life, the *Secunda secundae* of the *Summa theologiae*, is structured in terms of the cardinal and theological virtues. Some contemporary Thomists have therefore been eager to label him a 'virtue theorist' and to eschew the more traditional perception of him as a natural lawyer. Doing so has the added benefit of dissociating his work from putative legalism in moral theology.[6]

Nevertheless, the framework of the contemporary debate in virtue theory has generated a false dichotomy between Aquinas' appeal to virtues and to principles of the natural law. Neither virtues nor principles play a strictly reducible role in his moral and political theory. While a rigid and strictly deductive account of the moral life must not be attributed to St. Thomas, there is a place for the deduction of certain concrete norms for action from the general principles of the natural law in his system.[7] This conclusion runs contrary to some interpreters of his moral theory who reject the characterization of him as a natural lawyer. It is, however, the key to understanding his conception of normative limits upon state authority in political theory, and also a basis for acknowledging both liberal and communitarian concerns.

Thomistic natural law theorists such as John Finnis and Germain Grisez have been engaged in a dispute with proportionalists about whether natural law theory can provide a basis for certain moral absolutes.[8] The former aim to protect the pursuit of genuine goods by

---

[6] The most radical version of this argument, which will be examined in detail below, can be found in Daniel Nelson, *The Priority of Prudence: Virtue and Natural Law in Thomas Aquinas and the Implications for Modern Ethics* (University Park, Pennsylvania: Pennsylvania State University Press, 1992). A more moderate version of the view can be found in Daniel Westberg, *Right Practical Reason Aristotle, Action and Prudence in Aquinas* (Oxford: Clarendon Press, 1994), esp. pp. 229ff.

[7] See e.g. *Summa theologiae* I-II.95.2. See also John Finnis, *Moral Absolutes: Tradition, Revision, and Truth* (Washington, DC: Catholic University of America Press, 1991) and Germain Grisez, *The Way of the Lord Jesus Volume One: Christian Moral Principles* (Chicago: Franciscan Herald Press, 1983) (hereafter CMP).

[8] See e.g. John Finnis, *Moral Absolutes* and Germain Grisez, CMP, esp. chap. 6.

the maintenance of certain absolute moral requirements.[9] The requirements of right conduct retain their force because they protect genuine ways of seeking human fulfillment. In this way, natural law principles are complementary to human goods and virtues. Admittedly, some Thomistic natural lawyers have not appreciated fully the centrality of the virtues in Aquinas' account of moral and political life. With proper clarification, though, his appeal to virtue and law must not be regarded as at cross-purposes. Furthermore, the specification of a narrow but well-defined range of moral absolutes establishes normative limits upon political authority. Aquinas may thus respond sympathetically to liberal political theorists' concerns about abuse of state power while recognizing communitarian concerns about the common good.

Contemporary Virtue Theory

To many recent interpreters of his moral philosophy who are inspired by the seminal work of Alasdair MacIntyre, Aquinas is evidently a virtue theorist. Careful scrutiny, however, shows that drawing such a conclusion is neither simple nor obvious. The category of 'virtue ethics' is a modern invention, forged as a replacement for the once dominant deontological and consequentialist schools of thought. It has a history and is a product of certain localized disputes with its predecessors. Uncritical identification of Aquinas' moral philosophy with contemporary virtue theory is not only historically anachronistic, but it also deprives his synthesis of the golden mean between communitarian and liberal political theory.

Virtue theorists often assert that principle-based models of ethical and political decision-making lead to interminable disagreement. These thinkers do not hold that appeals to principles must be supplemented by appeals to virtues. Rather, they think that appeals to principles must be replaced entirely or seen as strictly derivative from the virtues, and also that ethical universals must give way to moral particularism.[10] This

---

[9] See e.g. CMP chap. 7 & 8, also John Finnis, *Fundamentals of Ethics* (Washington, DC: Georgetown University Press, 1983), esp. III.6, pp. 74ff.

[10] See e.g., John McDowell,"Virtue and Reason," *The Monist*, 62, 1979, reprinted in Roger Crisp and Michael Slote, eds., *Virtue Ethics*, Oxford Readings in

sharp dichotomy between the role of the virtues and moral principles is inadequate to capture the richness of Aquinas' position. We may tend to overlook this fact because renewed interest in the virtues was sparked by philosophers with certain sympathies for Aristotle and Aquinas. There is a temptation to assume that contemporary virtue theory is synonymous with the recovery of the historical tradition of the virtues. This assumption has produced some positive results, including a renewed sense of the importance of the virtues in Aquinas' moral philosophy and awareness that modern influences upon Thomistic natural law theory have pushed it in the direction of presenting Aquinas as a deontological theorist with a strictly deductive model of practical reasoning. If virtue theory is the answer to our Kantian discontents, then it may seem that liberating Aquinas from his position as a central figure in the natural law tradition will give new currency to his thought.[11]

Two important obstacles to this sort of reconstruction of Aquinas' moral philosophy are worth considering. First, some critics argue that virtue theories do not provide a basis for the resolution of putative interminable disagreements attributed to principle-based models of ethical discourse.[12] This point is bolstered by the fact that virtue

---

Philosophy (Oxford: Oxford University Press, 1998), pp. 141-162. See especially, p. 161, "If the question 'How should one live?' could be given a direct answer in universal terms, the concept of virtue would have only a secondary place in moral philosophy. But the thesis of uncodifiability excludes a head-on approach to the question whose urgency gives ethics its interest."

[11] See e.g. Nelson, *The Priority of Prudence,* "[Natural law's] force as a coherent and identifiable moral and political doctrine has long been spent.... As a result, Thomas Aquinas, the main character in the story, appears to have only historic interest. If, however, there is a different story that can be told about St. Thomas, a story that makes his usual appearance in the natural-law narrative a case of long mistaken identity with profound cultural consequences, then there may be reasons to include him in another story—that of the virtues —which deserves contemporary interest."

[12] See e.g., John Haldane, "MacIntyre's Thomist Revival: What Next?" in John Horton and Susan Mendus, eds., *After MacIntyre: Citical Perspectives on the Work*

theorists have not been very successful in deploying political theories based upon their ethical theories. Second, the attempt to deny a substantive role for the natural law in Aquinas' moral philosophy faces important and stubborn textual obstacles, many of which are connected with his treatment of the relation between ethics and political philosophy. Aquinas looks to natural law principles, for instance, and to the norms we derive closely from them, for a set of transcendent moral goods that can help to resolve problems of fundamental moral and political disagreement. The use of these principles has a distinguished history, influencing important developments in the birth of international law and more recently in the fight for civil rights in the United States through Martin Luther King, Jr.'s, "Letter from Birmingham City Jail."

Some interpreters opt for a middle way, arguing that Aquinas' moral philosophy cannot be captured by exclusive appeal either to virtues or to principles.[13] This chapter contends that is the most accurate view of Aquinas' thought and it gives him the theoretical high ground. His integrated conception of law and virtue can offer much to the contemporary political debate between liberals and communitarians. In order to support this conclusion, one must do three things: 1) determine more precisely what is the nature of virtue theory, 2) evaluate the arguments for treating Aquinas as a virtue theorist, and 3) apply the fruits of this analysis to his political theory.

Virtue Theory and Particularism

In their recent anthology collecting some of the most important work in the field, Roger Crisp and Michael Slote emphasize that an exhortation to live the virtuous life is not a sufficient condition for describing a theoretical position as a virtue theory.[14] After all, Mill and Kant could appeal to the virtues while subordinating them as *means* to the observance of universal rational norms. The virtue theorist, on the

---

of Alasdair MacIntyre (Notre Dame, Indiana: University of Notre Dame Press, 1994), pp. 91ff.

[13] See e.g. Westberg, *Right Practical Reason*, p. 12, p. 229.

[14] Crisp and Slote, *Virtue Ethics*, p. 2.

other hand, must "carve out his or her own niche."[15] Virtue itself must become the primary moral category. Concepts of duty and obligation must be regarded as derivative. As Crisp and Slote stress, "The virtue ethicist at least does not *need* such language."[16] To give principles a co-equal role in one's moral philosophy would render it subject to the repudiated struggles of predecessor theories. Hence, there is a built-in presupposition of tension between virtues and principles. Clearly, if Aquinas is a virtue theorist in the contemporary sense, it is necessary to free him from any intrinsic dependence upon natural law theory as a means of action guidance.

Rejection of principle-based approaches is closely connected to moral particularism, a point which can be seen most clearly in John McDowell's provocative idea of the "uncodifiability thesis."[17] According to McDowell, as long as we think of moral rationality as the attempt to formulate universal rules of conduct and to deduce particular conclusions from them, we treat virtue as a secondary concept.[18] He proposes an alternative model of practical rationality, one that he regards as inspired by Aristotle. McDowell models practical judgment on the notion of perception, specifically the perception of Lockean secondary qualities. What is unique in his conception is not merely the assimilation of practical judgment to perception. Visual metaphors abound in traditional accounts of the virtues. The crucial difference in his approach is the repudiation of any relation between ethical perception and moral universals. Secondary quality perception both reflects the world and requires an internal disposition in the agent. This discriminating ability is thoroughly cognitive, but it is not in any way syllogistic. The internal disposition of the agent is not a reasoning ability, but a rational sensibility. According to McDowell, agents can fail to be rationally responsive to the world around them. Like the perception of secondary qualities such as color, moral perception can be objective, even though the properties in question are not 'brutely

---

[15] Ibid.

[16] Ibid., p. 3.

[17] McDowell, "Virtue and Reason," in Crisp and Slote, pp. 148ff.

[18] Ibid.

there' in the world like primary qualities.[19] Although we do not literally see the moral qualities of our actions, we train our rational faculty to grasp the fitness or unfitness of our actions immediately and non-inferentially. It is not difficult to see that this conception of virtue is the result of the historical attempt to define virtue theory sharply in contradistinction to utilitarian and deontological appeals to the deduction of moral conclusions from principles.

The intricacies of McDowell's position and its full implications for moral epistemology are beyond the scope of the present consideration, but it is important to note that he deploys his perceptual analogy using the Aristotelian account of habituation to the virtues. The ability to judge practical truth is, according to McDowell, literally a process of acquiring certain habitual dispositions or sensitivities to perceive reliably the moral qualities of our actions.[20] This characterization of moral knowledge in terms of virtue construed as a rational sensibility is central to McDowell's "uncodifiability thesis" and his moral particularism. He insists that the perceptual model for knowledge can do without a conception of "stateable propositional content."[21] Thus, the familiar idea of practical reasoning in terms of which particular moral conclusions are deduced from general principles is no longer appropriate. For McDowell, a conception of morality in which virtue is regarded as the primary category and principles as strictly derivative, requires us to reject the syllogistic model of practical reasoning. He notes:

> This picture fits only if the virtuous person's views about how, in general, one should behave are susceptible of codification, in principles apt for serving as major premises in syllogisms of the sort envisaged. But to an unprejudiced eye it

---

[19] See John McDowell,"Values and Secondary Qualities," in *Morality and Objectivit*, Ted Honderich ed. (London: Routledge and Kegan Paul, 1985), reprinted in Geoffrey Sayre-McCord ed., *Essays on Moral Realism*, pp. 166-180.

[20] McDowell, "Virtue and Reason," p. 142.

[21] Ibid., p. 147.

> should seem quite implausible that any reasonably adult moral outlook admits of any such codification.[22]

We may be inclined to agree with McDowell that attempts to subordinate one's whole conception of what virtue requires to a set of rules is misguided. But, his thesis goes further; making the argument that to conceive of practical judgment in terms of universal principles is to introduce an unacceptable form of deontological codification. This more radical interpretation of the tension between virtues and principles has fueled recent developments in virtue ethics and has significant implications for virtue politics. One who wishes to read Aquinas as a contemporary virtue theorist must discount the significance of his talk of deduction of specific moral norms from universal natural law principles. Once this category of norms has been eliminated, Aquinas is left without clear theoretical distinctions that help to establish the limits of political authority.

Aquinas: Natural law and Virtue

Whether or not McDowell's specific target of criticism is Aquinas, it is clear that the Thomistic natural law tradition played an important role in the development of the position he seeks to undermine. We must remember that the sources of Aquinas' moral philosophy include not only Aristotle's *Nicomachean Ethics*, but also the Stoic and Augustinian traditions, as well as the Biblical basis of morality in the Decalogue and the concept of a covenant. These sources necessitate reconciliation of appeals to the virtues with the notion of universal and immutable laws. Members of the natural law tradition have therefore paid special attention to the process of eliciting (including deducing) specific norms from more general principles. It should be granted that some inferior presentations of his thought have tended to misrepresent Aquinas by overemphasizing the degree to which he regarded the moral and political process as deductively specified. In reaction against the legalistic excesses of their predecessors, some 'virtue Thomists' have embraced a position very much like that espoused by McDowell. It is therefore necessary to examine whether Aquinas fits the

[22] Ibid., p. 148.

stereotypical view of a natural lawyer and to what extent the revised description of him as a virtue theorist is apt.

Aquinas as 'natural lawyer'

There are far too many natural law interpretations of Aquinas to enumerate in this space. For the sake of simplicity, we will look briefly at three representative instances: a popular 20th century introduction to his moral philosophy, a traditional Latin manual of moral theology, and more recent work from the so-called "new natural law theorists" John Finnis, Germain Grisez and their collaborators. This survey will demonstrate that while the stereotypical view of Aquinas has been adopted by some interpreters, a more comprehensive picture of Thomistic natural law theory shows much greater subtlety and depth.

Perhaps the most striking case for the stereotypical view of Aquinas can be found in Austin Fagothey's *Right and Reason*, a popular English language introduction to natural law theory.[23] If one compares changes made between earlier and later editions of the text, Fagothey presents virtually a textbook case of the view coming under fire from virtue theorists. Fagothey's work is noteworthy because it served as a key text for a generation of North American college students and seminarians. Despite Fagothey's evident erudition, his work leaves much to be desired in regard to his interpretation of Aquinas on the relation between natural law principles and virtues. What is even more striking is that Fagothey attempted to correct this problem in later editions of the text. He erroneously thought that in doing so he was departing from the letter of Aquinas' moral philosophy in order to save its spirit.

In the preface to the third edition of the text, he notes that he has made certain minor emendations to his presentation of the presuppositions and methods of ethics in order to bring them up to date. Specifically, his intention is to be less dogmatic and to alter the appearance of a legalistic attitude toward moral choice from previous editions.[24] Whether these changes were made in light of the new

---

[23] Austin Fagothey, *Right and Reason: Ethics in Theory and Practice* (St. Louis: C.V. Mosby, Co., First Edition, 1953 [Third edition, 1963]).

[24] Fagothey, *Right and Reason*, Third edition, Preface.

climate in theology beginning to take shape at the Second Vatican Council, he does not say. His answer to this question would be instructive, since the Council was widely perceived as attempting to combat excessive legalism in moral theology and to restore the proper place of individual conscience and prudential judgment.[25] What we do know is that the emendations represent a major shift away from conceptualizing natural law theory as a deductive science toward an account of it in terms of the acquisition of certain virtues, especially practical wisdom.

In the first edition of the text, Fagothey had enumerated two primary methods of inquiry: the deductive or a priori approach and the inductive or empirical approach. Commenting upon the use of these two methods, he had asserted, "[T]he method of ethics is mixed, *with emphasis upon deduction.*"[26] In the third edition, the same sentence appears without the latter part about deduction, and it immediately adds, "It is no mere spinning of a string of conclusions from ideas found embedded in our minds with no reference to experience."[27] Fagothey continues with a curious series of paragraphs that attribute the empirical or inductive procedure in moral philosophy to Aristotle's *Nicomachean Ethics*. The deductive procedure is said to be proper to theological science and paradigmatic of the way Aquinas proceeds in the *Summa theologiae*.[28] Fagothey then asserts that Aquinas never wrote a properly philosophical treatise on ethics since he used the theological procedure of deduction rather than the philosophical method of induction.[29] Acknowledging that this latter method, putatively the procedure Aquinas prefers, is inappropriate to a philosophical treatise on natural law theory, Fagothey resolves to follow the philosophical procedure as more appropriate to his study.

---

[25] For a useful discussion of this point see Daniel Westberg, *Right Practical Reason*, pp. 3ff.

[26] Fagothey, *Right and Reason*, First edition, p. 25; emphasis added.

[27] Ibid., Third edition, p. 19.

[28] Ibid., pp. 19-20.

[29] Ibid., p. 20.

He inserts a paragraph in the chapter on natural law in the 3rd edition that muses, "There are some who look upon the natural law as a rigid and stifling box around their lives and cramping them into an unrelieved round of prescribed duties."[30] In an effort to dispel this myth about Thomistic natural law theory, Fagothey refers the reader to *Summa theologiae* I-II.94.4, the passage in which Aquinas grants that the universal principles of the natural law admit exceptions when we descend to matters of detail. This passage has been used more recently by proportionalists and 'virtue Thomists' to mount a critique of the stereotypical view of Aquinas' moral philosophy.[31] In the third edition of *Right and Reason*, this passage replaces a long discussion in the first edition of the necessity of demonstrating the immutability of the natural law.[32]

If we were to judge Aquinas' moral philosophy and the state of Thomistic natural law theory by the light of this once popular North American view, we would have to conclude that both were inclined toward the sort of deductive account of moral choice that virtue theorists aim to repudiate. Fagothey's presentation also tends to strengthen the case of virtue theorists within the Thomistic camp who complain that the tradition has seriously misread Aquinas, and that he is in fact a virtue theorist. The obvious evidence for their complain which is that, contrary to Fagothey's assertions, Aquinas gives relatively limited consideration to the question of the natural law and much more extensive and systematic consideration to acquiring the virtues in the second part of the *Summa theologiae*. While Fagothey's presentation of natural law theory fits the stereotypical mold, one should note that it is neither an accurate representation of Aquinas' moral philosophy, nor even of the whole manual tradition. Both points merit attention since some 'virtue Thomists' wish to discount the entire traditional reading of his work as seriously misguided. 'Virtue Thomists' are certainly correct to insist that Aquinas' method in moral philosophy is not primarily deductive. Both general and specific considerations support this view.

---

[30] Ibid., p. 136.

[31] See e.g. Nelson, *The Priority of Prudence*, pp. 125ff.

[32] Fagothey, *Right and Reason*, First edition, p. 164.

The second half of the second part of the *Summa theologiae*, for instance, provides a concrete treatment of the moral life organized in terms of the cardinal and theological virtues. Aquinas is eminently clear about the reasons for undertaking his study in this way. He notes that universal moral principles are less useful because of the concrete particularity of human actions.[33] Furthermore, he asserts that all moral matters can be reduced to the consideration of the virtues, and the various virtues and vices can be brought under the scheme of the seven cardinal and theological virtues, with their opposing vices.

It remains to be seen whether the reduction Aquinas has in mind here can be equated with particularism of the sort endorsed by John McDowell, but it is evident that the method of the *Summa theologiae* is not strictly deductive as Fagothey originally claimed.

Various specific considerations in the text strengthen this conclusion. For instance, in treating the virtue of prudence, Aquinas postulates its dependence upon both universal principles and the moral virtues.[34] The moral virtues enable the agent to judge rightly about the particular ends of his or her actions in light of their correspondence to the universal principles of action. The moral virtues therefore have an irreducible cognitive role to play in the moral life.[35] In his discussion of natural law, Aquinas refers to the contingency of particular actions for which he has previously argued that the guidance of the moral virtues is required.[36] He notes that the descent from general principles to particular cases admits of variation. While the natural law always prescribes virtuous actions, it does not provide complete guidance for all of the acts of the particular virtues.[37] Lest we come to identify that process with a further set of deductions, Aquinas notes that the process is sometimes deductive, but in many instances it is not.[38] From this sampling of texts, it is evident that Aquinas envisions a complementary

---

[33] See *Summa theologiae* (hereafter *ST*) II-II.prol.

[34] See *ST* II-II.58.5, also II-II.57.4.

[35] *ST* II-II.58.5.

[36] *ST* I-II.94.4.

[37] *ST* I-II.94.3.

[38] *ST* I-II.95.2.

relationship between principles and virtues in the moral life. Neither component can be eliminated in favor of the other.

Significantly, the same view of Aquinas' moral philosophy is held by a number of sources in the manual tradition. While 'virtue Thomists' grant that a few scholarly treatments of Aquinas' moral philosophy placed appropriate emphasis upon the virtues, the standard interpretation is that Thomistic moral philosophy has been excessively legalistic. This view conveniently and incorrectly supports the attempts to write off the traditional regard for the substantive role of the natural law in Aquinas' thinking.

The case of Prümmer's *Manuale Theologiae Moralis* provides a noteworthy counterexample.[39] This early 20th century manual of moral theology was a staple in pre-conciliar (and some post-conciliar) seminary programs. The general structure of the manual, like the second part of the *Summa theologiae* upon which it is based, is hardly legalistic. It deals concretely with the moral life in terms of the cardinal and theological virtues. A single tract in the first volume is devoted to the subject "*De legibus*," with a single sub-article concerning the natural law. The virtues in general are treated in another tract, with a separate tract devoted to each of the virtues individually.

Prümmer covers the traditional range of moral theology, including an extensive discussion of casuistry and probabilism. He makes use of the deductive model when describing the process of moral decision-making, but he pays special attention to the non-deductive role that prudence plays in conscience.[40] He specifically acknowledges the cognitive role of prudence and the moral virtues in choice. He postulates two other categories of practical theology, the mystical and the ascetical, which strengthen the impression that his view is far from legalistic. Prümmer's example demonstrates two important points: First, many traditional interpreters of Thomistic ethics paid attention to the virtues, which figure so centrally in Aquinas' own work. Second,

---

[39] See Dominicus M. Prümmer, O.P., *Manuale theologiae moralis: secundum principia S. Thomae Aquinatis*, Editio Decima (Barcelona: Herder, 1946).

[40] See Prümmer, Tractatus IV, "De conscientia," pp. 195ff.; also Tractatus X, "De virtute prudentiae et vitiis oppoditis," pp. 454ff.

the radical distinction between principles and virtues drawn by modern virtue theorists appears to be an exaggerated and artificial dichotomy from the point of view of Thomistic moral philosophy.

Turning to a contemporary example, John Finnis, and his collaborators Germain Grisez and Joseph Boyle, represent a recent version of Thomistic natural law theory that is intended to address challenges to natural law ethics and more generally to moral cognitivism arising from modern philosophy. Their theory is innovative because it eschews a conception of natural law ethics as a deduction from a philosophical anthropology and metaphysics. They have been accused of turning natural law theory into a version of Kantian formalism whereby ethical judgments are merely logical requirements of practical rationality. While, on occasion, they appear to embrace this viewpoint, Finnis has offered a vigorous defense of how their theory can acknowledge the real dependence of the moral order upon human nature.[41]

The so-called 'new natural lawyers' are aware of the importance of the virtues in ethical analysis. They do, however, appear to regard the role of the moral virtues as derivative from and perhaps even reducible to that of general principles. Their view of the latter point is not uniform, however. Whereas Grisez appears to emphasize a more strictly deductive model of natural law theory in his *Christian Moral Principles*, Finnis and Boyle have made remarks that suggest a more moderate view. Nevertheless, the moral virtues are not accorded the non-derivative cognitive status in the moral life that Aquinas appears to attribute to them.[42] Their position is summarized succinctly by Joseph Boyle in the following manner:

> . . .according to the natural law account, the moral virtues have an irreducible role in moral knowledge. As dispositions of character necessary for the developed capacity to make moral

---

[41] See John Finnis, "Natural Inclinations and Natural Rights: Deriving 'Ought' from 'Is' According to Aquinas," in L.J. Elders and K. Hedwig eds., *Lex et Libertas,* Studi Tomistici 30 (Vatican City: Pontificia Accademia di S. Tommaso, 1987).

[42] Cf. *ST* II-II.58.5.

> judgments correctly and easily they are necessary for mature, competent moral decision-making. But it is clear that the moral virtues do not constitute a source of moral knowledge independent of the knowledge of the universal principles of the natural law. It is true that the possession of the virtues adds to these principles what reasoning from them cannot provide, that is an ability to appreciate the moral significance of the emotional appeal of the particularities of possible actions. But these character traits would not be moral virtues unless they were shaped by the principles of the natural law.[43]

Although the virtues are an essential part of moral life according to proponents of the 'new natural law theory,' their cognitive function is derivative and limited.[44] For Aquinas, on the other hand, practical wisdom requires moral virtue both antecedently and consequently. The virtues enable cognitive insight into our grasp of both general principles and the applications of those principles to particular cases. As he notes in *Summa theologiae* I-II.94.4, natural law theory does not descend with apodictic certainty to all matters of detail. Consider, for example, ethical and engineering or business decisions made under adverse conditions. By definition, such instances involve circumstances where judgments must be made when we lack a decision procedure or algorithm for applying general principles to a particular case. Aquinas recognizes that only the virtues can help us to make rational but non-algorithmic decisions under circumstances in which no simple deduction is possible.[45]

Aquinas as 'Virtue Theorist'

The stereotypical picture of Aquinas as a natural lawyer does not do justice to his position, but calling attention to the importance of virtue in his thought does not thereby make him a virtue theorist. There are a

---

[43] Joseph Boyle, "Natural Law and the Ethics of Traditions," in Robert P. George, ed. *Natural Law Theory: Contemporary Essays* (Oxford: Clarendon Press, 1994), p. 14.

[44] Ibid.

[45] See e.g., *ST* I-II.95.2c.

growing number of interpreters who wish to take this additional step. Perhaps the clearest representative of this position is Daniel Nelson's *The Priority of Prudence.* In Nelson's view, if Aquinas is a natural lawyer, then interest in his moral philosophy cannot be anything more than antiquarian nostalgia:

> . . .even though natural law continues to figure in legal theory. . . its force as a coherent and identifiable moral and political doctrine has long been spent. Its claim as a compelling philosophical theory is understood, at least by most professional philosophers, to have been refuted. . . .[46]

According to Nelson, the tradition has seriously misread Aquinas. Recasting him as a virtue theorist will provide an alternative to those in Catholic moral theology who accept the repudiation of natural law theory, but who do not wish to become proportionalists.[47] Rendering Aquinas attractive to proportionalist moral theologians suggests just how far in the direction of particularism Nelson is prepared to push his reading of Thomas. For instance, an oft-repeated theme in the book is that virtue theory does not concern itself with universals, which are so abstract as to be of little or no value.[48]

Nelson's rehabilitation of Aquinas as a modern virtue ethicist is fraught with important difficulties, including textual obstacles that provide counterexamples to his thesis. He attempts to explain each of these away as insubstantial, using several different strategies: 1) he argues that natural law theory is an insignificant part of Aquinas' overall theory, having no essential epistemological role to play; 2) he argues that it merely serves as an explanatory device and not as a tool for guiding action; and 3) in at least one case, Nelson concludes that Aquinas occasionally lapses into use of stereotypical natural law talk.

In opposition to the deductive model of practical reasoning, Nelson stresses that for Aquinas moral judgment depends upon the experience of particular circumstances. Prudence looks to the singular, not to

---

[46] Nelson, p. 8, also pp. 130-131.

[47] Ibid., pp. 133-134.

[48] Ibid., pp. 144-145, 46, 59, 72, 98,100,103.

universal principles.[49] Thomas does assert that prudence regards both the universal and the particular, and that it depends upon first principles. Nelson's strategy is to argue that this dependence is really of very little significance for Thomas.[50] As evidence for this claim, he points out that Aquinas does not offer an extensive treatment of how one is to reason from the first principles of the natural law to secondary precepts. Nelson argues that this explanation is lacking in Aquinas because Aquinas thinks it is, in principle, impossible to make this transition. The first principles of the natural law serve not as action-guiding postulates, but as an explanatory device for the structure of practical reasoning.[51] This provides a convenient way to dispose of the most serious textual obstacle to Nelson's position: Aquinas' repeated use of the natural *habitus* of *synderesis* in relation to prudence and practical reasoning. He argues that the general principles held by *synderesis*:

> . . .are so abstract and general that they are devoid of any meaning except that which they receive in conjunction with the operation of the cardinal virtues under the direction of prudence. . . . Natural law plays no significant epistemic function in making practical moral determinations.[52]

This line of argument allows Nelson to build a barrier between prudence's ability to see the moral qualities of particular acts and the natural law's provision of universal principles, which is not unlike McDowell's "uncodifiability thesis." Nelson concludes that Aquinas' use of natural law language may have some explanatory theological significance, but it adds nothing of importance to his virtue ethics.

Aquinas: Beyond Contemporary Virtue Theory

There are two lines of argument that militate against the acceptance of Nelson's particular categorization of Aquinas as a virtue theorist: 1) internal evidence in the text offers some important counterexamples,

---

[49] Ibid., pp. 144-145, et alia.

[50] Ibid., pp. 144-145, 96-97.

[51] Ibid., pp. 96-97, 144-145.

[52] Ibid., pp. 144-145.

and 2) saddling Aquinas with a virtue theory that embraces moral particularism and excludes the appeal to substantive moral principles faces significant theoretical difficulties. It is beyond the scope of the present analysis to give a detailed treatment of the latter arguments, so a brief enumeration of a few of them must suffice.

First, virtue theories are unable to meet the very challenge they pose against principle-based theories, namely, that the latter cannot eliminate irreconcilable moral disagreements, which are a common feature of modern ethical discourse. Virtue theorists are fond of pointing to the inability of consequentialism and deontology to resolve substantive moral disputes in order to guide action, because of the conflicting nature of the conclusions their principles entail. Many virtue theorists, however, embrace particularism and eschew transcendent moral principles in favor of prudential perception. Because of this, they lack the tools necessary to solve disagreements about virtuous perceptions, and are thus in no better position than their principle-based counterparts.

Second, Nelson's particularist interpretation of virtue theory leaves no room for a category of intolerable acts. Even virtue theorists such as Alasdair MacIntyre have come to recognize the need for such a category. Nelson's attribution of a position equivalent to McDowell's uncodifiability thesis to Aquinas is inconsistent with an account of universal moral absolutes, something that Aquinas clearly considers important.

Third, without a substantive distinction between exceptionless moral absolutes and the full requirements of virtue, it is impossible to deploy a political theory based upon the virtues that fixes concrete limits upon legislative authority and state power.

In addition to these general theoretical problems, Nelson's attempt to discount the importance of natural law in Aquinas faces some stubborn textual counterexamples. Two kinds of textual evidence militate against Nelson's view. First, Aquinas' conception of virtue cannot be separated from that of fundamental practical principles, and second, there is substantial evidence to indicate that he thinks the natural law provides a concrete source for the guidance of action.

With regard to the first point, Thomas makes numerous references to the natural *habitus* of *synderesis* which contains indemonstrable practical principles. He argues that the principles contained by *synderesis*, and indeed all the fundamental principles of the natural law, are formulable propositional realities.[53] Whatever else we may think about the relationship between fundamental natural law principles and concrete moral choices, this is incompatible with the uncodifiability thesis. Aquinas also maintains that there is a close relationship between principles and virtues, especially the virtue of prudence. For Aquinas, prudence provides the central link between intellectual and moral virtue.[54] Significantly though, he ties prudence to the virtue of understanding, and thus to the *habitus* of fundamental practical principles, noting that prudence must proceed both by universal and by particular knowledge. In a similar discussion of the same virtue in the treatise on prudence in the *Secunda secundae* (47.6), Aquinas directly references *synderesis*, arguing that it is *synderesis* not prudence that appoints the end to the moral virtues. Frequently, one finds that Aquinas refers to the central importance of principles when it comes to the exercise of practical wisdom. The virtue theorist may be tempted to dismiss these references. Nelson suggests that natural law principles exercise a purely formal role here, like the principle of non-contradiction, but it should be noted both that Aquinas often gives examples of syllogisms of prudence and conscience and that he offers general norms or principles which exercise a concrete action-guiding role.

Within Aquinas' treatment of the natural law, there are many further indications that he regards virtues and principles as intertwined, with principles having a meaningful role to play in the guidance of action. First, there is his general conception of law and the hierarchy of the forms of law, which has important implications for his political philosophy. While Nelson asserts that the dependence of the human law upon the natural law merely serves as an explanation for the existence of human agreement, for Aquinas the natural law

---

[53] See *ST* I-II.94.1c.

[54] See *ST* I-II.58.4.

provides a means both for explaining agreement and for securing it.[55] The determination of justice requires the exercise of political prudence, but there are concrete norms of respect for human persons that can be formulated and derived from the fundamental principles of the natural law. Questions 94.4 and 95.2, for example, in the *Prima secundae*, contemplate definite limitations in the process of descent from universal principles to individual choices. At the same time, however, they postulate certain transcendent moral absolutes that concretely guide action. Those action-guiding principles are captured, according to Aquinas, in the principles of the Decalogue.

In Question 95.2, for instance, Aquinas asks whether every human law is derived from the natural law. In responding to this question, he draws a distinction. Some human laws are derived from the natural law as conclusions from their proper premises, i.e., syllogistically. Others are specifications of the general principles, requiring the exercise of political prudence. Much of the substance of moral and political life is determined in the latter way, for, as Aquinas notes in Question 94.4, the more we descend to matters of detail, the more the general principles cannot be embodied in particular circumstances.

It is evident that Aquinas thinks there is a place in the moral life both for deductive reasoning and rational but non-deductive choices guided by virtuous habits. The former possibility is untenable for contemporary virtue ethicists such as Nelson, since it maintains the necessity and truth of the general principles of the natural law.

The conflict between contemporary virtue theory and Aquinas' conception of practical reasoning is significant. His discussion of murder provides an illustrative example: the prohibition against intentional killing is derived as a proper conclusion from the principle that one should do no harm.[56] The latter principle Aquinas takes to be a proximate negative corollary of his first principle of practical reason. In other words, do no harm is a *per se nota* first principle of the natural

---

[55] *ST* I-II.95.2c, for example, argues that the negative universal moral absolute regarding the prohibition of murder can be derived from the general principles of the natural law.

[56] *ST* I-II.95.2c.

law. He offers the same analysis of the precept against intentional killing in his discussion of the Ten Commandments.[57] The parallel treatment is noteworthy because he asserts that the precepts of the Decalogue are essentially the minimal specific content of the natural law. In discussion the Old Law, he draws a distinction between those principles which are absolutely required as preconditions of the moral life and those which conduce to the "well-being of perfect virtue."[58] The precepts of the Decalogue fall into the former class. They can and should be known by everyone since they are deducible directly from the first indemonstrable principles. They are also contained in divine revelation because of the fallibility of human nature in its fallen state. It is interesting to note that Aquinas restricts himself to the formulation of a certain small number of negative moral absolutes. The rest of the moral life is not amenable to this deductive procedure. Although the number of precepts is limited and their content is negative, they are nevertheless transcendent, exceptionless and action-guiding moral norms. Aquinas could not have discounted the importance of the Decalogue for the guidance of concrete moral choices. It was and is a critical Christian tool for the examination of conscience.

From this analysis, we can draw the following preliminary conclusions. Virtue theorists have pointed out correctly that not enough attention has been given to the centrality of the virtues in Aquinas' moral philosophy. Nevertheless, the anti-theoretical and particularist bent of contemporary virtue ethics is inconsistent with Aquinas' own version of the interrelation between virtues and principles. Despite the irreducible role that virtues play in the practical judgment process, Aquinas simultaneously maintains the deductive structure of natural law theory, especially for certain negative moral absolutes that define minimal universal standards for just human conduct.

---

[57] See ST I-II.100.1,3; I-II.99.2.

[58] *ST* I-II.100.2c.

Virtue Theory and the Limits of Political Authority

There are numerous lessons to be learned from the debate concerning whether Aquinas should be classified as a 'virtue theorist' or as a 'natural lawyer.' The first of these is that contemporary categories provide a sort of artificial dichotomy. The virtues have an irreducible role to play in his moral theory, but so do deductive reasoning, general principles and exceptionless moral norms. While this conclusion may disappoint virtue ethicists who endorse moral particularism, it provides Aquinas with a foundation to address the contemporary struggle between liberal and communitarian theorists over the limits of political authority and the nature of the common good.

Like his ethics, Aquinas' political theory cannot be classified neatly into one or the other competing camps. As an Aristotelian, he recognizes the political need to foster civic virtue and the common good, which runs contrary to procedural conceptions of justice and efforts to separate the specification of the right from the human good. Communitarians such as Alasdair MacIntyre, Richard Taylor and Michael Sandel have rightly pointed out the poverty of the liberal conception of the 'unencumbered self' and the procedural state. On the other hand, liberal political theorists wisely express reservations about investing the state with too much authority over the conception and pursuit of the good.[59] This is especially true of modern societies, which are more heterogeneous than their pre-modern counterparts.

Aquinas' position represents a compelling middle ground, offering to communitarianism a substantive theory of the good in terms of which justice must be defined and implemented, and offering to liberal political theory normative limits upon political authority. The boundaries of law and government are fixed largely by certain negative norms restraining external acts contrary to justice, which human positive law is especially suited for, given its coercive structure.[60] These negative norms provide moral absolutes, and they depend upon

---

[59] See e.g., Kymlicka, ch. 6, pp. 238ff.

[60] See ST II-II.79.2c; also John Finnis, *Aquinas: Moral, Political and Legal Theory* (Oxford: Oxford University Press, 1998), p. 170.

elements of natural law theory that have been shown to be integral to Aquinas' position. While offering a substantive approach to the common good, Aquinas is therefore able to meet the objections of liberal theorists against perfectionism in political theory.

In order to elucidate this dimension of Aquinas' thought, one must look briefly at his account of the limits on law and government. John Finnis' seminal work on Aquinas' political theory is helpful for this task. Finnis argues that Aquinas carefully limits political authority. He is correct about this point, but he also maintains that these limits render the specifically political dimension of the common good instrumental. Human positive law, despite apparent evidence to the contrary, neither directly instantiates a basic good nor intends the fullness of human virtue in citizens. Finnis concludes that Aquinas' conception of the role of the state in securing the common good is essentially no different from that of John Stuart Mill's position in *On Liberty.*[61] In contrast to Finnis' conclusion, Aquinas' normative limits on political authority are consistent with the state intending that citizens achieve the fullness of natural and supernatural goodness. For Aquinas, law and government must intend certain ends which they are not sufficient or competent to produce without cooperation. Just as human nature is not capable of its true end without the cooperation of grace perfecting nature, so too the law can intend mediately what it cannot produce immediately.[62]

There is an apparent difficulty with this thesis. Communitarians, such as MacIntyre and Sandel, who claim Aristotle and Aquinas as their intellectual compatriots, hold that rational agreement about moral principles presupposes a substantive shared conception of the human good.[63] Furthermore, there is textual evidence to indicate that Aquinas, following Aristotle, conceived of the appropriate goal of the state as the

---

[61] Finnis, *Aquinas,* p. 228.

[62] See *ST* I-II.5.5, *ST* I-II.96.3.

[63] I do not mean to assert that MacIntyre and Sandel are proponents of forms of communitarian political theory that cannot respond to the liberal objections concerning the limits of legislative and governmental authority. It is beyond the scope of this paper to adjudicate that debate. See Alasdair MacIntyre, "The Privatization of the Good," in *Review of Politics*, 52:1990, pp. 344-361.

production of virtuous citizens. If that is so, there would appear to be no intrinsic *theoretical* limits on what the state should do legislatively in order to produce that end. In order to demonstrate that Aquinas' views do not have these more radical communitarian implications, we should consider passages that appear to support a more radically unlimited conception of the state.

The most appropriate place to start is the "Treatise on Law" in the *Prima secundae* of the *Summa theologiae*. At the beginning of the treatise, Aquinas asks whether law in general should always be ordained to the common good (*bonum commune*).[64] Having established that it is a directive of practical reason (a1) and that the first principle in practical matters is the final end, he argues that law should concern principally the direction (*'respiciat ordinem'*) of activity toward the final end of happiness (a2c). Borrowing an analogy concerning parts and wholes from Aristotle, Thomas argues that the individual person is properly considered a part of the *communitas perfecta*, so that law should concern communal happiness (*felicitatem communem*). It is worth noting that he uses the more specific term *felicitas* to indicate the end of the state rather than the common term good (*bonum*), leaving no doubt as to the relation of law to happiness, which includes the fullness of virtue. Of course, there is room to argue that just what it means to *'respiciat ordinem'* is open to interpretation, but the plain sense of the text is hard to ignore in the absence of further considerations.

As if to add further strength to the assertion of the previous passage, Aquinas maintains in *ST* I-II.92.1 that it is an effect of law to make human beings good. He argues that if the legislator is virtuous and well-intentioned in accordance with the direction of divine justice, then the effect of law will be to bring its subjects to goodness *simpliciter*.

The overall sense of the argument in *ST* I-II.92.1 is, however, not an unequivocal endorsement of communitarian perfectionism. Aquinas notes that sometimes law habituates persons to virtue through coercion and fear of punishment, rather than through the production of internally virtuous dispositions. He grants that it is enough for the procurement of the common good that those who are not rulers be

---

[64] *ST* I-II.90.2.

merely obedient to the command of the law, presumably through fear of punishment rather than through an internal disposition to virtuous action. Thus, the law's direction to perfect virtue is in most cases more or less indirect. There are, at least, practical limits upon what states and rulers can reasonably expect of citizens in terms of virtuous conduct.

Another passage that appears to present the strongest case for the more radical communitarian reading of Aquinas is found in the *De regno*.[65] Aquinas' treatment of the office of the king is, by Finnis' own admission, one of the most difficult to square with his conclusion that the specifically political common good is instrumental. St. Thomas speaks of the purpose of law and government as to induce virtue and direct citizens toward happiness.[66] The language of the passage is most explicit in giving to the ruler not only the responsibility of directing citizens toward the imperfect happiness attainable in this life, but also toward eternal happiness.[67]

The passage is, however, in need of interpretation. Aquinas says that the ruler should promote the good life of the community in such a way as to make it *suitable for* (*congruit*) heavenly beatitude and should command those things that *lead to* (*du*) this goal. The sense of 'making life suitable for' and 'leading to' beatitude could well be interpreted instrumentally. Finnis points out that Aquinas offers an apparently instrumental analogy: The king is like the armorer who fashions an instrument so that a soldier can fight well.[68] But we must recall the point of that analogy. Aquinas is not comparing the instrumentality of the political community to the attainment of human virtue, but the attainment of human virtue as instrumental to the attainment of heavenly beatitude. If the analogy is meant to show that the actions of the political community aim only at a strictly instrumental good, then it will thereby diminish the intrinsic value of the attainment of happiness in this life as well. Furthermore, the strictly instrumental

---

[65] Finnis, *Aquinas*, p. 228.

[66] *De Regno* 2.4 [I, 15].

[67] Ibid.

[68] Finnis, *Aquinas*, pp. 231, 182.

reading of this passage is still theoretically consistent with arguing that legislators should promote human virtue.

It is certainly true that Aquinas regards the cultivation of human happiness (*felicitas*) as subordinate and instrumental to the attainment of eternal happiness (*beatitudo*), but it is also true that he regards the attainment of human happiness as good in itself. It is an intermediate good. So, it is true that the king cannot have as the immediate object of his actions the production of eternal happiness; nor does it turn out that production of human happiness can be the immediate object of his actions. But this need not rule out that *felicitas* and *beatitudo* are mediately intended by the king with the cooperation of other agencies, including grace. Aquinas says that the king should not only command what conduces to the good life of the community, but that having established that good life, he should also preserve it (*conservet*) and do what he can to make it better (*ad meliora promoveat*).[69] The plain sense of this passage is that the fullness of virtue of the citizens should be a part of the king's intention.

Finnis' responses to this line of argument includes some terminological cautions and an appeal to other passages where Aquinas distinguishes the role of divine and human government. He notes that St. Thomas makes an almost imperceptible shift from speaking of the good life of the multitude, which the king should promote, to speaking of the public good (*bonum publicum*).[70] Aquinas elaborates his explanation of the 'public good' in terms of the transgression of justice (*transgediendo iustitiam*) and disturbing the peace of others (*aliorum pacem perturbant*).

The terms 'peace' and 'the public good' are significant according to Finnis because they are synonymous with the limited and instrumental role of government, a point he discusses in several places throughout his analysis. One problem with Finnis' argument is that it is difficult to tell whether we should interpret the inclusivity of peace and the *bonum publicum* in terms of the role of the king in the passage or vice versa. Thus, Aquinas could be using *bonum publicum* in a narrow and strictly

---

[69] *De Regno* 2.4 [I, 15].

[70] Finnis, *Aquinas*, pp. 230, 181-2.

instrumental sense or in a broader and more inclusive way, depending upon which set of concepts we regard as fixing the scope of the others. The term 'transgression,' on the other hand, is especially significant, since Aquinas associates the sin of transgression (*transgressio*) with a vice opposed to justice that disposes the agent to violate the negative moral absolutes derived from the natural law.

The term 'transgression' has been transferred from bodily movements to moral acts. Literally, someone is said to 'transgress' who steps across a fixed boundary. The term applies to moral acts insofar as one should not cross the boundary established by negative precepts of the natural law.[71] These negative moral absolutes help to establish the boundaries of limited government and positive law.

There is some uncertainty about the correct interpretation of Aquinas' terminology here, since *transgressio* and *iustitia* have both narrow and technical senses as well as broader less technical meanings. Aquinas indicates that transgression may be taken technically to mean the specific vice which violates negative moral absolutes or more generally to mean any kind of vicious or sinful behavior.[72] Similarly, *iustitia* considered as a general virtue which relates persons to others collectively rather than individually can be considered to include the acts of all the virtues, whether they concern the individual or group good.[73] Furthermore, the text of the passage in *De regno* argues that the king's responsibility is not merely to restrain vicious transgressions, but also to induce virtue and to be solicitous for its improvement. Aquinas maintains that transgressions against justice are a chief impediment to the maintenance of virtue, but he does not restrict the intentionality of the ruler merely to the removal of obstacles or impediments. The very fact that Aquinas mentions both the negative purpose of law to restrain vice and its positive role of inducing virtue suggests that he thinks both roles are appropriate for the ruler. And yet, it is true that he is silent about any positive program for the development of full virtue in the citizens.

---

[71] *ST* II-II.79.2c.

[72] *ST* II-II.79.2.ad 1.

[73] *ST* II-II.58.5c.

From these observations we may draw the following conclusions: Finnis correctly emphasizes that the *De regno* calls for a narrower rather than wider scope for the role of law and government in the promotion of virtue. At the same time, the plain sense of these passages requires that we acknowledge Aquinas views the purpose of the legislator not merely in terms of the restraint of vice, especially injustice, but also in terms of the promotion of virtue. Finnis' anti-communitarian claim that, for Aquinas governments are theoretically and practically prohibited from legislating the fullness of human virtue is correct, but we must also reject the view that Aquinas has a merely procedural conception of justice in which the only purpose of government is to protect our liberty to pursue our own conception of the good.[74]

There is some reason to think that Finnis could ultimately concur with this conclusion, despite his bold claim that Aquinas' account is essentially identical to Mill's justice principle. Finnis grants that, for Aquinas, governments have an interest in inculcating virtues other than justice and the internal dispositions which all virtues require, for the sake of the political common good.[75] He also acknowledges a distinction between human law's "requirements" and its "legitimate objectives." He develops this point by differentiating between the good that the political community can attain, namely, complete virtue which is "unlimited," from the good that positive law can mandate and with which it can require persons to comply.[76] Finnis offers a distinction between the role of law and government, and the aims of the social order. He concludes that the "specifically political common good is *limited* and *in a sense* instrumental."[77] Where Aquinas falls on the spectrum between proceduralism and communitarianism for Finnis, therefore, depends greatly upon the "sense" in which the unlimited aspect of the common good can be said to form the deliberations of legislators and be intended by them. Given these qualifications, there is reason to hope that Finnis would ultimately agree with Alasdair

---

[74] Finnis, *Aquinas*, p. 182.

[75] Ibid., p. 183.

[76] Ibid., p. 185.

[77] Ibid., p. 187; emphasis added.

MacIntyre's observation that for a Thomistic political theory, "rational agreement on moral rules always presupposes rational agreement on the nature of the human good."[78] We should therefore concur with Finnis' insistence that there must be concrete normative limits upon political authority and state power, while maintaining that this does not require Aquinas to embrace a procedural conception of political life.

Normative Limitations upon the authority of Human Law

If Aquinas' political theory can articulate a fairly clear account of these limits, it can provide an attractive middle ground between the pitfalls of liberal proceduralism and communitarian perfectionism. As it turns out, Aquinas' retention of the deductive aspects of natural law theory in the form of certain negative moral precepts, alongside his appeal to the importance of *prudentia,* provides a critical component for his determination of the appropriate limits of political authority. This result should not be altogether surprising since some contemporary interpreters have tended to discount this aspect of his natural law theory in their efforts to label him a virtue ethicist.

This connection between Aquinas' ethics and politics can be articulated very briefly by examining two points: first, his account of the factors limiting the authority of human law, and second, the close connection between these factors and the nature of positive and negative moral precepts.[79] There are many practical limits upon what it is reasonable for governments to legislate. Aquinas suggests two such limits: the need to bring human beings gradually as opposed to suddenly into a virtuous state, and the fact that most human beings, given the present condition of human nature, would be unable to meet the tough standard of full virtue. Thus, he thinks it is unwise for human law to attempt to eradicate completely such vices as excessive drinking and prostitution, even though these constitute vicious moral acts. In some particular political community, it is conceivable that these pragmatic limitations could be set aside. The counsels of perfection

---

[78] MacIntyre, "The Privatization of the Good," p. 345.

[79] As Finnis points out, Thomas discusses those limiting factors primarily when differentiating divine law and human law. Finnis, *Aquinas,* p. 183.

applying to the common life of a particular religious order might constitute a case in point for Aquinas.

The primary normative limitation upon positive law, however, comes from the nature of human acts and habits. Human acts involve external performances and internal intentional states. Positive law exercises control over human acts by regulating external behavior through coercion or the threat of coercion. Since human legislators cannot regulate or produce internal dispositions through the threat of external coercion, it is beyond the competence of positive law to judge internal dispositional states. Virtues and vices are habits or internal dispositional states that incline agents to act well or badly. It is therefore beyond the competence of human law to command all the acts of the virtues not only because human beings would have a hard time fulfilling such a demanding request, but also because human law is theoretically incapable of judging anything besides external actions and their consequences.

Since all human actions involve external manifestations and internal intentional states, we may wonder how it is possible for positive law to prohibit any vicious act or to enjoin any virtuous one. Aquinas' answer is that there are certain intolerable acts which should not be done, regardless of the state of mind of the agent. As Finnis has pointed out, Aquinas may lack the modern terminology of natural rights in his philosophical vocabulary, but he does have the concept of certain exceptionless just and unjust external acts which do not depend upon the state of mind of the agent for their character as right or wrong, enjoined or prohibited.[80] The regulation of such external acts belongs to the special competence of human law.

As it turns out, these negative moral absolutes correspond to certain moral norms that Aquinas regards as deducible from the primary principles of the natural law.[81] The negative precepts fix the boundaries that human beings cannot justly cross in the moral life.[82] The difference between negative and positive precepts of the law is fairly clear: the

---

[80] See Finnis, *Aquinas*, pp. 137ff.

[81] Ibid., p. 138.

[82] *ST* II-II.79.2c.

negative precepts forbid vicious acts, and the positive precepts enjoin the acts of the various virtues.[83] The negative precepts bind always and in every instance; the positive ones are always binding but not on every occasion.[84] The negative precepts are especially suited to the universal applicability of human law while the fulfillment of positive precepts requires the prudential discernment of the individual moral agent.

Aquinas: Both Virtue theorist and Natural Lawyer

The foregoing considerations lead us to a substantive conclusion. The contemporary categories of virtue and principle-based ethical theory are inadequate to capture the true nature of Aquinas' moral and political philosophy. Thomas is not merely a 'natural lawyer' in the stereotypical sense of the term. The stereotypical sense of this term is, in fact, a product of the influence of early modern philosophy upon the scholastic tradition of interpreting Aquinas. The notion that Aquinas regards the moral life as fully specifiable in terms of deductions from natural law principles is a caricature of his position. At the same time, the particularist bent of contemporary virtue theorists is contrary to the genuine sense in which Aquinas thinks certain moral conclusions are deducible from the general principles of the natural law. These conclusions are represented by the negative moral absolutes that he associates with the Decalogue. While this result is unacceptable to virtue theorists like John McDowell, who hold that particular moral judgments are uncodifiable, it strengthens Aquinas' ability to offer an account of the virtues that leads to a coherent political theory. His simultaneous focus upon virtues and principles allows him to provide an account of political life that acknowledges the need both for a substantive account of the common good and for principled limits upon the legitimate extent of political authority. Aquinas' account of the virtues thus retains the appropriate unity of *moralis philosophia* in its original sense.

---

[83] *ST* II-II.33.2c.

[84] *ST* II-II.79.3.ad 3.

JACQUES MARITAIN AND NATURAL RIGHTS: THE PRIORITY OF METAPHYSICS OVER POLITICS

David Klassen

Much of the discussion in recent years among philosophers about the rights of the person has been framed by the "liberal-communitarian debate" which became the subject of anthologies beginning in the1980s, and which traces its origins to questions arising out of the publication of John Rawls's *A Theory of Justice* in 1971.[1] The main tenets of "liberalism," as represented by thinkers such as Rawls and Ronald Dworkin, include the importance of individual rights and a belief that the individual is the originator and ultimate bearer of value. In contrast, the term "communitarianism" has been applied to the views of those who stress the importance of communal and public goods, and who hold that values are rooted in the customs and traditions of communities.[2] Within that framework of contemporary discourse, some commentators – for the most part Catholics who are sympathetic to communitarianism – have claimed that Jacques Maritain's theory of the natural rights of the human person, put forward decades earlier in works such as *The Rights of Man and Natural Law* (*RMNL*), *The Person and the Common Good* (*PCG*) and *Man and the State*

---

[1] See Michael Moreland, "Jacques Maritain, Thomism and the Liberal-Communitarian Debate," *The Failure of Modernism: The Cartesian Legacy and Contemporary Pluralism*, ed. Brendan Sweetman (Washington, D.C.: The Catholic University of America Press, 1999), pp. 141-54. Note 4 at p. 142 gives a brief summary of the debate and cites some major contributors and anthologies.

[2] See *The Oxford Companion to Philosophy*, s.v. "communitarianism" and *The Routledge Encyclopedia of Philosophy*, s.v. "community and communitarianism" for more detailed discussion of the meaning of "communitarianism" and "liberalism" in the contemporary context. I have chiefly relied upon *The Oxford Companion* for the definitions given. According to the *The Routledge Encyclopedia*, those who have been described as "communitarians," such as Alasdair MacIntyre, Charles Taylor and Michael Sandel,"for the most part avoid the term."

(*M&S*),[3] is a liberal aberration that is in conflict with his otherwise communitarian political philosophy.

I intend to show how Maritain's doctrine of natural rights is supported and justified by his philosophical understanding of the person and to answer those who have accused him of inconsistency in advocating both personal rights and the importance of the community and the common good. If I am correct, Maritain's critics of recent years have failed to appreciate his metaphysics of the human person, and hence they have not understood the way in which his doctrine of natural rights transcends the purely political categories of communitarianism and liberalism. For Maritain, the individual person is not the originator of value, as is the case for liberalism; nor is value relative to the community or bestowed upon a person by the community, as is the case for communitarianism. A person's value, according to Maritain, is derived primarily from having a spiritual personality in the image of God and from being in relation to the absolute and divine order.

I. Criticism of Maritain

A seminal work in a line of articles in which Maritain has been criticized for failing to present a coherent view of person and society is Frederick J. Crosson's "Maritain and Natural Rights" (1983). Crosson contends that Maritain's attempt to defend democracy and human rights led him to "assertions which were internally inconsistent as well as inconsistent with the basic context of political philosophy in which

---

[3] Quotations from Maritain's works are cited in the text with the abbreviations listed below, and the works are referred to in the text by the same abbreviations:

RMNL: The Rights of Man and Natural Law (New York: Charles Scribner's Sons, copyright 1943, publication 1949).

PCG: The Person and the Common Good (Notre Dame, IN: University of Notre Dame Press, 1966; copyright 1947 by Charles Scribner's Sons, copyright 1946 by *The Review of Politics*).

M&S: *Man and the State* (Chicago: University of Chicago Press, 1951; Washington, D.C.: The Catholic University of America Press, 1998).

he worked."[4] Michelle Watkins and Ralph McInerny, in an article entitled "Jacques Maritain and the Rapprochement of Liberalism and Communitarianism," cite both Crosson and Alasdair MacIntyre to support their case that "Maritain sought to synthesize two inherently incompatible political doctrines."[5] According to Watkins and McInerny, such liberal concepts as freedom and human rights are "at the theoretical level in serious tension, if not inconsistency, with his overall communitarian framework."[6] Similarly, Deborah Wallace agrees with Crosson's critique insofar as she says that Maritain is not faithful to Thomas Aquinas' theory of natural law when Maritain proposes rights that are said to exist prior to community bonds.[7]

Although the issue of Maritain's fidelity to Aquinas has been raised by some critics and will arise incidentally in this essay, I do not intend to focus on it. I am more interested in the internal consistency and plausibility of Maritain's own thought, and in examining the way in which his doctrine of natural rights is supported and justified by his philosophical understanding of the person.

II. Maritain's arguments for the natural rights of the person

The rights themselves are said by Maritain to be correlative to the person's obligations to fulfil his or her necessary ends under the natural law, as will be seen in the second argument discussed below. They include rights that belong to the natural law strictly speaking and which are universal and invariable in the nature of things, including

---

[4] Frederick J. Crosson, "Maritain and Natural Rights," *Review of Metaphysics* 36 (June 1983), p. 911.

[5] Michelle Watkins and Ralph McInerny, "Jacques Maritain and the Rapprochement of Liberalism and Communitarianism," *Catholicism, Liberalism and Communitarianism*, ed. Kenneth L. Grasso, Gerard V. Bradley and Robert P. Hunt (London: Rowman & Littlefield Publishers, Inc., 1995), pp. 151-72 at 152.

[6] Ibid., p. 170.

[7] Deborah Wallace, "Jacques Maritain and Alasdair MacIntyre: The Person, the Common Good and Human Rights," *The Failure of Modernism*, pp. 127-40 at 137. Cf. Crosson, pp. 903-04, 907, 909, 911.

the rights to existence, to personal freedom in the sense of being an agent responsible for one's acts before God and community, and to the pursuit of perfection in the moral life. A second tier of rights, including the right of private ownership of material goods, belongs to the law of nations or *jus gentium.* Such rights are known through rational knowledge and follow in a necessary manner from the natural law strictly speaking. The third tier of rights, such as the "freedom from want," corresponds to requirements of the *jus gentium*, but such rights are contingent in that they are to be fulfilled by the positive law in particular circumstances that vary in different societies (*M&S*, 97-101; *RMNL*, 79-80).

Maritain gives two main arguments in the following passage for concluding that the human person is by nature endowed with rights:

> The human person possesses rights because of the very fact that it is a person, a whole, master of itself and of its acts, and which consequently is not merely a means to an end, but an end, an end which must be treated as such. The dignity of the human person! The expression means nothing if it does not signify that, by natural law, the human person has the right to be respected, is the subject of rights, possesses rights. These are things which are owed to man because of the very fact that he is man. The notion of right and the notion of moral obligation are correlative. They are both founded on the freedom proper to spiritual agents. If man is morally bound to the things which are necessary to the fulfillment of his destiny, obviously, then he has the right to fulfill his destiny; and if he has the right to fulfill his destiny he has the right to the things necessary for this purpose. (*RMNL*, 65)

The first argument is from the nature of the person. Maritain says that the person, who is an end and not a means, and who has dignity, must be treated accordingly. Therefore, according to natural law, the human person is the subject of rights. This argument depends on two main premises: (1) that the person is, in its essential nature, characterized by attributes such as self-mastery, being a whole and not a part, and being an end and not a means, and hence has a high degree of perfection and dignity;[8] and (2) that in the nature of things those very attributes entail the possession of rights. In other words, the argument presupposes a high view of the human person, and that in the nature of things the good inherent in the person demands or calls for a fitting response on the part of others, giving rise to rights. In sections III and V of this paper, I will discuss how Maritain arrives at the qualities he attributes to the person. For now, let it be noted that there is an underlying optimism on his part, which is apparent not only in his high view of the person, but also in his belief that there is a natural law wherein the good is respected and personal dignity is accorded rights.

The second argument, based upon the moral obligations of the natural law, specifies that the rights in question pertain to the teleology of the human person. The natural law requires the human person to put itself in tune with certain necessary ends, as Maritain explains several pages earlier:

> This means that there is, by very virtue of human nature, an order or a disposition which human reason can discover and according to which the human will must act in order to attune itself to the necessary ends of the human being. The unwritten law, or natural law, is nothing more than that (*RMNL*, 61).

Because the person has the *obligation* to act in accordance with his necessary ends and thereby to fulfil his destiny, Maritain reasons that the person has the *right* to fulfil his destiny and a *right* to the things necessary to do so. He presupposes a rational order in the universe, wherein the person is not burdened with obligations that cannot be fulfilled. As with the first, Maritain's second argument for the existence of rights is grounded in an optimistic view of the nature of things.

---

[8] As to perfection of the person, Maritain at *PCG*, p. 32, note 24, quotes Aquinas: "'Person signifies what is most perfect in all nature – that is, a subsistent individual of a rational nature' *Sum. Theol.*, I, 29, 3."

III. The person's direct relationship to the absolute and divine order

The most important reason given by Maritain for the dignity of the person, and thus for the rights of the person according to the first line of argument stated above, pertains to the direct relationship of the person to the order of the divine and of sacred things, which he also calls the "absolute." It is in this aspect of Maritain's thought that we find the strongest statement of his high view of the person, here evidenced near the beginning of *RMNL:*

> To say that a man is a person is to say that in the depth of his being he is more than a part and more independent than servile. It is to this mystery of our nature that religious thought points when it says that the human person is the image of God. The worth of a person, his liberty, his rights, arise from the order of naturally sacred things, which bear upon them the imprint of the Father of Being, and which have in Him the goal of their movement. A person possesses absolute dignity because he is in direct relationship with the absolute, [in] which alone he can find his complete fulfillment. His spiritual fatherland consists of the entire order of things which have absolute value, and which reflect in some way, an Absolute superior to the world and which draw our life towards this Absolute (*RMNL*, 4).

In telling us that the dignity of the person, and hence its rights, arise because of the person's direct relationship with the absolute order of sacred things and God, rather than being conferred upon the person by the community or mediated by the community, Maritain argues that rights arise prior to the political community. Some commentators, who are mentioned at the beginning of this paper,[9] have therefore criticized Maritain for promulgating a doctrine of "pre-political" rights that is contrary to the teachings of Aquinas. Maritain, nevertheless, claims to be following St. Thomas when he says that the dignity of the human person is derived from the person's direct ordination to God as its ultimate end (*PCG*, chap. II, 15-19, notes 7 and 8). Moreover, Maritain's

[9] For criticism of Maritain's doctrine of "pre-political" rights, see Crosson, p. 909, Watkins and McInerny, pp. 168-69, and Wallace, pp. 136-37.

understanding of rights that arise out of the relationship of the person to the divine might more accurately be called "trans-political" rather than "pre-political," because he argues for rights that claim a priority of transcendence, rather than a temporal priority over the political order.

IV. Metaphysics of the person

Maritain's metaphysics of the person, set forth in the third chapter of *PCG,* is based upon the hylomorphic doctrine of Aquinas, according to which "the human soul, together with the matter which it informs, constitutes one substance, which is both carnal and spiritual" (*PCG,* 36). According to Thomistic hylomorphism, human persons and all corporeal beings are individuated by matter. The soul, which Maritain describes as "a metaphysical energy," is also called the form of the body and is the animating principle which determines the species of the corporeal being. The matter, including already formed matter from what Maritain calls "germinal cells, with all their hereditary content," makes the corporeal being an individual which has a certain quantity and position in space (*PCG*, 35-37). The human being is a special case of corporeal being with a rational and immortal soul.

The soul and body do not each exist on their own as complete beings, but rather soul and matter are "two substantial co-principles of the same being, of one and the same reality, called man" (*PCG,* 36).[10] Nevertheless, Maritain makes a distinction between the way each of the co-principles finds expression in the human being in his discussion of "two poles." There is a material pole, which Maritain associates with *individuality* and with Pascal's teaching that "the self is detestable." The spiritual pole, on the other hand, is associated with *personality* and with the teaching of St. Thomas that person signifies "what is most perfect in nature."[11] This distinction should not, however, be taken to mean that the soul *is* the person, which Aquinas himself denies even with respect to the soul in its separated state, on the ground that because it retains its unibility to matter, the separated soul is not truly an

[10] The co-principles are soul (i.e., form) and matter, not soul and body. The body may be understood as ensouled matter.

[11] *Supra,* note 7.

"individual substance."[12] The person is properly understood to be the whole human being, the unity of soul and matter, as Maritain points out in his discussion of the individual and the person: "One and the same reality is, in a certain sense an individual, and, in another sense, a person. Our whole being is an individual by reason of that in us which derives from matter, and a person by reason of that in us which derives from spirit" (*PCG*, 43).

Maritain's metaphysics of the person attributes to the human being as individual those traits which can be associated with *individualism* in a negative sense. Most or all of the *positive* traits that might ordinarily be associated with individuality are attributed to the soul, which is the principle of "personality" as opposed to "individuality" in the sense Maritain uses the words. By using those terms as he does, Maritain is able to build upon and develop the Thomistic metaphysical tradition and, in so doing, to emphasize the distance between what he means by *personalism* and any form of narrow *individualism* that would be inconsistent with a communitarian framework. While proclaiming fidelity to the doctrine of individuation by matter, Maritain's metaphysics nevertheless identifies designated matter as the principle of individuation only in a limited sense, primarily with respect to quantity and location.[13] The soul, as has been pointed out, is the principle of unity and identity which for Maritain determines the human person to be "that which it is."[14]

---

[12] Aquinas, *Summa Theologiae* (herein cited as *ST*) I, q. 29, a. 1, ad 5: "The soul is a part of the human species; and so, although it may exist in a separate state, yet since it ever retains its nature of unibility, it cannot be called an individual substance, which is the hypostasis or first substance, as neither can the hand nor any other part of man; thus neither the definition nor the name of person belongs to it."

[13] *PCG*, p. 37: "Corporeal beings are individual because of 'matter with its quantity designated.' Their specific form and their essence are not individual by reason of their own entity but by reason of their transcendental relation to matter understood as implying position in space."

[14] *PCG* pp. 35-36. "In every being made of matter, this pure potency bears the impress of a metaphysical energy – the 'form' or 'soul' – which constitutes with it a substantial unit and determines this unit to be that which it is." See

V. The spiritual personality as the basis of human dignity and human rights

Let us now return to Maritain's first argument for natural rights: "The human person possesses rights because of the very fact that it is a person, a whole, master of itself and of its acts, and which consequently is not merely a means to an end, but an end, an end which must be treated as such" (*RMNL*, 4). In the next few paragraphs, I will examine Maritain's reasons for saying that the person is a whole, a master of itself and its acts, and an end not a means. This examination will show that each of the aspects of the person that is referred to as a reason for dignity and rights relates to the spiritual pole of the human being rather than to material individuality. Most importantly for the purposes of this paper, the reader will see that for Maritain dignity and rights are rooted in a person's ability and ordination to reach out and communicate and to act for the sake of the greater good, thus distinguishing his theory of human rights from any form of individualism that would conceive of the person as a self-enclosed unit whose rights are in tension with the good of the community.

The human person is a *person*, Maritain tells us, "by virtue of the existence of its soul." The spirit is "the root of personality" (*RMNL*, 3). Not confined to a merely physical existence, the human person has subjectivity, an aspect of what Maritain calls "spiritual superexistence," which is disclosed not only in the person's interiority to self, but also in his "communications of knowledge and love" (*RMNL*, 3; *PCG*, 40-41). Through knowledge, the person is a microcosm that encompasses the universe and therefore is a *whole not a part*. Through love, the person can give freely of itself to others who are in a sense "other selves" (*RMNL*, 3; *PCG*, 41). Through communications both of knowledge and love, the person is "directly related to the absolute" (*PCG*, 41-42). The

---

also *PCG*, p. 36: "Because each soul is intended to animate a particular body, which receives its matter from germinal cells, with all their hereditary content, from which it develops, and because, further, each soul has or *is* a substantial relation to a particular body, it has within its substance the individual characteristics which differentiate it from every other human soul."

direct relation to the absolute is, as has been noted, at the heart of Maritain's understanding of the dignity of the person.

Communications of knowledge and love not only give evidence of the person's subjectivity, but they also show the person to be *master of itself* and of its acts and to exercise existence for itself (i.e., to be *an end, not a means*). Maritain's account of how the capacity to bestow oneself in love implies a subsisting spiritual being that exists for itself and which is endowed with freedom and self-mastery, is as follows:

> To bestow oneself, one must first exist; not indeed, as a sound, which passes through the air, or an idea, which crosses the mind, but as a thing, which subsists and exercises existence for itself. Such a being must exist not only as other things do, but eminently, in self-possession, holding itself in hand, master of itself. In short, it must be endowed with a spiritual existence, capable of containing itself thanks to the operations of intellect and freedom, capable of super-existing by way of knowledge and love (*PCG*, 39-40).

In Maritain's understanding, self-mastery does not arise from or give rise to the right of an individual to exercise instrumental control over its environment or over other persons. It exists by virtue of and for the sake of bestowing oneself in an act of love. Self-mastery in this sense is intimately related to the person subsisting and exercising existence for itself. If the self were merely a relation to others, to the community, or even to God, as sound is related to the air or an idea to the mind, and did not subsist and exercise existence for itself, then it would have nothing of its own to master and nothing to bestow in love. This is part of what Maritain means when he says that the person is an end and not a means. He also quotes Aquinas to support his contention that each human person is willed and governed by God for its own sake:

> For the individual that is governed only for the sake of the species is not governed for its own sake, whereas the rational creature is governed for its own sake.... Accordingly, rational

> creatures alone are directed by God to their actions for the sake, not only of the species, but also of the individual.[15]

It should be noted, however, that Maritain says that being willed and governed for its own sake does not prevent the individual person from being made first for God, secondly, for the order and perfection of the created universe, and only thirdly for itself. He says that being made for its own sake means that the person is made "for the action (immanent and spiritual) by which it perfects itself and accomplishes its destiny" (*PCG*, 17, note 7).[16] He therefore does not suggest that the person is willed for its own sake in the sense of being made for the arbitrary exercise of its freedom, without regard for the common good. Here Maritain parts company with contemporary liberalism. The individual human person is an end, not a means, created for its own sake, but *not only* for its own sake. In Maritain's view, the person is willed and governed for its own sake - and therefore has rights - in order that it may freely bestow itself in love for the sake of God and for the perfection of the created community. The view that the person is willed, governed, and has rights in order to bestow itself in love reminds us of the argument for rights based upon the existence of obligations and of the correlation of rights and obligations. It also illustrates Maritain's contention that there is no conflict between human rights, as he conceives them, and the common good of the community, because those human rights exist insofar as they enable the person's contribution to the common good.

VI. Political philosophy

Recall that at the beginning of this essay I referred to articles which criticize Maritain for an alleged inconsistency between the basic communitarian framework of political philosophy and the supposedly liberal notion of "pre-political" rights of the person. In addressing that criticism, one might first emphasize that although Maritain does present the reader with a political philosophy, it is not *only* a political philosophy. Everything that Maritain says in regard to natural law,

---

[15] *Summa Contra Gentiles* (herein cited as *SCG*) III, 113; as quoted at *PCG*, p. 19, note 8.

[16] Maritain in his footnote 7 cites *ST* I, q. 65, a. 2, and Cajetan's commentary.

natural rights, politics, society and the common good is built upon his metaphysics of the person and upon his understanding of the person's direct relationship to the absolute and the divine. His critics, insofar as they consider him to be a communitarian, mistakenly attribute to him the view that a person's humanity and dignity are derived from the political community and that the natural law is ordered to the community rather than the community to the natural law.[17] But Maritain himself emphasizes that it is our common human nature, not society, the community or the individual will, that determines the content of the natural law. "I am taking it for granted," he says, "that there is a human nature, and that this human nature is the same in all men" (*RMNL*, 60; *M&S*, 85). After citing the precept that "we must do good and avoid evil, " which he calls "the preamble and principle of natural law," Maritain says, "Natural law is the ensemble of things to do and not to do which follow therefrom in *necessary* fashion, and *from the simple fact that man is man*, nothing else being taken into account" (*RMNL*, 62-63). For Maritain, as for Aquinas, natural law is "a participation in Eternal Law," which manifests the order of Divine

[17] Crosson, for example, says that "Maritain of course stands with Thomas Aquinas on the ordering of natural law to the community" (Crosson, p. 897). And Crosson asks whether "the concept of pre-political, inviolable rights can be made consistent with the premise that man is by nature a political animal, i.e. that he *becomes human* and can attain fulfillment *only* through the political community" (p. 911; emphasis added). Crosson misunderstands Maritain insofar as he supposes that Maritain, in speaking of man as a political animal, means to say that it is *only* the community and not man's nature that makes him human. Similarly, Watkins and McInerny attribute to Maritain (in speaking of his "communitarian" side), and themselves appear to endorse the view, that it is the "community that granted the person his dignity in the first place" (Watkins and McInerny, p. 167), that "it is the community and the state that enable this person to become human in the first place" (pp. 168-69) and that "human beings are defined by their political and communal interactions" (p. 169).

Reason (*M&S*, 96).[18] The ultimate end of the eternal law is not a human good such as the common good of the community, but "God Himself."[19]

While acknowledging that "man is a political animal," by which he means that "the human person craves political life" (*RMNL*, 6), Maritain maintains that human nature, and therefore human dignity and human rights, are prior to political society by being its preconditions. According to Maritain, "society is born, as something required by nature, and (because this nature is *human* nature) as something accomplished through a work of reason and will, and freely consented to" (*RMNL*, 6).

VII. Conclusion

Because it is based upon a metaphysical understanding of the human person and of the person's relation to absolute and divine things, Maritain's doctrine of natural rights avoids the purely political realm of the "liberal-communitarian debate" of the last twenty or thirty years. Critics of Maritain who claim to have found tensions and inconsistencies between his doctrine that the person has "pre-political" dignity and rights and the "communitarian" aspects of his philosophy have, in my opinion, not given sufficient attention to his metaphysics.

Maritain's metaphysics of the person allows him to avoid the alleged inconsistencies and also provides a plausible foundation for his doctrine of natural rights. His affirmation of the spiritual personality, which is the basis of his high view of the person and of the person's dignity and rights, is in turn firmly grounded in experiences of subjectivity and of communications of love and knowledge, which form part of everyday human life. Because the rights he affirms are correlative to obligations to contribute to the common good, and because the common good is defined as the good of persons who are not mere parts, there is no conflict in Maritain's model between the

---

[18] See *ST* I-II, q. 91, aa. 1-2.

[19] "But the end of the Divine government is God Himself, and His law is not distinct from Himself. Wherefore the eternal law is not ordained to another end" (*ST* I-II, q. 91, a.1, ad. 3).

two. The common good "presupposes the persons, and flows back on them, and, in this sense, is achieved in them" (*PCG*, 51). If Maritain is correct in claiming that there is no inherent contradiction between rights of the individual person and the common good, then the contemporary "liberal-communitarian debate," at least with respect to the issues treated in this paper, suffers from a false dichotomy brought on by an inadequate understanding of the person as nothing more than a political actor.

Ralph McInerny, in a tribute published subsequent to the article he co-authored with Watkins, asks whether we have unjustly lost the optimism that was Maritain's, and he recommends *M&S* as an invitation to rethink the way we pose the basic questions of political philosophy.[20] In answer to the question McInerny poses, one might respond that there is no less reason for optimism in our day than in Maritain's, when Stalin ruled the Soviet Union and Hitler Germany. The invitation to rethink our political philosophy ought to be accepted. It is time once again for political philosophy to seek its roots in a deeper understanding of the human person and of the person's place in nature and before God. The timeless metaphysical questions addressed by Maritain need once again to be considered.

---

[20] McInerny's tribute to Maritain is found on the back cover of the 1998 paperback reprint of *M&S*, where McInerny is identified as Director of the Jacques Maritain Center, University of Notre Dame. It reads in part: "He devotes particular attention to the concept of rights, since, historically, rights theories were fashioned to supplant the natural law theory to which Maritain as a Thomist gives his allegiance. Maritain provides an ingenious and profound theory as to how natural law and natural rights can be complementary. For this reason alone, his theory remains a fundamental contribution to political philosophy, but it is filled with other gems as well. Was Maritain too optimistic in his appraisal of modernity? Or have we unjustly lost the optimism that was his? *Man and the State* is an invitation to rethink the way we pose the basic questions of political philosophy."

THE AMBIGUITY OF AUTONOMY

Ralph Nelson

Two political positions seem paradoxical given the common use of the term "liberal democracy." On the one hand, Isaiah Berlin is surely noted as an outstanding liberal philosopher, though he seldom discussed the problems of democracy as such. By endorsing negative freedom and criticizing various formulations of positive freedom,[1] he seems to undercut any democratic conception of freedom, although he doesn't criticize democracy. Yves R. Simon, on the other hand, is surely a democratic philosopher who is critical of liberalism in a number of passages throughout his work. At a very early age he was negative about liberal ideology,[2] and this persisted in his later writings. I am not suggesting that this was an obsession with him. Simon did not reject those civil liberties associated with liberalism. Nor was he a conservative, though this term often designates but a libertarian liberal. Although the liberalism that he discussed was French liberalism, there are references that indicate that John Stuart Mill was also envisaged. Simon realized that contemporary liberalism differed in important ways from the older variety.

Now Simon did not, and in fact could not, know of the contemporary form of liberalism, styled by some of its commentators with the useful title of "deontological liberalism" that surfaced in the 1970s and has dominated American political philosophy since that time. I say it is a useful title, for it sharply contrasts the new current with the older liberalism, from Bentham to Dewey, which was undeniably teleological. Deontological in this context does not designate a duty ethics, but one that asserts a priority of the right over the good, or of rights as trumps of collective goals, or of rights as opposed to end-

---

[1] Isaiah Berlin, *Four Essays on Liberty* (London and Oxford: Oxford University Press, 1969), pp. 118-172. See also F. A. Hayek's comparison of liberalism and democracy in *The Constitution of Liberty* (London: Routledge and Kegan Paul, 1960), p. 442, n. 2.

[2] Yves R. Simon,"Libéralisme et démocratie." in *La Démocratie* 5ème année, 1.10 (25 fevrier, 1924), pp. 429-433 is the earliest expression, and the most extensive is "Beyond the Crisis of Liberalism" in *Essays in Thomism,* Robert E. Brennan, ed. (New York: Sheed and Ward, 1942), pp. 263-86.

result principles. It is clear from the writings of the principal representatives of the new tendency (Rawls, Dworkin, Nozick, and Larmore) that it is opposed to many of the ideas central to Simon's moral and political philosophy. I think of the set of ideas such as the common good, authority, and autonomy. These constitute key concepts for Simon from 1940 onward, yet each of them is contested by leading contemporary thinkers.

Let us take first the notion of the common good, which Simon states "dominates the whole political philosophy of St. Thomas,"[3] and, from the context in which it was stated, dominates Simon's viewpoint as well. But the common good is an extremely controverted notion, sometimes seen as a synonym for a collection, sometimes as indefinable, sometimes as simply vapid. The foremost American theorist of democracy, Robert Dahl, has explored the difficulties of this concept. If we take his earliest version of *Modern Political Analysis*,[4] we find that the conception hardly figures at all, and I believe that reflects empirical political theory at the time. Yet a quarter of a century later, in *Democracy and Its Critics*,[5] he expends considerable energy in wrestling with the concept of the common good;[6] it is certainly an issue for him in a way that it was not previously. However, Dahl is an exception. Liberal political philosophers by and large are certainly negative about the concept, for it is based on a teleological approach that they reject, and that has consequences that they suspect.

Secondly, as one commentator on Simon has mentioned, the role of authority in democratic society has been a "too-often neglected problem."[7] It has been rare for liberals to devote much attention to it,

---

[3] Yves R. Simon,"Thomism and Democracy" in *Science, Philosophy, and Religion, Second Symposium*, Lyman Bryson and Louis Finkelstein, eds. (New York: The Conference of Science, Philosophy, and Religion, 1942), vol. 2, p. 258.

[4] Robert A. Dahl, *Modern Political Analysis* (Englewood Cliffs: Prentice-Hall, 1963).

[5] Robert A. Dahl, *Democracy and Its Critics* (New Haven and London: Yale University Press, 1989).

[6] Ibid., pp. 73, 116, 118, 218, 224, 280, and 308.

[7] Thomas A. Spragens, Jr., in a review of *Freedom and Community* in *American Political Science Review* 43.2 (June, 1969), p. 561.

but there is a notable exception. I refer to a rare instance of a liberal consideration of authority, that of Richard Flathman, *The Practice of Political Authority: Authority and the Authoritative.*[8] Discussing the nature of political authority, Flathman distinguishes substantive-purposive theories from formal-procedural ones, clearly concluding that the latter is the better of the two. When he explains that the substantive-purposive type theory emphasizes purpose or function, it is clear that Simon's account belongs here. If Flathman gives priority to the formal-procedural concept, he does not completely reject the other concept. He goes on to relate authority to individual agency and argues that the two are compatible. However, in a subsequent essay, Flathman stresses the dangerous character of authority as he understands it: "Authority will cease to be suspect only when we create for ourselves a politics of high citizenship in which we no longer have reason to suspect it. In my judgment, however, authority is on principle suspect, on principle objectionable."[9] So even this recent liberal effort ends in a deep mistrust of the very notion of authority.

The third member of this set of concepts, autonomy, is the main subject of this paper. In order to specify the meaning of autonomy for Simon, one must first identify other meanings of freedom that are presupposed by it. Only after developing Simon's account of autonomy will we be able to make a comparison with the dominant liberal notion.

For Simon, freedom is a continuum, starting in its initial form of voluntariness, then in its state of free choice and, finally, in its completion as autonomy. It is observable that there are theorists who will define freedom in its initial form as Thomas Hobbes does, when in his controversy with Bishop Bramhall he defines liberty (freedom) as "the absence of all the impediments to action, that are not contained in the nature, and in the intrinsical quality of the agent."[10] And if Isaiah

---

[8] Richard Flathman, *The Practice of Political Authority: Authority and the Authoritative* (Chicago: University of Chicago Press, 1980).

[9] Richard Flathman, "Citizenship and Authority: A Chastened View of Citizenship" in *News for Teachers of Political Science* (Summer, 1981), p. 17.

[10] Thomas Hobbes, "The Questions Concerning Liberty, Necessity, and Chance Clearly Stated and Debated between Dr. Bramhall and Thomas Hobbes" in

Berlin's treatment of the subject is more nuanced, he also sees freedom as the freedom from constraint, as negative freedom. That there is an initial form of freedom, as freedom from constraint, restraint, or compulsion, does not seem to be in dispute. The whole issue of free choice, however, has generally been contested. Many liberals accept free choice as the final form of freedom, and often identify it, or confuse it, with autonomy.

Simon wants to argue that there are indeed three forms or states of freedom, and, in the course of defending his position, he sets out a number of features that contrast sharply with deontological liberalism. His treatise on free choice - actually the second version of his argument[11] - attempts to counter the objections to free choice based on theories of determinism, universal causality, and indifference; that is, he seeks to dispel the notions that free choice violates the principle of determination,[12] sets out an exception to causality, or equates free choice with passive indifference.

His main assumption is that the will has a fundamental orientation: "Adherence to the comprehensive good [*bonum in communi*] intuitively and intelligently grasped is the most voluntary, the least constrained, the least coerced, the most spontaneous of all actions."[13] This orientation is not to be confused with free choice, though it is its ground. Free choice is "freedom from necessity."[14] So based on the determination of the will to the comprehensive good, Simon has to show how the will escapes necessity. The analysis bears on the relation between intellect and will, on their mutual causality. "There is no

---

The English Works of Thomas Hobbes, ed. Sir William Molesworth, (Aalen: Scientia Aalen, 1962), vol. 5, p. 367.

[11] The first version was *Traité du libre arbitre* (Liège: Sciences et lettres, 1951).

[12] For the determinist argument, see Ted Honderich, *How Free Are You?: The Determinism Problem* (Oxford: Oxford University Press, 1993), and Ilham Dilman, *Free Will: An Historical and Philosophical Introduction* (London: Routledge, 1999), p. 121.

[13] Yves R. Simon, *Freedom of Choice*, ed. Peter Wolff (New York: Fordham University Press, 1969), p. 27.

[14] Ibid., p. 28.

freedom of the will without freedom of judgment."[15] He examines the question of determination, then the question of causality in the broad Aristotelian sense of the term, and then the use of the term "indifference" in regard to free choice. Simon believes that he has resolved this last difficulty by distinguishing between active and passive indifference. While active indifference stems from abundance, passive indifference stems from deficiency, as in the extreme case of prime matter. "By reason of its being a living relation to the comprehensive good, the will invalidates the claim of any particular good to bring about a determinate judgment of desirability."[16] Free choice is a "dominating indifference."[17] If this dominating indifference, or superdetermination, as he calls it, means that no particular good has an irresistible attraction, it also means that the free agent can invest its own determination to the good as such in a particular good. In this way Simon finds sense in the expression "the power of putting his happiness where he pleases."[18]

We usually think of voluntary action and free choice in regard to personal agents and to the conditions under which these agents are free. Simon understandably deals with autonomy in a collective setting in his first foray into the topic, *Nature and Functions of Authority*.[19] Simon realizes that for many the relation between authority and autonomy is antinomic; that is, as one progresses, the other declines. That is certainly the way in which the two principles are often seen. Yet, Simon wants to maintain that these principles properly understood are complementary. This proper understanding relies on a functional analysis of authority in which a sharp distinction is drawn between the

---

[15] Ibid., p. 98.

[16] Ibid., p. 103.

[17] Ibid., p. 120.

[18] Ibid., p. 158.

[19] Yves R. Simon, *Nature and Functions of Authority* (Milwaukee: Marquette University Press, 1940). The same year Simon gave a paper featuring many of these themes which is included in *Freedom and Community*, ed. Charles P. O'Donnell (New York: Fordham University Press, 1968), Chapter 2. For a treatment of the topic, see Vukan Kuic, *Yves R. Simon: Real Democracy* (Lanham, Maryland: Rowan and Littlefield, 1999), Chapter 5.

essential function of authority and its substitutional function. The latter in its parental form, for instance, aims at its own disappearance. However, the essential function of authority, its task in achieving the common good "of a united multitude,"[20] will not disappear.

Autonomy in this social and political context means self-government. If the emphasis is on political government, autonomy also holds for various social organizations. The way in which a political system combines the two principles of authority and autonomy brings in a third term - hierarchy. What Simon clearly has in mind is a political order in which, at each level, authority and self-government are assured, rising from the lowest to the highest, the national or central system. This is commonly known in Catholic social thought as the principle of subsidiarity,[21] but subsidiarity is not a term used by Simon.

The progress of the social sciences will not change the need for this essential function of authority, in spite of the high hopes once held to the contrary, when it was believed that advancing knowledge would preclude the role of authority. Simon ends the first part of the booklet by summarizing the "endeavor to proportion exactly authority and liberty in any given situation."[22] In *Philosophy of Democratic Government*, his political *magnum opus*, Simon describes the relation this way: "Thus autonomy renders authority necessary and authority renders autonomy possible - this is what we find at the core of the most essential function of government."[23]

At the end of *Nature and Functions of Authority*, Simon refers to Jacques Maritain's *Freedom in the Modern World*[24] on the concept of terminal freedom, obviously of great influence on what is to follow.

---

[20] Ibid., p. 17.

[21] *Catechism of the Catholic Church* (Liguori, Missouri: Liguori Publications, 1994), paragraph 1885.

[22] Yves R. Simon, *Nature and Functions of Authority*, p. 41.

[23] Yves R. Simon, *Philosophy of Democratic Government* (Notre Dame: University of Notre Dame Press, 1993), p. 71.

[24] Jacques Maritain, *Freedom in the Modern World*, trans. Richard O'Sullivan (New York: Charles Scribner's Sons, 1936).

"The process through which this terminal liberty is secured consists in an interiorization of the law. The virtuous man is no longer subjected to the law, since the law has become interior to him and rules him from within."[25] If Maritain's formulation of terminal freedom owes its inspiration to the Pauline epistles, I would suggest that Simon's idea has been taken over from Emile Durkheim. Of him Simon says that "despite his system [Durkheim] was in certain senses a profound moralist."[26] And it is apparent from Simon's writings that he was well acquainted with the French sociological tradition and had studied under one of Durkheim's disciples.[27] What did he find in Durkheim that was particularly worthy of attention?

As a sociologist, Emile Durkheim described the process by which social norms and values become adopted by members of the society. This process of interiorization by which these norms and values are made one's own is solely designed to account for a socially-derived ethics. What Simon does, I believe, is to argue that the formulation of interiorization of the law is proper to moral autonomy as such. That is, what Durkheim posits as particular is really universal.

Now Simon relates this interiorization to the acquisition of the moral virtues. I would not simply classify his position as a virtue ethics, as proposed, for instance, by Elizabeth Anscombe, [28] because the virtues are involved in the achievement of autonomy, not just in some vague sense of flourishing. Self-mastery can only be advanced by the cultivation of the moral virtues, according to Simon.

Simon presents an elaboration concerning "the general laws of the quest for autonomy."[29] The first point he makes consists in the

---

[25] Yves R. Simon, *Nature and Functions of Authority*, p. 43.

[26] Yves R. Simon, *Community of the Free*, trans. Willard R. Trask (Lanham, Maryland: University Press of America, 1984), p. 28.

[27] Simon's thesis at the Sorbonne, *Mémoire sur Charles Dunoyer*, was directed by Célestin Bouglé, a close friend of Durkheim .

[28] G. E. M. Anscombe,"Modern Moral Philosophy," in *The Collected Papers of G. E. M. Anscombe* (Minneapolis: University of Minnesota Press, 1981), vol. 3, pp. 26-42.

[29] Yves R. Simon, *Community of the Free*, p. 30.

rejection of individualism, by which he indicates the position that the aim of political action is the good of individuals distributively considered rather than the common good. Since autonomy is interiorization of the law, and law is directed to the common good, this conclusion follows. Notice the Durkheimian resonance of the remark that "any will to emancipation which is foreign to the sense of the common welfare is directed toward anomy rather than autonomy."[30] The communal search for autonomy leads Simon to examine membership in various organizations, such as labor unions, in which we pursue the interiorization of the law together with others. Not only must we resist any form of despotism, but we must also be aware of group egoism. Loyalty to these lower forms of society should not blind us to the hierarchy of natural societies at the top of which is humanity itself. Another way of saying this is that a universalist ethics should prevail over every form of particularism.

Throughout his writings on the subject of autonomy, Simon stresses what the conquest of freedom entails. First of all, he always emphasizes what a difficult task this is, what effort and sacrifice it requires. And its realization means "the power of choosing good alone."[31] We shall see how this aspect of Simon's theory of autonomy runs contrary to some of the strongest convictions held by contemporary liberal philosophers.

What do liberal political philosophers have to say about the meaning of autonomy and its implication? John Rawls connects autonomy with his conception of the original position, the veil of ignorance, and the principles we would select under relative conditions of ignorance. "Thus acting autonomously is acting from principles that we would consent to as free and equal rational beings, and that we are to understand in this way."[32] In *A Matter of Principle*,[33] Ronald Dworkin

---

[30] Ibid.

[31] Yves R. Simon, *Nature and Functions of Authority*, p. 42. "Just as an individual person, through virtue, protects himself against the risk of making wrong choices" in *Freedom and Community*, p. 46.

[32] John Rawls, *A Theory of Justice* (Cambridge: Harvard University Press, 1971).

[33] Ronald Dworkin, *A Matter of Principle* (Cambridge: Harvard University Press, 1971).

defends the notion of a right to moral independence (a right to follow one's opinion about the right way to live) and relies on the egalitarian character of Kantian morality. Alan Gewirth refers to "the familiar etymological idea of autonomy as setting one's law for oneself, by 'law' meaning rules of [moral] conduct."[34] Such "requirements are self-imposed and are therefore products of the agent's own autonomy."[35]

So if we are to accept the representatives of deontological liberalism, the liberal conception of autonomy that dominates much of what is considered liberal political philosophy is derived from Kant, and ultimately from Rousseau. This view claims that freedom consists in self-imposed laws, or rules if you prefer. Freedom is a property of the mature moral agent. Among the ideas canvassed as expressing the core of liberalism are the primacy given to freedom over equality, and the distinction between private and public morality, neutrality, and autonomy. It seems that autonomy is the best candidate for expressing the core of liberalism.[36] For the dominant kind of liberalism, autonomy is a postulate, an attribute, a pre-supposition of the individual agent. It is a given, not requiring any demonstration. It is often singled out as the liberal notion of the good, like Kant's good will, the only thing that is good without qualification. Liberals object to what they view as attempts to have other people's morals imposed upon them, that is, rules of conduct not of their own choosing. Leaving aside the question of whether or not this principle is consistently held, one realizes that there is no doubt that liberal philosophers have vehemently opposed a number of moral and political rules that have been part and parcel of the culture for a very long time. These rules are of considerable importance because they concern matters that are literally of life and death, as well as involve venerable institutions. The reasons for the liberal rejection of these rules are found in their understanding of what autonomy or free choice consists in.

---

[34] Alan Gewirth, *Self-Fulfilment* (Princeton: Princeton University Press, 1998), p. 34.

[35] Ibid., p. 56.

[36] Among others who reached this conclusion, I would mention Patrick Neal, *Liberalism and Its Discontents* (New York: New York University Press, 1997).

To what extent is the liberal notion of autonomy equivalent to free choice?[37] One has the impression that the liberal feels truly autonomous when there are options before him, not legally prohibited, between carrying the unborn to term or not, between ending one's life or not, or being aided in doing so, or between being "married" to a person of the same sex or not. That liberal political philosophers are in favor of legalized abortion goes without saying. A noteworthy brief was presented to the United States Supreme Court several years ago by six moral philosophers, all liberals acting collectively as *amicus curiae*, defending assisted suicide as a human right.[38] The introduction was by Ronald Dworkin, and two of the signatories were philosophers usually thought of as ideological opponents, namely, John Rawls and Robert Nozick. That the argument was addressed directly to the United States Supreme Court is characteristic of recent recourse by liberals to judicial decision-making over appeals to legislatures.

In Canada, judges on the appellate courts of two provinces, Ontario and British Columbia, have ruled that the existing definition of marriage as between a male and a female is contrary to the equality provisions of the Charter of Rights and Freedoms, although the institution is not mentioned therein. There were liberal commentators who preferred to see the judgment as an expansion of human autonomy. In the United States there are liberals who now propose some kind of civil union for homosexual couples, and perhaps some who would follow the Canadian judicial precedent.

And then we come to the way in which liberal philosophers have generally confronted any attempt to combine, if not relate, freedom and virtue. In his survey of modern political systems, William Bluhm organizes his treatment on "the counterpoint of 'virtue' and 'freedom'."[39] "They signify totally different ways of conceiving the

---

[37] Alan Gewirth, *Self-Fulfilment*, p. 193.

[38] The text can be found under the heading "Assisted Suicide: The Philosophers' Brief with an Introduction by Ronald Dworkin" in *The New York Review of Books*, 44.5 (March 27, 1997), pp. 41-7.

[39] William Bluhm, *Theories of the Political System*, 3rd edition (Englewood Cliffs: Prentice-Hall, 1978), p. 13.

entire political process."[40] When he later discusses some writers who supposedly reunite these values – like Kant and Rawls – his argument is not very convincing. Then Thomas A. Spragens, Jr., in his aforementioned review of *Freedom and Community*, when he takes issue with Simon's idea of freedom as choosing the good alone, declares that "surely it is an excessive contraction of the notion of freedom that leads to the belief that any guarantee against the risk of a wrong choice is purely advantageous to freedom as such."[41] But perhaps the liberal position has been most strongly put by Shadia Drury when she views the relation between freedom and virtue as antinomic. "If we choose freedom, as liberal societies do, then we must be willing to put up with a certain degree of vice. It is impossible to have both perfect freedom and perfect virtue at the same time."[42]

I will conclude by enumerating, in summary form, what I consider to be the salient features of the dominant liberal conception of autonomy, how it differs from Simon's conception, and why there is an ambiguity between the liberal use of the term and that offered by Simon.

1. Inspired by Kant, the liberal conceives of autonomy as expressing the viewpoint of the moral legislator.
2. Autonomy is taken to be an attribute of the individual agent. If rights are considered part of autonomy, they may be understood as trumping any collective goal. Even when not associated with a theory of human rights, autonomy as an assumption is often identified as the basic good of liberal ethics.
3. For all intents and purposes, this notion of autonomy is the same as free choice, and it implies options unimpeded by legal prohibitions.

---

[40] Ibid.

[41] Thomas A. Spragens, Jr., in a review of *Freedom and Community* in *American Political Science Review* 43.2 (June 1969), p. 561.

[42] Shadia B. Drury, *Leo Strauss and the American Right* (New York: St. Martin's Press, 1997), p. 109. Cf. Charles Larmore, *The Morals of Modernity* (Cambridge: Cambridge University Press, 1996), pp. 3 and 11.

4. If this idea of autonomy need not completely exclude virtue, the liberal remains wary of the identification of the two.

Now I come to the reason for the title of this paper. Ambiguity consists in the use of a term having two or more possible meanings. I think that I have shown that when one speaks of Simon's conception of autonomy and compares it with that of the liberals, they are at odds on all relevant points. For Simon, we are subject to the law, but we must make it our own. We are not treated as law-makers. For Simon, autonomy is not posited, but is a conquest. It is not individualistic, but communal. It is not opposed to virtue, but is achieved through it. And if it involves free choice, it is not identical with it. For starting from its initial form, freedom advances through our choices and stable dispositions on the way to terminal freedom. If Simon's account is preferable to the liberal one, it is because it offers a better explanation of the dynamism of the moral life and incorporates free choice, virtue, and moral perfection.

The Common Good: Why is it Good? Why is it Common?

James Schall, S.J.

> A society of human beings . . . is one whose parts have an action independent of the whole, for here the part governs itself. Such a whole has merely unity of action; for this union is brought about by the collaboration of parts that are self-governing. Therefore, if these parts are ordered to the common good as to their chief good, this direction is not accomplished except by self-government. In Aristotle's doctrine, the action of the ruling element in the political community is in no sense divorced from the participation of the citizen. — Charles N. R. McCoy[1]

> The principal part of the common good is contained within our souls. — Yves Simon[2]

> For the good of the species is a greater good for the singular than its singular good. This is not therefore a species prescinded from individuals; it is the singular itself, which, by nature, desires more the good of the species than its particular good. The desire for the common good is in the singular itself. —Charles De Koninck[3]

I

The terms "common good," "commonweal," "general welfare," or "greatest good" are themselves frequently heard in politics, ethics, literature, the press, theology, and philosophy. They may or may not be exactly interchangeable. Words need content and context. These terms continue to bear a note of high mindedness, of something more excellent - even "divine," as Aristotle said. St. Thomas's famous

---

[1] Charles N. R. McCoy, *The Structure of Political Thought* (New York: McGraw-Hill, 1963), p. 53.

[2] Yves Simon, *A General Theory of Authority* (Notre Dame: University of Notre Dame Press, 1980), p. 126.

[3] Charles De Koninck, "On the Primacy of the Common Good," *The Aquinas Review*, 4, 1, (1997), p. 18. This edition of *The Aquinas Review* reprints De Koninck's original essay, together with I. Th. Eschmann's critique of it, "In Defense of Maritain," and De Koninck's reply, "In Defense of Saint Thomas."

definition of law was precisely, "an ordination of reason, by the proper authority, *for the common good*, and promulgated" (I-II, 90, 1). The common good is an end to be chosen and brought into reality. It contains a reason or order worth putting into effect, if not already in place. Once in effect, it is a dynamic, not static, concept. A common good must be an on-going accomplishment. This is part of its excitement and nobility.

All actual human common goods, as prudentially reasonable configurations, can degenerate or increase. In either case, a "common" good will still be actively needed to achieve what is possible in the circumstances for those who participate in it. The particular good would be less itself, less good, if it were not also involved in a common good because the common good is composed of particular goods. A less than perfect good is still a good. Even a lesser evil has something to be said for it.

Idealists often become tyrannical because they seek to impose their systems apart from the nature, reason, and will of those of whose common good they are. The "common good" in general parlance is not wholly exempt from this danger, almost as if we could conceive it apart from those who might compose it. The principles of the "lesser evil" and the "greater good," moreover, are themselves elements of the common good in actual historic circumstances. The common good does not cease to function if some or most are not good.

The common good is sometimes said to be "opposed" to the private or particular good, but not in a way that denies that some goods are really private. Common good includes private goods as private. The common good is designed to keep genuine private goods precisely private and this for the common good itself. Private goods, as such, are good to have. The common good does not absorb private goods without itself at some point ceasing to be itself any longer a good. Private goods are good like all good. Good, divine and human, while remaining what it is, causes or incites whatever is good to be more good. What makes it possible to have private goods is itself a good, a common good.

Private goods themselves exist as goods, as realities. The order of things in which particular goods fall enables them to contribute to a greater good. Foundations of houses really do hold them up, and they really are not doors or second stories of the same house. "Privacy" or closed goods, however, those that proclaim their good over against their being, against what they are, turn in on themselves. They produce a loneliness or isolation about them. They cannot stand the test of common being and its order from which and into which good flows or ought to flow.

Thus, it may be a common good, say, to have a free market system in which good quality apples can be grown by anybody and sold at a fair price to any purchasers who want them. But the apple, on eating it, is my particular good or perhaps my particular ill if it is too green so that a stomach ache ensues. The eaten apple is not a "common good," yet there is something common about all private goods. It is good that I am healthy, to which good the apple contributes a real, if tiny, element. "An apple a day keeps the doctors away." But it is also good that there are doctors in case I am not, after eating the apple, healthy. It is even good that there are lawyers and police in case someone, unbeknownst to me, deliberately poisons my good apple or, like Augustine, steals the produce of my fruit trees. Perhaps this symbolism is why the Fall is famously pictured as involving the willful eating of an apple!

The common good is not some separate "vision" or "thing" conceived to be standing apart from or imposed on those for whose "good" it is said to be "common." Many a totalitarian mind has been inflamed by a dream of the "common good," by a way of "making" or "forcing" people to be good apart from their desire or ability to participate in the said scheme that will, presumably, eradicate all their problems. Indeed, I suspect that many a totalitarian is really a mystic gone wrong, intellectually wrong, because he wants to do so much good that he cannot trust or foster the participation of those whose good he so longs to implement. In this sense, we might argue that much of our difficulties do not arise from "evil" spreading its wings, but from "good" that has misunderstood its own condition.

"The common good touches the whole man, the needs both of his body and his soul," John XXIII writes in *Pacem in Terris*. He continues:

> Hence it follows that the civil authorities must undertake to effect the common good by ways and means that are proper to them; that is, while respecting the hierarchy of values, they should produce simultaneously both the material and spiritual welfare of the citizens.... In our Encyclical, Mater et Magistra, we emphasized that the common good of all 'embraces the sum total of those conditions of social living whereby men are enabled to

achieve their own integral perfection more fully and more reasonably' (#57-58).

The common good is here pictured as something to be "effected," or brought about; that is, it does not just happen, but, while being something implicitly given in human nature as something to be accomplished, it remains the result of thought, decision, and action. It does not come into being by itself as if it were a superior being that had its own separate reason, will, and capacity to act. The common good is to be suffused within the minds and wills of those for whom it is common, both rulers and ruled.

Evidently, there are ways to attempt to bring about a common good that are "improper." This sobering reminder means that we must have some philosophical criterion to distinguish between what is and what is not a "proper" manner of bringing about this common good. The common good must really be a "good," something that is worthy of being desired. What is "not good" is recognizable, though still under the light of the good. Establishing the proper means, institutions, and purposes applicable to any political society is what natural law and political philosophy are about. Spiritual and material well-being are to be sought and brought into reality together. Thus, we do not seek one then the other. Even here, however, there is a priority of rank--"Seek ye first the Kingdom of God, and all these things will be added to you." "Man does not live by bread alone." "Remember, keep holy the Sabbath Day." "If you did this to the least of my brethren, you did it to Me."

The common good is more "divine" than the particular good. *What is* is good. Good is good. Making things better is "more good," or better, provided we know what "better" is. The good has the note of superabundance about it. The common good makes it possible for us to be more fully ourselves, as if we could not be really or fully ourselves without it. Goodness is both something of substance and something of acting. Denying being the possibility to be "fully good" is not good.

II

The common good is said to embrace "the sum total of conditions of social living." Apparently, we could have all these "conditions" and still not have a real common good. Men still must "achieve" by themselves what is called an "integral perfection" and do so both reasonably and fully. It is almost as if we are warned not to bury the one talent instead of using it to create more. What is "good" can evidently always be rejected, unless it is what is "goodness itself," which we never encounter as such in this life. Charles N. R. McCoy remarks that the common good cannot be achieved "divorced from the participation of the citizens." This participation itself, however, can be toward the less virtuous or less good, as well as toward a greater good. The subject matter of all ethics and politics must, as Aristotle said, include the objective judgment of the moral status of the act about to be effected. Is it good or bad?

Thus, "doing good" has its dangers if it means always doing something for others rather than allowing or encouraging them to do something for themselves. Charity begins at home. It ought not to take the place of home. "Doing good," in the sense of ourselves fulfilling ourselves by doing good for and in place of others, can be a very dangerous and selfish action. We may want others to be poor *so that* we can help them. It is better to teach a man how to fish than simply give him food, granted that sometimes this latter may be all we can do. This participation of others in causing the good, including their own good, is itself a major element in the common good. But it seems possible to have a good constitutional order in which citizens choose not to abide by its rules or conditions. This preference is how a private good can be opposed to a common good, precisely when it neglects its relation to the common good by its private acts. The common good includes the private good. The private good is only private within its relation to what is common. But the common good is not an "alternative" to the private good. We want what is good to be in fact good.

No "sum total of human conditions" can work automatically apart from human participation and choice. Otherwise, the pursuit of the good becomes the pursuit of being taken care of, not of ourselves acting. The choosing and the thinking that goes into choosing – Aristotle's deliberation and decision – themselves are elements of the "sum total," without which the common good cannot exist. That such a rejection or failure to effectuate what is good is possible seems to be a matter of human observation. We can only deny that it happens if, on some basis or other, we deny our experience.

In theory, and perhaps indirectly, we deal here with the problem of evil, which is itself never another good "being," but somehow is always a lack of being in what is good, particularly in the case of a moral good.

Why the complete good is impossible or unlikely in this world has, in part, to do with free will and the Fall, which in turn has to do with the question of whether we are only political beings, that is, with the question of whether a practical happiness in this world is the only happiness there is. The mislocation of the highest good constitutes one of the objects of study of political philosophy. Indeed, it is one of the criteria that define good and bad regimes. But man is something more than a political animal. The good to which he is finally oriented is itself the cause of the other goods that he chooses. The lesser or finite goods often appear as alternatives to his highest good. It is the thesis of the common good that this is not necessarily the case, or better, that it is not necessary that what is good must be used badly, even though it can be so used. The fact that it can be used badly is the drama of our existence, as it also implies, again, that it need not be used badly.

III

Behind the notion of a common good, in the political sense, is the question of the ontological nature of the city in contrast to the ontological being of the individuals that compose the city by their prudence, actions, and passions. The city is not a substance, a "being," though it is "of being," that is, it has a distinct reality. Usually society is put in the ontological categories of action, passion, and primarily relation – *ad aliud*, according to how its members stand to one another. It deals with how human beings relate to one another reciprocally as others in a chosen, legal order. There is a certain tendency in the Hegelian tradition of viewing the state itself as a substance, as a separate being that transcends its parts: the Spirit marching through the world. The state, however, is not a substance. It is a unity of actions. Indeed, its parts are related to the whole as precisely parts.

The whole can only be the whole if the parts are parts. It is in the interest of, that is, to the good of the whole, that parts be what they are. Parts derive their whole justification from the prior nature of the whole and its good. We do not first conceive the hand, and then construct the human being to go with it. The whole human being, which has a hand as an integral part of *what it is*, comes first. Conceived this way, the parts may be expendable, for "the good of the whole." In medicine, this is the principle that we use to justify the amputation of defective limbs. Even though they perform some specific act that no other part could perform, the parts only exist because of and for the sake of the whole. The whole itself, however, may have an action that transcends the actions of each part, while including them. This principle, however, does not deny that once a part is gone, say a limb is amputated, the whole must from then on limp. It is really missing some good due to it.

Thus, in the case of the common good of a human society, the "parts" of which it is composed are not just parts. Maritain calls them "wholes." Society is made up of parts, each of which is a substantial whole.[4] Though they are said to be by nature social and political beings, human beings are also said to transcend the whole political order, as if each human being, by being himself, is implicitly ordained to this higher purpose by his own proper activities, activities that are not that of the polis as such. The fact that lesser goods must be achieved first or more gradually is no argument against this priority. This higher ordination, in fact, is what limits the state to be itself, a unity of order, a relation, not a being. That is, the state does not exhaust human purpose or the destiny of its members. By being itself, it is ordered to a higher end.

This view was traditionally expressed in terms of the primacy of the contemplative life. Human beings, as persons, are said to have an end that is higher than the state and for which the state also exists. The common good, thus, wants lesser goods to be achieved as goods. It is, if you will, a theory of abundance, not a theory of parsimony. The common good that is the political common good is itself a "lesser good" in comparison to the end of the "wholes" that make it up. The immortality of the *polis* – it lives on as its members are replaced via

---

[4] Jacques Maritain, "The Person and the Common Good," *The Social and Political Philosophy of Jacques Maritain*, edited by Joseph W. Evans and Leo R. Ward (Notre Dame: University of Notre Dame Press, 1976), pp.82-88. "The human person's vocation to goods which transcend the political common good is embodied in the essence of the political common good. . . . The direct ordination of the human person to God transcends every created common good – both the common good of the political society and the intrinsic common good of the universe" *Man and the State* (Chicago: University of Chicago Press, 1951), p. 149.

birth and death – is itself subordinated to the immortality of the soul. Through the immortality of the soul, and more particularly through the resurrection of the body, the personal destiny is achieved that constitutes the real good to which human beings, from their beginning, are ordered.

IV

The term "person," however, is not without its own problems. It is a term that arises originally from Greek drama. The "persona" was the mask worn by an actor to hide his own personality and to imply or to indicate that of the character he was portraying. Later, "person" was defined by Boethius as a subsistent being of a rational nature. The mask became the being it represented, as it were. The rational subsistent being, by being itself, could, through its reason, "be" other things not itself, all other things. The person meant both itself and what was not itself. It indicated an autonomy, that this thing had its own life, source of action, and grounding in being. It was that for which other things existed. Person was the highest sort of being.

"Person," moreover, was the term that came to be used in theology to describe the three "subsistences" in the Trinity. The word must always be seen in the light of that background. The inner life of God was revealed to contain both an otherness and a unity. The term "person" described this diversity. It was said to be a "substantial relation," meaning that one person of the Trinity was *not* the other, but that each, nonetheless, was in or of one nature, one God, not three gods. Moreover, the whole inner being of each person was seen to be related to or defined by his relation to the other persons. The Son was from the Father. No one knew the Father but the Son. The Christian understands that love and friendship, while agreeing with Aristotle on these topics, arose precisely out of this background. "Greater love than this no man has who lays down his life for his friend" (Jn. 15:13). The very irreducibleness of each person of the Trinity combined a sense of otherness and identity that prevents anything from being isolated in itself, or contrariwise, from being totally absorbed so that it no longer remains itself.

Person came to describe the absolute uniqueness and irrepeatability of certain beings, rational beings. In a famous controversy between Charles De Koninck and I. Th. Eschmann, ostensibly over the proper interpretation of the common good, the question was asked about the accurate understanding of person or "personalism." In what sense was the "person" considered to be independent or autonomous? The crux of this controversy remains of considerable, if not more, importance today. The term "person," with its philosophical adjuncts, namely, "rights, " "dignity, " and "values," has come to mean almost the opposite of what the term "person" meant in that philosophy that understood God as a common good. That is, God was known as that good to which all things are ordained, so that our good as persons is itself ordained to this common good that is God, in which all things are good.

What happened in the meantime is that the term "person" came to be conceived not as merely a subsistent being of a rational nature, but rather as a fully autonomous being whose reality was exempt from precisely anything but itself. To be a person meant to be dependent on nothing but oneself. The description of personal autonomy was posed or defined in the terminology of "rights," "values," and "dignity" in such a way that person had no relation either for its own given being or for its own good, to any order outside of itself. "Dignity" meant this self-declared autonomy. "Rights" meant whatever content we chose to put into the definition of person. Thus, it has happened that precisely the words that have been most used to establish the proper understanding of what it is to be a human being have been, largely, co-opted so that they mean almost the opposite of their original intent.

"But Christianity actually has a deep resistance to the concept of human rights," Robert Kraynak has written.

> As shocking as this may sound today, there are numerous and profound reasons why this is so. In the first place, Christianity places duties to God and duties to one's neighbor before individual rights and cannot easily accept the proposition that people have the right to pursue happiness as they see fit, especially if that right leads to societies that are indifferent to God.... Today the term "person" refers to a human being with a duty to forge his or her own identity or moral personality by an assertion of the will.... In recent years... "person" has become a

> moral (not metaphysical) term applied to human beings, meaning a rational and free agent who possesses inherent dignity and rights.[5]

Through this understanding of the term "rights," it becomes almost impossible actually to do anything for anyone, as whatever anyone needs or wants ought to be his by "right." So if he does not have what he wants, or thinks he wants, however he defines it, it is someone else's fault or someone else's duty to provide. Rights have no independent source or content than what the subject wills. The emphasis on "dignity" means that we are allowed or encouraged to do what we want. The definition of democracy has come to mean the protection of our "right" to do what we choose, wherein what we choose constitutes the dignity of our person. Nothing has a "claim" on our will except a negative understanding of the common good that deprives the word "common" of any meaning. There is, strictly speaking, nothing to be held in common as participated in by others.

V

In his essay on the "Good," Jörg Splett maintains that failure to keep together the relation of good to both reason and will occasioned:

> the real disappearance of the proper reality of the good in rationalism, which culminated in Spinoza's conception of the *amor intellectualis*. But it also gave rise to an irrational philosophy of values, which especially in its modern form separates *esse* and *bonum*, knowing and willing (or "feeling") in a dualistic way and never envisages the antecedent unity in being as well as in consciousness. The appeal to a merely irrational "feeling" is a simple rejection of a positivist denial of the objectivity of the good....[6]

---

[5] Robert Kraynak, *Christian Faith and Modern Democracy* (Notre Dame: University of Notre Dame Press, 2001), pp. 153-54.

[6] Jörg Splett, "Good," *Encyclopedia of Theology: The Concise Sacramentum Mundi*, edited by Karl Rahner (New York: Seabury, 1975), pp. 581-82.

Splett dubiously implies that this failure to "keep together" good and being was the fault of St. Thomas and Aristotle, even though they were very careful to explain the relation of will to reason and to *what is.*

Splett, however, seems to be right to link the notion of "value" to a "disappearance of the proper reality of the good in rationalism." If good has no reality, if it disappears, then human choice has no proper object. Reason goes its own way and does not provide, as in Aquinas, something worthy of desire or will. The term "value," which we usually associate with Max Weber's sociology, is what connects "rights" to "person." Value is what happens to will left to itself. Since there is no "good" either revealed in the ontological being of the subsistent human being or in the universe in which he acts, the person has the sublime need to create himself, to give himself content, substance. "Value" is a modern word. It provides ends unrelated to reason or to *what is.*

According to this view, no person has any content to his own being except that which he gives himself. Once he gives himself something, he has a "right" to it. His dignity is constituted by the fact that he is autonomous. He has no "intrinsic" dignity, as the "right" to abortion indicates. Neither truth nor good arise out of common being from whence the diversity of things first comes. Hence, the social enterprise is not in pursuing and willing a "common good" composed of wholes that reach to ordered being, but in defending a private good which is self-constituted, giving itself rights, autonomy, and value.

Charles De Koninck's original essay on the common good, since it was an attack on personalism, was understood by some, notably by Father Eschmann, to be an attack on Maritain, something that De Koninck vigorously denied. But De Koninck did attack an understanding of dignity and person that was exactly the opposite of what such words had originally meant. He writes: "It must not be forgotten that the philosophers responsible for modern totalitarianism did not deny the dignity of the human person; on the contrary, they exalted this dignity more than ever before."[7] De Koninck wished to show that this modern conception of man is based on a principle of

[7] De Koninck, "On the Primacy of The Common Good," p. 11.

autonomy quite opposed to a view of person whose good is seen to be linked to the good of others, to a common good.

To make his point in terms of the common good, De Koninck uses the example of the fallen angels. Of Satan, De Koninck writes, dignity consisted:

> in the exaltation of his personal dignity and of the proper good of his nature; he preferred his proper good to the common good, to a beatitude which was participated and common to many; he refused this latter because it was participated and common. Even though he possessed his natural happiness and the excellence of his person by no special favor, but rather by a right founded on his creation itself – to God he owed his creation, but all else belonged properly to him; by this invitation to participate he felt injured in his proper dignity.[8]

To conceive dignity after the manner of Satan, then, is what De Koninck understands to be the "personalist" or "Pelagian" error, the error of an autonomy closed to a higher good. It prefers the sufficiency of the good one self-creates. It relates to nothing other than to one's self.

"The dignity of created persons is not without ties, and the purpose of our liberty," De Koninck affirms, "is not to overcome these ties, but to free us by strengthening them. These ties are the principal cause of our dignity."[9] The fact that we are not totally complete in ourselves is not a defect in us. What we are is not a defect in reality precisely because of a common good in which we also participate. To love is to be bound. The only alternative to this being bound is not to be bound, which is a form of rejection of the good of others. "The sin of the angels was practically a personalist error: they preferred the dignity of their own person to the dignity which they would receive through their subordination to a good which was superior but common in its very superiority."[10] The fallen angels thus appear as adversaries to the

---

[8] Ibid.

[9] Ibid., p. 12.

[10] Ibid., p. 13.

common good precisely by preferring their own good as unrelated to any good other than themselves. This is the "personalist" error. Because of their angelic choice, the world is deprived of their good as diffusive among many, while they are deprived of any good that they might have received.

De Koninck thinks that the personalist error is the Pelagian claim of self-sufficiency for our destiny. In a subtle observation, he seeks to explain more exactly how the totalitarian notion of dignity opens the way to the denial of dignity. De Koninck observes that there is a speculative error involved here. He means that something more ominous is at work here than the sin of the angels, which was a purely practical error. The angels knew they were not God. In the case of man, the speculative error is such that, in practice, it results in our enslavement in the name of human "dignity." The devil refused to participate in any good but his own. "The denial of the higher dignity which man receives through the subordination of his purely personal good to the common good would ensure the denial of all human dignity."[11]

Thus, it is 1) a denial of human dignity to isolate human existence from the destiny or orientation to a common good that is not simply one's own creation. 2) It is a high good to receive a good beyond one's own good, as it were, to "be" more than we "are." 3) To close the finite human good from all other good ends up by undermining human dignity, which consists precisely in its capacity to will the good of others.

De Koninck has concentrated on a version of personalism that has, in fact, become predominant in the culture, the personalism of the autonomous man who gives himself his own dignity and even his own consciousness. Values and rights are what this man wills, not what he has received by reason of his being *what he is.* Thus, he does not "have" rights or values by nature. He gives them to himself. In effect, the person is left with no inherent defenses against a totalitarian version of the "common good" that would seem to counteract the chaos that comes from universalizing rights and values that have no common

---

[11] Ibid., pp. 13-14.

basis in objective reality. Any order is better than the chaos of rights-practices that have no unity other than arbitrary will. This analysis seems to be why De Koninck holds that modern totalitarian theories consider themselves to be on the side of human "dignity" and human "personhood." They save personalist theories on their own grounds, on the grounds of a will predetermined to nothing but itself, but with the power to enforce its order. The "denial of all human dignity" resulted from the denial of any openness to the common good. Human dignity is based on something more than the will's own act of affirming only itself as the basis of this dignity.

VI

To understand what is at issue here, one must see why the "common good" is not merely a collection of individual goods. Individual goods, to be themselves, have a relation to the common good that is, particularly in the case of rational beings, interior to them. The common good is not only unachievable apart from the wills and intellects of members of the community, but it is also achieved best when it is voluntarily and even happily participated in. Clifford Kossel states the principle well: "The immediate objective of civil law," he writes,

> is to establish social unity and peace by establishing an order of justice in which all the citizens and lesser societies may have security in their goods and be enabled to share in the fruits of social cooperation according to their contribution. This very order is the first common good, but it is ordained to a further end, the virtuous life of the citizens. Law immediately takes care of the external order and the external acts required for that order. But by its directive and coercive power, it aims ultimately to lead the citizens to act from true interior virtue by habituation to these acts. Yet it cannot by itself effect this. Hence while the very establishment of law and order makes possible the liberty by which individuals and lesser communities can carry on their proper functions, it also stimulates and calls for their free cooperation in actually bringing about the virtuous life and communion in that life through the communication of their

goods with one another. This is civic friendship, the final aim of the legislator.[12]

It is important to sort out's position here. The "first common good," as he calls it, is the order of law and justice that provides a framework within which free people can act rationally to secure the greater goods made available by the multitude.

But this "first common good" is itself insufficient. There is, as it were, a "second" common good, to which the first common good points. We are not directly loved or made content by a "framework of law," however useful it may be. Citizens are ultimately to act not because of law or coercion but because of virtue, within the law. This position means that they act out of friendship and not merely out of justice. The law evidently, as Aquinas says, points to friendship but it cannot by itself produce it. A civil society is the context for many things of which it itself is not capable of either knowing or fostering. These are properly higher goods. Because of this, the civil society is a reflection of the nature of the good itself, in the goods that it makes possible. This possibility also implies that the good that is capable of being produced in the city is a reflection of the proper common good and an embodiment of it after its own manner. At the same time, it is not that highest good to which the wholes that are "persons" in the ontological sense are ordained, a good they do not themselves create or make.

Yves Simon in making this point in another way, observes that in one lifetime very few people can be excellent in more than one or two capacities, if that.[13] This is so because in order to acquire many, if not most perfections, we need a lifetime of training and practice, particularly in the higher things. This limitation is not a bad thing in itself, and it is a fact. Thus, if we are going to have available to us goods other than those we can perfect ourselves, we will have to allow or encourage others to effect them. This result has nothing to do with we

---

[12] Clifford G. Kossel, "The Moral Views of Thomas Aquinas," *Encyclopedia of Morals,* edited by V. Ferm (New York: Philosophical Library, n. d.), p. 21.

[13] Yves Simon, *A General Theory of Authority* (Notre Dame: University of Notre Dame Press, 1980), p. 28.

ourselves being well-rounded persons. The very condition of the individual human being is to be lacking many things that are either necessary or worthy to have. This is the point of Plato's observation about specialization and, to some degree, of Adam Smith's understanding of a market.

If we ask, "Why is the common good, good?" the answer seems to be that we want a world in which a variety of perfections can exist and be available in their respective ways to those who do not have them. This desire includes particularly the goods of the mind, of truth and of beauty. It is "good," in other words, that we have goods of all orders brought into being by others. It is not a failure on my part if I, even because I lack time, talent, or opportunity, cannot do what someone else can do. If we all did the same things, what would be available to us would be those same things that we all did by ourselves, a very narrow world. Kossel's point is rather that these particular things work themselves out in an atmosphere beyond justice if they are really to work or be present at all.

It is in this context Simon recalls that Aristotle points out that the common good is more "divine" than the particular good. Simon notes that "divine" for the Greeks meant that a thing is imperishable, a point made by Hannah Arendt in *The Human Condition.* We have a certain experience of imperishability in two ways – in the case of the persistency of the species and in the continuity of communities. Individuals enter into life and leave it constantly. The species, not as an idea but as a concrete reality, exists in actual individual beings within the species who are continually replaced. "The law of generation and corruption covers the whole universe of nature," Simon writes:

> This law is transcended in a very proper sense by the incorruptibility of the species and the immortality of human association. The masterpiece of the natural world cannot be found in the transient individual. Nor can it be found in the species, which is not imperishable except in the state of universality; but in this state it is no longer unqualifiedly real. Human communities are the highest attainments of nature, for they are virtually unlimited with regard to diversity of perfections, and virtually immortal. Beyond the satisfaction of individual needs the association of men serves a good unique in

> plenitude and duration, the common good of the human community.[14]

The "masterpiece of the natural world," as Simon graphically calls it, is the real, active common good when it actually and through its "parts" provides goods.

Simon uses the term "imperishability" both to designate the living species in operation – that is, little fishes replace big fishes ad infinitum so that some fish actually exist at any given time– and to designate that aspect of a community that analogously carries on down the time so that we can say that a nation lasts longer than the lives of its individual members. To understand a species "in the state of universality," that is, as an essence, means that it exists in this form only in the mind. This is what Simon means by saying that it is "not unqualifiedly real," whereas real fish in a real pond are unqualifiedly real, though they are not the whole or abstract species whose form they bear to make them formally what they are.

VII

If the common good is "good" precisely because it enables the abundance of being to come into effect through the actions of its parts, each of whom has his own internal principle of action, then why is the common good "common?" De Koninck has pointed out that the "desire" for the common good is in the singular itself. And Simon remarks that "the principal part of the common good is contained within our souls." In *Genesis,* we read that it is not "good" for man to be alone. What does "not being alone mean?" After all, we do not want it to mean that we do not remain ourselves. We are the ones who want the good that comes from our not being alone. We may recall the title of a book of some years back, *The Lonely Crowd*, which implied that the mere presence of others did not prevent us from being lonely. There would have to be some way for us, while remaining ourselves, to become the other.

Basically this is what knowledge and will are about. "Thus God, a purely and simply universal good, is the proper good which all things

---

[14] Ibid., p. 29.

naturally desire as their highest and greatest good, the good which gives all things their entire being."[15] Nature is suffused with intellect. "It is thanks to this participation in intellect that every nature tends principally towards a universal good."[16] This observation suggests that intellect itself is open to the order of things.

De Koninck writes, "[T]he common good is not a good other than the good of the particulars, a good which is merely the good of the collectivity looked upon as a kind of singular."[17] We do not know or love a particular, and then, in addition, love something else called the "common good." Such a common good would really belong to no one; whereas, the very point of the common good is that it is also ours. The common good is the good of the particulars, but the particulars know that this good is also the good of others. If their particular good does not include this awareness that others know this truth or will this good, then their isolation will be complete. Thus,

> the common good is better for each of the particulars which participate in it, insofar as it is communicable to the other participants; communicability is the very reason for its perfection. The particular attains to the common good precisely as common good only insofar as it attains to it as to something communicable to others.[18]

Love of others includes a common good.

While it is true that we cannot, properly speaking, "do" anything for God, it does not follow that we cannot imitate the order of God. "It is the created common good, of any order, which imitates most properly the absolute common good."[19] This is why the common good is good. "But God, Who is the most perfect good, tends toward the good of being as a whole. And thus not without reason is it said that good as such is diffusive; for the more a being is good, the more it spreads its goodness

---

[15] De Koninck, "On the Primacy of the Common Good" p. 18.

[16] Ibid.

[17] Ibid., p. 17.

[18] Ibid., p. 16.

[19] Ibid., pp. 19-20.

to beings, which are further from itself."[20] And this is why the common good is common.

[20] Ibid., p. 20.

FREEDOM AND SATISFACTION

Romanus Cessario, O.P.

Freedom and Punishment! If you had lived in Boston since January 2002, it would be difficult to avoid thinking about punishment. Why? Because those who have received punishments include priests, Bishops, and even the Church herself. Similar scenarios have emerged in other cities throughout the United States as the former ways of treating clerics accused of external unchastity with minors rapidly lost standing in the public eye. There is no need to rehearse the specifics of what has come to be known in the United States as the scandal of clerical sexual abuse. One thing should be noted, however: the story-line, as Mary Ann Glendon likes to observe, has been almost entirely scripted by a secular press that exhibits no manifest sympathy for the Church or her teachings.[1] Unfortunately for many persons, the Church to this day has not succeeded in getting her own story out. Even many good Catholics remain confused. And we all still await a sound analysis of the events that have occurred since a local Boston newspaper first covered the story in its first Sunday edition of 2002.

Take the case of Cardinal Bernard Law; born in Torreòn, Mexico, Law is the son of Bernard A., a pioneering aviator, and Helen Stubblefield Law. His early education was mainly acquired in the United States Virgin Islands. As valedictorian of his high school class in Charlotte Amalie, Law reflected early on the importance of Catholic social teaching: "Never must we let bigotry creep into our beings." While an undergraduate at Harvard, Law participated in Catholic intellectual life at St Paul's Church, Cambridge, and concretized his plans to study for the priesthood. He was ordained a Catholic priest in 1961 and began his service to the Church in Vicksburg, Mississippi. As the civil rights movement of the 1960s reached its height, he was

---

[1] Reuter's news service reported on Friday, October 10, 2003, that Pope John Paul II's top aide said earlier that day that the media had exaggerated the sex scandal that has shaken the U.S. Roman Catholic Church and unfairly tainted thousands of priests with overzealous coverage. "The scandals in the United States received disproportionate attention from the media," Secretary of State Cardinal Angelo Sodano told Reuters in an interview. "There are thieves in every country, but it's hard to say that everyone is a thief."

assigned to take over the diocesan weekly, *The [Jackson] Mississippi Register*. Forthright articles such as "Everyone is Guilty," which appeared a week after the slaying of NAACP leader Medgar Evers, signaled his unequivocal commitment to the cause of racial justice and brought threats to his personal safety.

In 1973, Bernard Law was installed as Bishop in the diocese of Springfield-Cape Girardeau, Missouri. His tenure there was marked by commitment to both ecumenical and inter-religious dialogue, especially with the Missouri Jewish community. His assistance in resettling Vietnamese refugees who were arriving at Fort Chaffee occasioned the beginning of his long-standing involvement with the U.S. Vietnamese community, both Catholic and Buddhist. In 1984, Law was called to assume responsibility for the densely populated archdiocese of Boston, and the following year he received the cardinal's red hat from Pope John Paul II. As Boston's Cardinal, he soon became a leading voice in defense of Catholic teaching on human life, on the dignity of marriage, and on social justice. His strong stands on social issues made him a prime target when a rash of lawsuits brought the glare of publicity to clerical sexual abuse.

Prior to Law's tenure in 1984, public records show that there had been an average of about twenty-seven incidents per year of sexual abuse of minors by Catholic clergymen. For the years 1984 through 1992, the number of incidents dropped to an average of about ten a year. As the sociological ramifications of the problem became apparent, however, Law initiated the expression, "zero tolerance," and for the last two years of his service to Boston, there were no reported incidents. Though Law had followed the same psychiatric advice and had implemented the same protocols that were observed nationwide by both Catholic and other religious and benevolent groups when faced with the sexual abuse of minors committed to their care, the firestorm of criticism that erupted in Boston was especially intense. In 2002, he resigned to give the Church in Boston a chance to heal. On 27 May 2004, Law was named archpriest of the papal basilica of St. Mary Major, one of the oldest churches in Rome. Subsequent investigations reveal that what came to be regarded as the incautious re-assignment of abusive priests at one time represented a carefully monitored program of hoped-for rehabilitation and that Law, like countless religious leaders and public school superintendents, had acted on what they believed to be the best available medical advice at the time.[2]

Some persons argue that it will require decades to obtain an objective evaluation of what happened in 2002 and after, and even longer to render an accurate theological interpretation of them. One thing is clear: theological truth has not been well served during this period of reaction to allegations of clerical misconduct. Even the language used to describe the alleged malefactions prompts one to construe them from a secular point of view. Take for example the word "abuse" itself. I should have thought that Catholics would want to be more specific about the kind of vice that a person may commit, and so would prefer to speak about the "unchastity" of certain clerics rather than about "sexual abuse." The word "abuse" remains open to diverse and even subjective interpretations, signifying a genus while leaving the nature of the moral species undefined.[3] Consider as well that the accepted secular therapies to treat victims of sexual abuse differ in significant ways from the sacramental remedies for the sin of unchastity. But it is premature to pursue these kinds of discussions under conditions such as those illustrated by a feature story that ran in an October 2003 daily edition of *The Boston Globe*: "Victims agonize over church deal. Struggle with moral, legal questions about accepting settlement."[4]

Let me emphasize that it is not my intention to take advantage of this occasion to defend the established prudence that until the provisional approval of the Dallas Charter by the Holy See had governed the handling of unchaste and other priests who fell short of embodying the moral qualities that the exercise of their office requires

---

[2] For further information, see *Boston's Cardinal. Bernard Law, the Man and His Witness*, ed. Romanus Cessario, O.P. (Lanham, MD: Lexington, 2002).

[3] Just as we do not seek merely generic diagnosis from a physician, likewise we should not rest in merely generic descriptions of concrete moral disturbances and defects. This is especially true when those descriptions are so abstract and vague as to be ideologically and rhetorically manipulable.

[4] The 8 October 2003 story by Ralph Ranalli appeared on the first page of the "City & Region" section, B1, B6.

of them. I do think, however, that the Church's jurisprudence, which had been developed over centuries, along with the pastoral discretion that accompanied it, merits a second look. Although one may point to specific instances where this classical prudence was poorly implemented for diverse reasons, it still may be argued that the old dispensation succeeded better to uphold the common goods of both Church and polis than the practices now in force. In any event, the past several years have been a difficult period for the Church in our nation.

Most of the reasonable commentary on the unchastity of clerics has included calls for healing. Journalists of all persuasions agree that healing is desirable. Plaintiffs' lawyers argue that they seek prompt healing. Those who are aggrieved beg for healing. Bishops pray for healing. And finally, arbitrators determine the financial cost of procuring healing. In Boston alone, that cost will probably exceed one hundred million dollars. On 16 July 2007, *The New York Times* reported that after the 660 million dollar settlement by the archdiocese of Los Angeles, the sum paid by the Church in the United States has exceeded two billion.[5]

I

Aquinas recognizes the punishment called "damnum," which is one that costs a person his or her wealth.[6] On the other hand, the clerical sex abuse crisis in the United States has occasioned one of the most significant transfers of funds from the Church to other entities since the sixteenth-century Protestant reform. One hears different ethical evaluations of cash payments made by the Church to compensate those who allegedly have been harmed by clerics. Some persons consider such payments justifiable indemnification for injuries suffered; whereas, others wonder about the rightness of assuming large-scale tort liability in cases that involve allegations of varying degrees of sexual intimacy with plaintiffs who may be as old as seventeen years of

---

[5] "The Catholic Church in the United States has so far paid more than $2 billion in settlements and legal judgments to victims of sexual abuse and their families." See http://www.nytimes.com/2007/07/16/us/16abuse.html?_r=1&oref=slogin.

[6] See *Summa theologiae* IIa-IIae q. 108, art. 3.

age. Still others question a system that enriches by tens of millions of dollars contingent-fee lawyers who pocket one-third or more of everything they recover for their clients.[7] However one morally evaluates the present adjudication of abuse claims, there emerge other questions that transcend those usually associated with negotiated settlements or court judgments. Among these questions are those that pertain to the doctrine of the two powers - that of the political authority, and that of the Church.

One of the lessons that has been learned since 2002 is that, even in the United States, it is difficult to separate Church from State. One only has to recall the headlines: "Attorney General seeks to screen seminary candidates." "Judge orders priests' files handed over to plaintiffs' lawyers." "Re-assignment of abusive priests under grand jury scrutiny." John Courtney Murray, of course, never envisaged this turn of events when he developed his thesis that the First Amendment to the United States *Constitution* ensures the best political arrangement for the Church to carry on her specific work.[8] To quote loosely one American cardinal, "We have lost a lot of freedom." Because they fear liability risks, Bishops, for example, are not free to assign even those clerics who have repented sincerely of isolated sins committed many decades ago.

This turn of events should not have come as a surprise to the careful observer of the evolving position of the Catholic Church in the American experiment.[9] One of the problems that Catholics face and

---

[7] The argument for allowing lawyers to work on a contingent-fee basis appeals to equity; the practice, it is said, enables those without the funds to hire a lawyer to pursue their claims against entities that would respond only to civil suit. European countries, fearing that it would multiply litigation, generally do not allow the practice. I am not aware of any studies that examine the ethics of the practice when used against the Church.

[8] It is noteworthy that Europeans find it very difficult to grasp why the Church as a corporate entity, incorporated for example as a diocese or a religious province, should be held responsible for the actions of one of her ministers.

[9] I originally made this point at the 2003 Dallas National Catholic Bioethics Center workshop for Bishops, where I acknowledged the invaluable assistance of Professor Mary Ann Glendon in composing the following three

that has left Catholics in the United States less well-protected than the non-hierarchical churches that stem from sixteenth-century reform movements, is the uneven way that the provisions for free-exercise and non-establishment of religion as guaranteed by the First Amendment have been developed by the Supreme Court and within the public consciousness of our nation. In short, Americans are more attuned to recognize the privileges that free-exercise brings than those that attach to non-establishment. That the concerns of non-Catholic churches have dominated interpretive legal developments surrounding the First Amendment may help to explain this circumstance.

Discussion of First Amendment privileges of course belongs to specialists.[10] It seems, however, that the emphasis on free exercise by individuals has neglected or put at risk the associational rights of members of religions like the Catholic one where free exercise by individuals is inextricably related to the freedom of their religious institutions to govern themselves. The framers of the Constitution understood this well, but a narrow view of free exercise was introduced by the Supreme Court in the 1940s. At the same time, the situation for Catholics was worsened by the Court's extremely expansive interpretation of the establishment language to strike down almost every form of public assistance to religious institutions. Again, this has had a disparate impact on the Catholic Church which, more than others, has supplied health care and education and poverty relief to members of the polity. The Supreme Court's message to Catholic institutions engaged in this sort of work has been in effect: "Strip yourself of all religious insignia and don't express your religion if you want any help from the state – shut up and do the work!"

---

paragraphs that discuss the Church's present liability in the American republic. See my "Cooperation, *Veritatis splendor*, and the Luminous Mysteries," in *Walk as Children of Light: The Challenge of Cooperation in a Pluralistic Society*: Proceedings of the Nineteenth Workshop for Bishops, Dallas, Texas, ed. Edward J. Furton (Boston, Massachcuttes: The National Catholic Bioethics Center, 2003): 47-67.

[10] For instance, Philip Hamburger takes up the question in his *Separation of Church and State* (Cambridge, Mass.: Harvard University Press, 2003).

Though there are some signs that the legal situation is improving, we are not in as good a position as we should be to take full advantage of the provision of the Constitution that was meant to protect free exercise within institutions as well as by individuals alone. It is reasonable to inquire to what extent this lacuna has affected the Church's ability to respond to the challenges occasioned by the unchastity of certain clerics. Let me propose at this juncture, without entertaining further considerations, that the full implications of free exercise have not been discussed in the appropriate disciplines, which are not exclusively theological (perhaps they have not been even sufficiently envisaged), and let me propose as well that this deficiency has left the Catholic people with a truncated comprehension of how to protect Catholic institutions, including the hierarchical structure of the Church herself.

Indeed, Catholics have become so accustomed to look at Catholic life and institutions as parts of a larger, generally Catholic-friendly environment that many Catholics are willing to give changing public sentiments the benefit of the doubt. These Catholics too easily transfer the optimism of the "supernatural existential" to American society as a whole. This illusion that the Church in the United States was still able to assume, let alone rely on, the antecedent goodwill of the American public or, for that matter, of the Catholic population, was shattered brutally in the January 6, 2002, edition of *The Boston Globe*. The paper's front-page exposé on how the Church had dealt with unchaste clerics gave Boston Catholics the chance to demonstrate that they were no longer ready to make accommodations for the failures, albeit shameful ones, of the clergy, even though they were still expected to recognize in these men God's anointed ones and in the Bishops who supervised them the guarantee of true religion. Subsequent events and discourse confirm that the character of Holy Orders and the grace of episcopal "governance" number among the chief casualties of Catholic doctrine that have resulted from what in the United States we now call "The Crisis in the Church."[11]

---

[11] The Post-Synodal Apostolic Exhortation, *Pastores gregis* (October 16, 2003) of Pope John Paul II explains this grace: "The Bishop, by virtue of the office that he has received, is thus invested with an objective juridical power meant to

In late summer of 2003, the punishment of priests in Boston reached a certain tragic denouement. John Geoghen, one of the men charged with long-term sexual misconduct toward pre-pubescent children, was brutally murdered while being held in a maximum security cell as he awaited his appeal on a decade-old charge of improperly touching a young boy in a Boston-area public swimming pool. There exists a general agreement among sympathetic observers that the guilty verdict and the sentence of some ten years that he originally received support the view that the public administration of justice does not work evenly in the midst of an adverse political environment.

There is another consideration that merits our reflection. It is commonly accepted that child molesters, as the Miguel Piñero drama *Short Eyes* vividly portrays, do not fare well in prison.[12] Priest child molesters fare less well. The reason turns on the exercise of spiritual authority that priests enjoy in the communion of the Church. When they have been sentenced to prison terms, policemen, judges, political figures, and others who have exercised authority in civil society customarily find themselves detained in special prisons. Those who administer civil justice understand that public figures require protection in jail in order to avoid suffering reprisals from other prisoners who may recognize in these persons representatives of the civil authority that is responsible for their own incarceration or that upholds a public order that malefactors find inconvenient. The same potential for resentment also develops when those who have exercised spiritual authority and have upheld an ecclesial order face

---

be expressed in authoritative acts whereby he carries out the ministry of governance (*munus pastorale*) received in the sacrament" (no. 43).

[12] The play *Short Eyes* by Miguel Piñero takes place in the day room of a House of Detention. The cast of actors are mostly made up of Blacks, Puerto Ricans and a few Whites. They are young convicts. An accused child molester is brought into the cellblock. He is called a degenerate by a guard. A child molester (or in prison slang a "short eyes") is considered the most despicable of people. Mr. Piñero, while serving a five year sentence for armed robbery in Sing Sing Prison, started writing the play. Marvin Felix Camillo read some of Miguel's work and asked him to sign up in his drama workshop in the prison. In the early 70s, Joseph Papp produced the play *Short Eyes* at the Lincoln Center in New York City.

incarceration. But no special provisions exist to accommodate priest-prisoners. The historical solution for this problem includes their confinement in an ecclesiastical prison. The 1917 Code of Canon Law (*CIC* 120) still recognized the ancient *privilegium fori*, which required that ecclesiastical courts judge clerics in all contentious or criminal cases; for those found guilty, special confinement, usually in a monastery, was arranged. The Church for centuries maintained this privilege because, among other reasons, experience had shown that many laymen were inclined to oppress the clergy.[13]

The study of the historical evolution and present status of the *privilegium fori*, one of four clerical privileges once recognized in universal law by the Church, falls under the competency of professional jurists and canonists.[14] While these privileges have been eliminated in the Code of 1983, the rationale for the *privilegium fori*, which dates from at least the fifth century, merits some fresh consideration in light of the mistreatment of clerics that continues to make headlines even in the secular press.[15] One historical motivation for such reconsideration may be found in Martin Luther, who in order to assail the public identity of the Church, complained deeply about the *privilegium fori* in his 1520 "An Open Letter to The Christian Nobility of the German Nation Concerning the Reform of the Christian Estate."[16] I recognize, of

---

[13] Johannes Baptist Sägmüller has observed: "This [privilege] secures the clergy a special tribunal in civil and criminal causes before an ecclesiastical judge. The civil causes of clerics pertain by nature to the secular courts as much as to those of the laity. But the thought that it was unseemly that the fathers and teachers of the faithful should be brought before laymen as judges, and also the experience that many laymen were greatly inclined to oppress the clergy (c. 3 in Vito de immun., III, 23), led the Church to withdraw her servants even in civil matters from the secular courts, and to bring them entirely under her own jurisdiction." See *The Catholic Encyclopedia,* 1911 ed., s.v. "privileges," vol. VII, p. 438.

[14] For a brief commentary, see John E. Lynch, C.S.P., *Canon Law Society of America Commentary* (1985): 199, who also discusses the *privilegium canonis*, the *privilegium immunitatis*, and the *privilegium competentis.*

[15] Theodosian Code 16, 2, 41.

[16] "An Open Letter to The Christian Nobility of the German Nation Concerning the Reform of the Christian Estate," by Martin Luther (1520), introduction

course, that special juridical treatment for clerics would be difficult to justify under our constitutional form of government, unless a concordat between the United States and the Holy See would provide otherwise,[17] which is an unlikely prospect in the immediate political future of our country. At the same time, to recall the *privilegium fori* serves to remind us that safeguarding the public identity of the Church, and therefore the true freedom of the Catholic religion and her adherents, is something that requires provisions that cannot be taken for granted within the American democracy.

---

and translation by C. M. Jacobs, *Works of Martin Luther: With Introductions and Notes*, Volume II (Philadelphia: A. J. Holman Company, 1915): "See, now, how Christian is the decree which says that the temporal power is not above the 'spiritual estate' and may not punish it. That is as much as to say that the hand shall lend no aid when the eye is suffering. Is it not unnatural, not to say unchristian, that one member should not help another and prevent its destruction? Verily, the more honorable the member, the more should the others help. I say then, since the temporal power is ordained of God to punish evil-doers and to protect them that do well, it should therefore be left free to perform its office without hindrance through the whole body of Christendom without respect of persons, whether it affect pope, bishops, priests, monks, nuns or anybody else. For if the mere fact that the temporal power has a smaller place among the Christian offices than has the office of preachers or confessors, or of the clergy, then the tailors, cobblers, masons, carpenters, pot-boys, tapsters, farmers, and all the secular tradesmen, should also be prevented from providing pope, bishops, priests and monks with shoes, clothing, houses, meat and drink, and from paying them tribute. But if these laymen are allowed to do their work unhindered, what do the Roman scribes mean by their laws, with which they withdraw themselves from the jurisdiction of the temporal Christian power, only so that they may be free to do evil and to fulfill what St. Peter has said: 'There shall be false teachers among you, and through covetousness shall they with feigned words make merchandise of you' (2 Peter 2:1)."

[17] Lynch, *Commentary*, observes that "for the most part the special treatment of clerics has had little application in recent times, though some concordats did arrange for the imprisonment of convicted clerics in a monastery" (199). The United States, however, did honor the *privilegium immunitatis*, which "claimed that clerics were exempt from military service and from those duties and public civil offices alien to the clerical state" (ibid.).

II

In his 1975 study, *Surveiller et Punir: Naissance de la prison*, Michel Foucault, points out that "a convicted criminal could become after his death a sort of saint, his memory honored and his grave respected."[18] He goes on to recount the case of a certain Tanguy, who was executed in Brittany about 1740, and who had begun, before his conviction, a long satisfaction ordered by his confessor. "Was this," asks Foucault, "a conflict between civil justice and religious penitence?"[19] Let Foucault's question serve as a transition to the theme of Christian satisfaction, which discussion requires, however, that we first consider the virtue of vengeance.

In his treatise on justice, which occupies questions 57-122 of the *secunda-secundae*, Saint Thomas Aquinas includes a discussion of the virtue of vengeance (in Latin, *vindicatio*). Although some, if not most, people would find it difficult to think of vengeance as a virtue,[20] for Aquinas this virtue falls among those joined (*adjunguntur*[21]) to justice because, while people "lack the fullness of justice by reason of the debt rendered," they still render what is morally due as this obligation arises from the demands of a virtuous life.[22] We discover that Aquinas considers two grounds upon which to establish the debt of justice. "The distinction between legal debt and moral debt," writes T. C. O'Brien, "is prominent in 2a2ae, 80-118. The meaning of legal debt remains constant, a debt determined by positive law or private contract to the acquittal of which the debtor is bound by law."[23] The meaning of moral

---

[18] Michel Foucault, *Discipline & Punish. The Birth of the Prison*, trans. Alana Sheriden (New York: Vintage Books, 1995), p. 67.

[19] Foucalut, Discipline, p. 67, who found the case in A. Corre, *Documents pour servir à l'histoire de la torture judiciaire en Bretagne*, 1896.

[20] I am grateful to Jesuit Father John McIntyre of Boston College for having read an earlier version of this paper and for supplying helpful criticisms.

[21] *Summa theologiae*, IIa-IIae q. 80, art. 1: "Dicendum quod in virtutibus quae adjunguntur alicui principali virtuti. . . ."

[22] IIa-IIae, q. 80, art. 1.

[23] Blackfriars edition of the *Summa theologiae*, vol. 41, *Virtues of Justice in the Human Community*, ed. T.C. O'Brien (1972), Appendix I, "Legal Debt, Moral

debt, as O'Brien goes on to explain, contains variations based on the way that Aquinas interprets texts from Aristotle's *Nicomachean Ethics*. One differentiation, however, remains central to distinguishing the virtue of vengeance from the restitution that constitutes the act of commutative justice. It occurs in reply to a question that is raised in the first argument of question 80, the question where Aquinas treats the potential parts of justice, *de partibus potentialibus justitiae*. Vengeance, it is alleged, "seems to pertain to commutative justice, since it is the virtue which seeks to compensate injuries."[24] In replying to this assumption, Aquinas makes the following distinction: "Vengeance in so far as it is an act of public authority involving a judge's sentence, is an act of commutative justice; the vindication, however, which a man takes on his own initiative and in accord with the law, or which he seeks to obtain from a judge, is an act of a virtue annexed to justice."[25] This means that to determine the virtuous mean of vengeance, a person committed to virtue is required to evaluate a very particular instance of "moral debt," one that concerns redressing wrongs.

The four articles that comprise *Summa theologiae* IIa-IIae q. 108, which is about vengeance, explain in succession: (1) That the virtue of vengeance does not cover-up hateful retaliation, but rather aims to accomplish a good both by correcting or at least restraining a wrongdoer, or by relieving others from further harm that he may cause, and by maintaining a just order and by doing honor to God; (2) that this virtue is a specific one since it matches up to a distinct natural inclination (*inclinationem naturalem determinatam*) to get rid of what is harmful; (3) that the virtuously vengeful person may employ means suitable to persuade those who do not love virtue for virtue's sake but still may fear receiving the punishment due to the non-virtuous; and (4) that vengeance, while principally restorative, since it inflicts a

---

Debt," p. 316. This essay provides the basic distinctions necessary to understand Aquinas's organization of the potential parts of justice, the virtues of truth, gratitude, vengeance, liberality, and friendliness. The reference to q. 118, which excludes prodigality (q. 119), the excess vice of liberality, is probably a typographical error.

[24] *Summa theologiae* IIa-IIae q. 80, obj. 1.

[25] Question 80, art. unic., ad 1um.

punishment and so restores the balance of justice, may also accomplish preventive or medicinal objectives. Even the good, Aquinas observes, can suffer the loss of temporal goods, and this loss providentially works toward their betterment in virtue.

Question 108 supplies an overture to a Christian view of punishment. Aquinas's discussion of vengeance begins by envisaging a specific virtue of the Christian life, which like gratitude measures the repayment of deeds done by other persons: gratitude with the good done to us; vengeance with the evil. The discussion of vengeance, however, ends by airing general considerations that today some would place under the heading of theodicy, or consider as answers to the question, "Why bad things happen to good people?" Aquinas supplies the principle that governs the only valid Christian response to this question: "Since spiritual goods are of supreme importance, while the temporal are of slight moment, a person who is sinless at times suffers the loss of earthly goods; this is the meaning of the many hardships of life inflicted by God to humble and test us."[26] (Is he thinking of Christ as the prototype of one who is sinless?) To return to vengeance itself, we discover that this virtue represents a good quality in a man who, in light of all relevant circumstances, observes a due measure in redressing wrongs.[27]

Like every virtue, vengeance possesses its contraries. The vices opposed to vengeance are two; one exceeds the due measure by excess, whereas the other falls short of the due measure by defect. Aquinas suggests no name for the vice of those who fail altogether to inflict punishment. He may have judged it to be a less serious fault than the excess vice which is called cruelty or the sin of *saevitiae* – ferocity, or he may have had in mind the Catholic practice of granting indulgences. Indulgences benefit those to whom punishment is due, but who are spared enduring some or all of what is prescribed because of a recognized sacramental association with Christ's redemption.[28] This

---

[26] *Summa theologiae* IIa-IIae q. 108, art. 4.

[27] *Summa theologiae* IIa-IIae q. 108, art. 2, ad 3um.

[28] Indulgences rely on what is called the *thesaurus ecclesiae,* the deposit of good works that the saints have accumulated on account of their union with

latter explanation gains a certain plausibility when one notes that the only text of Scripture that Aquinas adduces in support of the nameless vice of defect with respect to vengeance is Proverbs 13: 24: "He who spareth the rod hateth his son." (*Qui parcit virgae, odit filium suum.*) This sapiential axiom, of course, envisages child rearing.

We are brought to conclude that the virtue of vengeance is required to moderate the natural inclination to eliminate what we consider harmful to ourselves and to those whom we love so that this inclination does not develop into the vicious quality of cruelty. That what today we would call emotion plays a part in this moderation is made clear when Aquinas, in *secunda-secundae* q. 159, discusses cruelty not as a sin against the virtues allied to justice but against a virtue allied to temperance, namely, clemency. We find ourselves deeply immersed in the rich moral psychology that Aquinas develops when he holds the *Nicomachean Ethics* in one hand and the Bible in the other.

Let's return to Boston. It would be difficult to gainsay that John Geoghen did not himself become a victim of a cruelty that expresses the excess of virtuous vengeance. In July 2007, a Boston newspaper reported having received in 2005 a macabre video in which Joseph Druce, the convicted murderer of John Geoghan, re-enacted choking the priest with a pair of gym socks, using Geoghan's own sneaker as a tourniquet to tighten the noose. Then, according to the video, Druce climbed on top of his cell cot and jumped off repeatedly, showing how he crushed the priest's frail body. Again in 2007, a video appeared on the Internet which purported to expose "The truth about officers allowing J.G. to die through their neglect." More than 9,000 persons are reported to have accessed this video. Some left comments, including this one: "One less irredeemable monster on the planet. Good work Mister Druce!"[29]

Christ . For further information, see my "St. Thomas Aquinas on Satisfaction, Indulgences, and Crusades," *Medieval Philosophy & Theology* 2 (1992): 74-96.

[29] See relevant stories in the *Boston Herald* for 6, 7 & 9 July 2007, respectively, "Security video from Geoghan slay hits Web," "Prison slay video remains online: Union says exposure poses risk for guards," and "New prison video posted under priest killer's name."

III

No Christian theologian who considers justice and the virtues related to it should fail to remember that Christ himself has fulfilled all justice.[30] "If God is for us, who is against us? He who did not spare his own Son but gave him up for us all, will he not also give us all things with him?" (Rom 8:31, 32). Some theologians, however, have questioned whether vindictive justice can serve as an instrument to accomplish the holy will of God. Notwithstanding, Aquinas upholds the well-known insight of Saint Anselm's *Cur Deus homo?* though he offers a radically different account of satisfaction than does the Archbishop of Canterbury.[31] The Common Doctor achieves his new interpretation of satisfaction, in short, by appealing to the nature of Christ's priesthood and of his priestly sacrifice on Golgotha.

The tradition that we identify with Saint Anselm accepts that an act of human justice could not satisfy by itself for the offense caused by the sin of the human race. Christ alone embodies the perfectly just man, and so he alone is capable of offering the sacrifice that fulfills what is due to God. In offering his own sacrifice of worship on the Cross, Christ fully propitiates the divine justice and once again inaugurates the reign of divine glory in the world. The tradition calls this work of the God-man satisfaction.

Aquinas enlarges on the theme that satisfactory punishments do honor to God and perfect the spiritual well-being of believers who voluntarily accept punishment as salvific. In other words, he defines

---

[30] For instance, see *Summa theologiae* IIIa q. 46, art. 1, ad 3um: ". . .hominem liberari per passionem Christi conveniens fuit et misericordiae et justitiae ejus. Justitiae quidem, quia per passionem suam Christus satisfecit pro peccato humani generis; et ita homo per justitiam Christi liberatus est." "The liberation of man through the passion of Christ was consonant with both his mercy and his justice. With justice, because by his passion Christ made satisfaction for the sin of the human race, and man was freed through the justice of Christ" (Blackfriars edition of the *Summa theologiae*, vol. 54, *The Passion of Christ*, ed. Richard T.A. Murphy, O.P., p. 7).

[31] For further discussion, see my *The Godly Image: Christ and Salvation in Catholic Thought from Anselm to Aquinas*, Studies in Historical Theology VI (Petersham, MA: St Bede's Publications, 1990).

satisfaction in terms of self-appropriation. That is, to the extent that the culpable party has achieved a certain freedom, he realizes it by way of self-appropriation of the values involved in satisfaction.[32] The mystery, of course, is that Christ takes on himself the sin of the human race while he himself remains sinless. All other members of the human race discover freedom through their participation in his "superabundant satisfaction,"[33] that is, by uniting themselves to the sacrifice of the race realized in the Golgotha-event.

Christian satisfaction, as the aforementioned example of Tanguy illustrates, can inform the lives even of Christian malefactors or criminals. The Church today still recognizes penalties or sanctions (Book VI in the current Code).[34] Fundamentally, they are of two kinds: one is medicinal (for the reform of the individual) and the other is expiatory (for repairing the public good). Penalties supply various means of achieving equilibrium: they keep things in balance or get things right. As we have observed, however, the natural inclination to redress wrongdoing can lead to excessive vindication by enacting a measure of retaliatory punishment that would qualify as a cruelty.[35] Clemency always becomes the Christian. To think about punishment only in terms of penalties, even medicinal ones, is to overlook the truth that in the Christian Church satisfaction enjoys a preeminent role in restoring justice.

---

[32] As theology professors like to say, by becoming more of what we already are by grace, the human person finds his perfection. The essentialist noun "satisfaction" really works in the Christian scheme of things as an existentialist verb. That is, satisfaction points less to a price to be paid than to a work to be embraced.

[33] See *Summa theologiae* IIIa q. 48. art. 2: "superabundans satisfactio."

[34] For recent discussion on how the Church imposes penalties, see *Il processo penale canonico*, ed. Zbignew Suchecki (Rome: Lateran University Press, 2003).

[35] In an address of September 8, 2003, in Dublin, then Archbishop Renato Martino, president of the Pontifical Council for Justice and Peace, reported that the Holy See considers the goal of prisons to be the rehabilitation of inmates. His views, which emphasized "the absolute respect for the dignity of the person sentenced and his rehabilitation in society," were directed to those who bear the responsibility for staffing prisons, and may be interpreted to address the proclivity for institutionalized cruelty in prisons.

If we take seriously the satisfactorial transformation of punishment, then in the Christian commonwealth punishment meted out to the malefactor should appear in a new light. Saint Thomas considers that even an innocent person can transform punishment into something meritorious by voluntarily accepting the penalty as a work of satisfaction. "Punishment pure and simple," he writes, "is not the desert of the virtuous man; still it is possible that punishment as expiatory be exacted of him. To make due satisfaction for offences either to God or to man is itself matter for virtue."[36] How much the more, then, is this true for one who deserves punishment. The Church, in fact, still encourages priests to pray after imparting sacramental absolution: "[M]ay. . . whatever good you do or evil you endure be cause for the remission of your sins. . . ." This liturgical prayer, known to Aquinas himself, sacramentalizes everything that is burdensome, that runs against the grain, even the vengeance that may befall those whose offense is involuntary (as explained in *Summa theologiae* IIa-IIae q. 108, art. 4).[37]

More than others in the past, Pope John Paul II has emphasized that virtue and freedom are correlatives. Since virtue enables one to possess the truth about the human good, it also ensures that a person enjoys the gift of true freedom, which is identified with the possession of charity. The one who loves the most, is the one who is most free, which is why the Pope insists that Christ on the Cross reveals the authentic meaning of freedom.[38]

---

[36] *Summa theologiae* Ia-IIae q. 87, art. 6, ad 2um. This article and the commentary supplied by T. C. O'Brien in vol. 27 of the Blackfriars edition of the *Summa theologiae* explains how "the notion of punishment is modified to include satisfaction because of Christ's redemptive Passion and the consequences of this on the Christian life."

[37] See my discussion of this prayer in *Godly Image*, pp. 107-108.

[38] For example, consider what is emphasized in Veritatis splendor, no. 85: "The Crucified Christ reveals the authentic meaning of freedom; he lives it fully in the total gift of himself and calls his disciples to share in his freedom." Compare this description of freedom with what Aquinas says in Summa theologiae IIIa q. 48, art. 2: "Christus autem ex charitate et obedientia patiendo majus aliquid Deo exhibuit quam exigeret recompensatio totius

To bring these remarks to a conclusion, I will draw together some observations: (1) Those who, in any forum, require or administer punishments that offend against the dignity of the human person fall short of living out virtuous vengeance. (2) Vengeance, as the example of John Geoghen's prison murder illustrates, can easily give way to the correlative vice of cruelty or ferocity. (3) The Christian Church witnesses to the mystery of Christ's expiation for the sins of the world and to the marvelous transformation of punishment that his satisfaction makes available to all. (4) In those persons liable to the punishment of original sin, promoting authentic freedom requires that all forms of punishment be taken up into the mystery of Christ's satisfaction. (5) In other words, there should exist, contrary to what Foucault may have thought, no conflict between civil justice and religious penitence.

When this view of satisfaction comes to inform how every believer regards the punishment of wrongdoers, we may be in a position to garner the real lessons for which divine providence has permitted the present "Crisis" to befall the Church in the United States. It is possible to anticipate at least one such lesson from the *Catechism of the Catholic Church.* In the commentary on the petition of the "Our Father," "And forgive us our trespasses," we read: "In refusing to forgive our brothers and sisters, our hearts are closed and their hardness makes them impervious to the Father's merciful love; but in confessing our sins, our hearts are opened to his grace" (2840). Another text from the *Catechism* makes the connection between grace and freedom: "By the working of grace the Holy Spirit educates us in spiritual freedom in order to make us free collaborators in his work in the Church and in the world" (1742). Satisfaction made in the spirit of Christian virtue ensures that those who have sinned regain their spiritual footing, so to speak, and once

---

offensae humani generis: primo quidem propter magnitudinem charitatis, ex qua patiebatur." "Christ, suffering in a loving and obedient spirit, offered more to God than was demanded in recompense for all the sins of mankind, because first, the love which led him to suffer was a great love...." Blackfriars edition of the Summa theologiae, vol. 54, The Passion of Christ, ed. Richard T.A. Murphy, O.P., p. 79.

again find themselves ready to take up freely the works of holiness incumbent on each Christian.

Religious Freedom as Catholic Crisis

John Conley, S.J.

In retrospect, Vatican Council II's *Declaration on Religious Freedom* (*Dignitatis Humanae*) appears to be an anodyne document. It is comparatively brief: only 7,000 words. Its status as a simple declaration, rather than as a decree or constitution, suggests its secondary importance within the conciliar corpus. Its cautious affirmations on "the right of the person and communities to social and civil liberty in religious matters" (*DH* subtitle) pale in comparison with John Paul II's robust defenses of religious freedom as the keystone of human rights. At the time of its gestation and promulgation, however, the declaration appeared anything but minor. It underwent nine different drafts from its first preconciliar, preparatory version to the definitive version promulgated on December 7, 1965. During conciliar debate in the aula, the schema on religious liberty provoked 120 oral interventions, 600 written interventions, and two "explosions" on October 12 and November 19, 1964, when the schema was withdrawn from final consideration. During the final vote on December 7, 1965, a determined minority of seventy conciliar fathers voted against the declaration. The fringes of traditionalist schism still brandish the document as proof of the council's alleged heresy,[1] while leftward dissidents insist that the document's defense of liberty of conscience within civil society tacitly affirms the freedom of theologians to dissent from Church teaching.[2]

In fact, the tumultuous history of the redaction and approval of *Dignitatis Humanae* indicates that the question of religious freedom represented a particularly grave crisis for the Catholic community in the 1960s. I will argue that this crisis occurred on at least three levels: the philosophical, the hermeneutical, and the moral. Furthermore, I will argue that this collective crisis of conscience and the awkward

---

[1] For a representative attack on the orthodoxy of the declaration, see Mark A. Pivarunas, "The Doctrinal Errors of *Dignitatis Humanae*," www.cmri.org/95prog2.htm.

[2] For a justification of intrachurch dissent through an appeal to religious freedom, see Roger Haight, "Four Gifts of the American Church to the Universal Church," www.cta-usa.org/conf2002talks/haight.html.

ways in which *Dignitatis Humanae* attempted to address it continue to haunt the Church in her internal efforts at ecclesiastic unity and in her external efforts to act as a prophetic witness to national governments and to international institutions.

Methodologically, I will complement citations of the actual text of *Dignitatis Humanae* with extracts from pertinent addresses by conciliar fathers.[3] The published proceedings of the council provide crucial contextual evidence for the crisis that shook the Catholic community during the prolonged dispute over religious liberty.

Philosophical Crisis

At the center of the conciliar debate over religious liberty is a fundamental dispute on the nature of the proper relationship between truth and freedom. Two major schools of thought clashed on how the Church should articulate this dialectic.

For the minority school, any declaration must begin with the rights of truth, especially the unique rights of the true religion and the religious duties of the state that derived from this truth in the areas of public worship, repression of error, and the protection of the salvation of Catholic subjects from non-Catholic and anti-Catholic proselytism. In his intervention in the conciliar debate, Cardinal Browne of the Curia underlined this starting point:

> 1. The greatest dignity of humanity resides in its elevation to the supernatural order. This truth demands that we protect those who profess the true faith from the preaching of other religions that are not founded on supernatural faith. We must especially say this for Catholic nations. 2. We may not accord equal rights to all religions. 3. Rulers and citizens can recognize which is the true religion and embrace it; authorities of Catholic nations know that the protection of religion is the greatest good

---

[3] The primary source used in this paper is the official proceedings of Vatican Council II: *Acta synodalia Sacrosancti Concilii Oecumenici Vatican II*, 5 volumes (Vatican City: Typis polyglottis Vaticanis, 1970); hereafter cited as *ASVII*. The declaration *De libertate religiosa* is found in *ASVII*, vol. 4, part 7, 663-73. Translations from the Latin are the author's own.

> for their citizens. 4. The diffusion of other religions in these countries is a violation of public morality, since it opposes the rights of Catholics and places their faith in peril.[4]

The minority school readily conceded that in the pluralist societies that characterized the contemporary world, it was necessary to tolerate both religious pluralism and a secular state as lesser evils to conserve a key social good, like civic peace. But this tolerance is never a matter of right, since error, like evil, has no rights. In his intervention, Cardinal Ottaviani of the Curia explained why the minority could not accept the conciliar thesis of a "right" to religious freedom:

> The true and the false are not equal and cannot exercise the same rights, but here [in the schema] they are placed on the same level. The same occurs in the treatment of correct and erroneous consciences. Thus we end up recommending what is only tolerable.[5]

Essentially, the minority position reprised the distinction between thesis and antithesis developed by Bishop Dupanloup,[6] affirmed by Leo XIII, and taught in manuals of moral theology until the council. According to this distinction, the ideal (thesis) of church-state relations always remains the official recognition of the Catholic Church by the civil power (with the defense of the Catholic faith of its citizens by the state), since only the Catholic religion has been mandated by God to teach and save humanity; however, in actual historical situations (hypothesis) where practicing Catholics are a minority, the Church can obviously accept the tolerance of religious error as a lesser evil. In his intervention, Archbishop Marcel Lefebvre used this distinction: "The Catholic Church alone has a right properly speaking to freedom. For the

---

[4] Michael Cardinal Browne, "Oratio," *ASVII*, vol. 4, part 1, 404.

[5] Alfredo Cardinal Ottaviani, "Oratio," *ASVII*, vol. 4, part 1, 300.

[6] Félix-Antoine-Philibert Dupanloup (1802-1878), bishop of Orléans, argued that the controversial positions on church-state defended by Pius IX in his *Syllabus of Errors* only represented an ideal (thesis) for Catholics. In the actual modern world of religious pluralism, Catholics could support a nonconfessional state as a tolerable if less perfect regime (hypothesis).

other communities or religions, it is necessary to examine each specific case with its particular circumstances."[7]

The majority school rejected the very starting point of the minority's argument. First, the defense of the rights of truth was a chimera. It is the person, not an abstraction, who is the subject of rights and duties. In his intervention, Cardinal Heenan of Westminster challenged the fallacious starting point: "It is quite clear that it is perfectly absurd to speak of error having no rights or of truth having rights. Rights concern persons and not things."[8] This primacy accorded the human person (who still has an obligation to seek and adhere to truth in the religious domain) instead of the abstract truth justified a clear affirmation of the individual's right to religious freedom instead of the limited affirmation of tolerance in pluralist societies.

Second, the majority contested the competence of the state in the religious domain. It is the human person who is properly speaking the subject of God's call to salvation and who must render an account of the response to this call, not the state as such. Moreover, the minority theses on the religious duties of the state dangerously confused the competence of the state with that of the Church, a confusion that has often destroyed the freedom of the Church throughout history.

The doctrinal confrontation on religious freedom did not admit of an easy solution. For the minority current, the proposed defense of religious freedom was an attack on the unique rights of the true religion in civil society. It even threatened the very status of the Catholic religion as the one true religion founded by God. To respond to the concerns of these fathers, the Secretariat of the Council, under the influence of Paul VI, introduced two amendments to the preamble of the declaration during the final deliberations over the text in 1965.

The first amendment states: "The Council declares that God himself has made known to the human race the way by which, in following it, people may obtain salvation and arrive at beatitude. We believe that this one true religion subsists in the apostolic and Catholic Church" (*DH*

---

[7] Archbishop Marcel Lefebvre, "Oratio," *ASVII*, vol. 4, part 1, 410-11.

[8] John Cardinal Heenan, "Oratio," *ASVII*, vol. 4, part 1, 295.

no.1). Obviously no conciliar father would deny this affirmation in itself, but this isolation of the truth of the Church, placed apart from its dialectic with human freedom, ran against the grain of the very structure of the argument of the declaration.

The second amendment affirmed "the moral duty of the human person and of associations regarding the true religion and the unique church of Christ" (*DH* no.1). This passage on the duty of associations disturbed the majority current because the ambiguous word "association" might suggest that civil society, this very particular association, possessed special duties toward the Catholic Church.

It should be recognized that this insistence by the minority on the religious duties of associations was salutary. It underscored the fact that the search for and the adhesion to religious truth were not the isolated affairs of an individual in his or her private liberty. They were also the affairs of families (*DH* no.5), of intermediate groups (*DH* no.4), and of the larger society (*DH* no.6) in which the conscience of the individual is formed and expresses itself. The rights and duties of these diverse associations cannot be reduced to the sum of the rights and the duties of the individual person in his or her religious quest. Despite these last-minute alterations, *Dignitatis Humanae* marks a capital shift in ecclesial reflection: the rights of the person seeking truth displace the alleged rights of truth as the central focus of the truth-freedom dialectic in the civil sphere.

Hermeneutical Crisis

Narrowly tied to the doctrinal conflict on religious freedom was the conflict concerning the interpretation of earlier declarations of the magisterium on the issue, especially those issued by the papacy. Several nineteenth-century popes had categorically condemned religious freedom and related civil liberties. In *Mirari vos* (1832), Gregory XVI taught:

> From this infected source of indifferentism flows this absurd and erroneous maxim, or rather this madness, that one must assure and guarantee freedom of conscience to anyone at all. We are preparing the path to this pernicious error by the full and

> unlimited freedom of opinion that is spreading near and far to the detriment of both religious and civil society.[9]

The encyclical underlines the duty of Christian rulers toward the Church:

> May our dear brothers in Jesus Christ, the princes, support by their assent and their authority the hopes we have formed for the salvation of religion and of the state. May they consider that their authority has been given to them, not only for temporal government, but to defend the church, and that all that is done for the advantage of the church is also done for their power and their tranquility.[10]

In *Quanta Cura* (1864) Pius IX reaffirmed this position:

> As a consequence of this absolutely false idea of social government [materialism], they do not hesitate to support this erroneous idea, which could not be more fatal to the Catholic Church and to the salvation of souls, which our predecessor of happy memory Gregory XVI called a madness: namely, that freedom of conscience and of worship is a right proper to each individual and that it must be promulgated and assured in every well-constituted state.[11]

His *Syllabus of Errors* (1864) reiterated this condemnation of religious freedom in its censure of freedom of worship, freedom of conscience, and the separation of church and state.

Since the era of Leo XIII (with the generalized use of the "thesis-hypothesis" principle), the Church largely accepted religiously neutral regimes as a necessity in societies marked by religious heterogeneity. But this tolerance did not abolish the lingering ideal of a confessional state recognizing and protecting the Catholic Church; it seemed only a pragmatic and prudent concession. Even on the eve of the council, the teaching of Pius XII on church-state relations expressed the ambiguity

---

[9] Gregory XVI, *Mirari Vos*, no. 14.

[10] Ibid., no. 23.

[11] Pius IX, *Quanta Cura*, no. 3.

of the Church attempting to accept *de facto* civil religious neutrality but unwilling to endorse *de jure* religious freedom.

> The church considers as an ideal the unity of a people in the true religion and complete harmony of action between this religion and the state. But she also knows that sometimes events are developing rather in the other sense, that is to say toward the multiplicity of religious confessions and conceptions of life in the same national community where Catholics constitute a more or less strong minority.[12]

This magisterial heritage on religious freedom raised a grave historical problem for the conciliar fathers: how can one declare a right to religious freedom that was the object of multiple and categorical condemnations of the modern magisterium, condemnations, moreover, that were rooted in the Church's centuries-old teaching on the rights of the true religion and the duties of Christian rulers?

The key for the solution to this impasse lay in the hermeneutic of the development of doctrine. According to this hermeneutic, descendant from the pioneering work of Cardinal Newman,[13] it was necessary to situate the doctrinal declarations of the magisterium in an historical process of progressive clarification, maturation, and adaptation as the Church proclaimed the gospel across the centuries. According to this developmentalist perspective, changes in doctrinal texts follow two complementary rules: one of continuity and one of change.

In his intervention, Bishop de Smedt of Bruges, the reporter for the schema on religious freedom, clarified the meaning of these rules. Continuity means that "this doctrine and this concern of the church are faithful to themselves and always clearly remain themselves," while change signifies that

---

[12] Pius XII, *Ci Riesce*, no. 6 [1953].

[13] Often cited by drafters of and commentators on *Dignitatis Humanae*, John Henry Cardinal Newman's *Essay on the Development of Doctrine* (1845) provided the general orientation for the declaration's developmentalist hermeneutic .

> The ecclesiastic magisterium adapts, expostulates, and defends its authentic doctrine according to the demands of the errors that arise and the needs born of the evolution of the human person and society. This progress leads the church to deepen its doctrine and to take a clearer view of it.[14]

This hermeneutic proposes a quasi-biological model of doctrinal development: what is in seed gradually matures by successive steps and evolutions.

In this perspective, the successive declarations of the magisterium on religious freedom constitute a progressive chain, wherein each pope fashioned adaptations of doctrine, all the while safeguarding certain values (the freedom of the Church, respect for dogmatic truth, opposition to indifferentism). In his intervention, Cardinal Shehan of Baltimore illustrated how this developmentalist interpretation could be applied to the magisterial patrimony of declarations on religious freedom:

> No one is arguing that the doctrine of this schema is found explicitly in the documents of Leo XIII, but we find in these documents a remarkable development in comparison with the doctrine commonly taught during the Middle Ages and in the period following the Reformation. By his teaching Leo XIII made the first steps on the path that his successors, especially Pius XI, Pius XII, and John XXIII, had to follow. By making the freedom of the church so central, Leo XIII led us to recognize that this freedom included the freedom of the human person. This is how Leo XIII opened the path to the teaching of Pius XI, who affirmed in the encyclical *Mit Brennender Sorge* (1937) that 'the human person has the inalienable right to profess his or her faith and to practice it in the desired manner.' Pius XII made a further step toward the doctrine of religious freedom. In his Christmas radio message of 1942, he includes among 'the fundamental rights of the person that must be known and promised' the right to the worship of God, public and private, and the right of religious communities to conduct public charitable activities. John XXIII,

---

[14] Bishop Joseph de Smedt, "Relatio," *ASVII*, vol. 3, part 8, 449.

especially in *Pacem in Terris*, pushed even further the development of teaching on religious freedom.[15]

This hermeneutics placed the solemn condemnations of religious freedom by the nineteenth-century popes in the middle of a slow maturation of the Church's doctrine: a progress in comparison with the theocratic theses of the medieval and early modern eras and a distant, imperfect ancestor of the doctrine of freedom of conscience in Pius XI or of freedom of worship in Pius XII.

Dignitatis Humanae not only employs the hermeneutics of development of doctrine to interpret the problematic history of church teaching on the issue, but it also explicitly avows its allegiance to this principle of interpretation: "This holy council intends to develop the doctrine of the most recent sovereign pontiffs on the inviolable rights of the human person and the juridical order of society" (*DH* no.1).

Undoubtedly this hermeneutic of development of doctrine was an effective tool in the conciliar debate on religious freedom. It ended a certain non-contextualist reading of magisterial texts that had long blocked the Church in her efforts to present a new teaching on the ensemble of questions dealing with church-state relations. It illuminated the general movement of magisterial teaching since Pius IX: a movement toward "the right of religious freedom" that grew with the passage of each decade. It contextualized the violent critiques of "religious freedom" in *Quanta cura* as the historically conditioned critique of the freedom offered by anticlerical states that suffocated the freedom of believers outside the narrow confines of worship. It discerned an intelligible continuity between the teaching of *Dignitatis Humanae* and the earlier papal condemnations in a common struggle against a "liberal" freedom founded on a narcissistic individualism characteristic of urban, cosmopolitan societies.

This hermeneutical approach, nonetheless, manifests several serious illusions. One cannot honestly explain the variations of the magisterium's teaching on religious freedom through the simple model of the progressive evolution of doctrine "since the beginning of the church." According to this epistemology, *Dignitatis Humanae* is simply

---

[15] Lawrence Cardinal Shehan, "Oratio," *ASVII*, vol. 4, part 1, 397.

the harmonious development of previous teaching. But is it not the nearly literal contradiction of a centuries-old condemnation of freedom of cult (and related religious liberties) condemned by the magisterium and the common theology of the Church? How did this freedom, solemnly condemned as a madness, turn into a sacred right?

The text of *Dignitatis Humanae* itself witnesses to this difficulty. Despite its declared intention to develop pontifical teaching (*DH* no.1), the declaration cites sources that fall into two distinct eras of ecclesiastic history: the pontifical writings since Leo XIII, especially since Pius IX (*DH* no.26), and the writings of the New Testament and the early fathers of the Church (*DH* no.33). These margins of the text are the eloquent witnesses of a certain bracketing of a substantial part of ecclesiastic history (namely, the Middle Ages and the modern period) in the reflection on religious freedom. Obviously one cannot easily integrate the pontifical condemnations of the nineteenth century in a declaration that appears to reverse the major tenor of these texts. Moreover, a contextualist reading of these condemnations risks an unconvincing interpretation of these texts that simply occults the serious ruptures in ecclesiastic teaching. If the condemnations of Pius IX aimed at the anticlerical liberals of the period, they also censured a Montalembert and a Lacordaire, ancestors of the Church's contemporary teaching on religious freedom. If the condemnations of Pius IX denounced subjectivism, they also clearly denounced the general principle of freedom of worship and related religious liberties.

More gravely, this hermeneutic risks justifying what is difficult to justify in the doctrinal history of the Church, for example, the pontifical justification of torture against heretics, defended by Innocent IV in his bull *Ad extirpando* (1252), ratified by Alexander VI, Clement IV, Urban IV, and Clement V at the Ecumenical Council of Vienne (1311).[16] This schema of a continual progress from the apostolic age to the contemporary period can only mask serious deviations in a doctrinal history marked by tragedy. In 1970, Paul VI underlined the inevitable confusion in this area before ecclesiastic history:

---

[16] For a discussion of the history of the Catholic Church's teaching on torture, see John J. Conley, S.J., *Torture as a Theological Problem*, unpublished M.Th. thesis, Weston School of Theology, 1985.

> We know that in the history of the church in the area of religious freedom there are pages that demand reservations and explications. But we joyfully approve the new teaching that better corresponds to the spirit of the gospel.[17]

To grasp the complex movement of the doctrine on religious freedom in the Church, one must use a hermeneutic of rupture in addition to a hermeneutic of development. The rise of the individual's right to religious freedom in ecclesiastic reflection is not the peaceful growth of a tree that patiently nurtures its fruit. Rather, the right proclaimed by *Dignitatis Humanae* is the result of a complex dialogue between the Church and liberal democracies regarding the demand for religious freedom. At the end of a quarrel of two centuries, this right, long condemned as an illusion and an error by the Church, becomes an integral part of its doctrine on human rights. But this right, so apparently exterior to the Church in the eighteenth and nineteenth centuries, has also undergone a profound transformation. Even if the Church warmly salutes the defense of religious freedom in international accords (*DH* no.15), the articulation, the foundations, the limits, and the practical implications of this right in *Dignitatis Humanae* remain specifically Christian and Catholic. Obviously this conciliar teaching on the right to religious freedom is not a creation *ex nihilo*. It recalls in a very specific way the Church's tradition: the neotestamentary teaching of respect for the freedom of listeners in evangelical preaching (*DH* no.11) and the patristic teaching on the freedom of the act of faith, as found in Tertullian and Lactantius (*DH* no.10). But this revival of the early ecclesiastic tradition on religious freedom simultaneously marks an abandonment of a more modern tradition that defended the confessional Catholic state as a theological ideal. Inevitably the appeal to tradition is partial.

Moreover, the teaching of *Dignitatis Humanae* does not simply spring from the past of the Church in an adaptation of its traditional doctrine to the demands of modern times, as a facile development of doctrine would suggest. It arises from a transforming encounter with liberal democratic society whose demand for religious freedom that seemed so

---

[17] Paul VI, "Audience of September 8, 1971," *Documentation catholique* (1971): 759.

foreign or even hostile to the Church during two centuries, has become part of the Church's convictions in her struggle against totalitarian societies in the contemporary period. Obviously this transformation is not a simple acceptance of the concept of religious freedom proposed by liberal democratic societies. The Church proclaims this freedom in accord with its own foundations, such as its apostolic and patristic sources and its dogmatic understanding of the liberty of the act of faith. Nonetheless, in this centuries-long controversy, the Church has surely learned something from her enemies concerning the justice of the demands for religious freedom and from her own distant sources of this freedom.

Ethical Crisis

The conciliar conflict over religious freedom was not an academic debate over the relationship between truth and freedom or a literary dispute over the proper interpretation of dusty magisterial texts. It was an examination of conscience on the actions of the Church in the area of religious freedom. This action in the past as well as in the present (in certain "Catholic states" such as Spain) appeared to make the Church an enemy of full religious freedom. Although the defense of the rights of the person had been a keystone of magisterial teaching since Pius XI, the burdensome history of the Church and the longstanding refusal to endorse the right to religious freedom scandalized non-Catholics and disturbed a large number of conciliar fathers. The terms "fault," "sin," and "reparation" repeatedly emerge in the bishops' interventions. As Bishop Baraniak stated in his intervention on behalf of the entire Polish episcopate,

> It would be good to recognize that tragically there has existed at the very heart of the church institutions that oppressed religious freedom. This would constitute a type of reparation toward those who suffered and at the same time prove the sincerity of the church in ecumenical dialogue.[18]

This crisis of conscience in the conciliar aula arose because of two particular problems: the accusation of hypocrisy levied against the

---

[18] Archbishop Antonius Baraniak, "Oratio," *ASVII*, vol.4, part 1, 306.

Church in her doctrine of "tolerance" and the persecutory history of the Church, especially in early modernity.

In nations where Catholics are a numerous minority, such as the Anglophone nations, non-Catholics accused the Catholic Church of flagrant hypocrisy in its position on religious freedom. Cardinal Heenan summed up this widespread accusation:

> Many non-Catholics imagine that on the question of religious liberty and tolerance, our position follows two different principles. When the church is weak and does not have the support of the civil power, that is to say when Catholics are in the minority, we are all for freedom. But when the church is strong, that is to say when Catholics are in the majority, we only talk about 'the rights of the truth.' They accuse us of suppressing the religious freedom of non-Catholics when we are strong enough to do it. In all honesty we must make an examination of conscience to see to what extent this accusation is justified.[19]

For many non-Catholics this accusation was symbolized in the religious policies of Franco's Spain. Under the Spanish civil constitution (reinforced by the concordat between the Vatican and the Spanish government), the Catholic Church enjoyed substantial privileges: recognition as the state religion; state funding for Catholic clergy; exemption of clergy from civil tribunals, even for the commission of civil crimes; the unique right of the Catholic Church to offer religious instruction in public schools; the unique rights of church tribunals in matters related to marriage. Moreover, Spanish non-Catholics suffered serious restrictions on their religious liberties: a civic ban on their public worship; a civic ban on their missionary activity; civic censorship, directed by the Catholic episcopate, on all religious publications and broadcasting. The occasional expulsion of Protestant missionaries from Spain only reinforced the suspicion, especially among Protestants in Western democracies, that the Church's obscure thesis-hypothesis casuistry on tolerance only masked a hypocritical will to power: in weakness she demanded freedom; in strength she demanded protection of the unique rights of the one true religion.

---

[19] John Cardinal Heenan, "Oratio," *ASVII*, vol. 4, part 1, 295.

Even graver was the painful ecclesiastic memory of her own complicity in religious repression, even persecution, especially in the late Middle Ages and during the era of the Reformation. With all the cautions on the different historical contexts behind these actions and on the distinction between individual Catholic sovereigns and the Church herself, the Church could not contemplate this violent history without consternation. In a warmly applauded address, Cardinal Beran of Prague, himself a political prisoner under the communist regime, touched the heart of this malaise:

> In my country the church seems to be expiating today the faults and sins that were committed in her name in the past against religious freedom. Such was the case in the sixteenth century with the burning at the stake of the priest Jan Hus or in the seventeenth century with the forced return to the Catholic faith of a large part of the people of Bohemia in virtue of the principle, *cujus regio, eius religio*. ['The religion of a region is that of the ruler of a region.'] This recourse to the secular power, wanting or pretending to serve the Catholic Church, has certainly left a wound in the heart of the population. This trauma has placed an obstacle to religious progress. It has furnished and still furnishes an easy argument for the enemies of the church to attack her.[20]

Dignitatis Humanae echoes this examination of conscience, but in a very subdued rhetoric:

> Although sometimes in the history of the people of God, traveling through the vicissitudes of human history, there have been ways of acting less in conformity with, even contrary to the evangelical spirit, the church has nonetheless always taught that no one can be led by constraint to the faith (DH no.12a).

This reference to "the vicissitudes of history" is most curious in a text that wants to underline the personal responsibility of every individual, especially in the religious domain. Moreover, this distinction between "the people of God" (whose actions occasionally contradict the gospel) and "the Church" (whose teaching always

---

[20] Joseph Cardinal Beran, "Oratio," *ASVII*, vol. 4, part 1, 393.

forbade constraint in the act of faith) occults the ethical problem posed by the Church's past. Didn't these lamentable actions by certain Catholics arise precisely because of, and not despite, the magisterium's teaching on the rights of truth, on the religious duties of princes, and on the necessity to exterminate heresy?

Despite this weakness, this passage of the declaration accurately expresses the paradox of the Church's history concerning religious freedom. On the one hand, the Church created certain principles, such as the freedom of the act of faith and the distinction between the two powers that are incontestable ancestors of religious freedom in modern liberal societies. On the other hand, by a centuries-long exaltation of the unique rights of the true religion in civil society and the necessity of the civil authorities to repress religious error, the Church created a persecutory history that for the majority of conciliar fathers could only be an object of regret and consternation.

Conclusion

A landmark in the defense of religious freedom and in the Catholic Church's patrimony of teaching on human rights, *Dignitatis Humanae* managed to resolve the philosophical, historical, and moral crises surrounding this issue in order to produce a consensus among the vast majority of conciliar fathers. But this consensus was achieved at the price of certain omissions, evasions, and remarkably sibylline phrases. At a distance of forty years, one can see the fragility of the argumentation supporting the defense of religious freedom.

The declaration provides a useful articulation of the relationship between freedom and truth in terms of a robust defense of human rights in the civic arena, but it avoids any discussion as to how this new approach to religious freedom in the civic forum affects the exercise of freedom within the Church's own internal forum. If it insists that conscience must be formed according to the objective demands of the moral order, it seems insufficiently attentive to the emerging phenomenon of a contemporary conscience that insists it can fabricate its own moral order by an act of will and desire. In succeeding decades, the allure of moral subjectivism, repeatedly alluded to by the conciliar minority, would become stronger than the conciliar majority apparently thought. The very existence of an objective moral order would become an object of dispute.

Its hermeneutic of doctrinal development also raises serious problems. This method of interpretation permitted the Church to understand its historical and current teaching on religious freedom as a dialectic of continuity and change; an ancient core of convictions regarding truth and freedom were dynamically adapted to the new reality of pluralist, liberal societies. An older, more static understanding of church doctrine has receded. But this evolutionary approach to church doctrine, that perceives only progress and maturation, in the Church's exposition of its basic teachings, dangerously masks the other, less triumphal side of doctrinal change. The evidence of rupture, reversal, contradiction, forgetting, and loss of primitive truths is simply ignored. A hermeneutic of conversion and retrieval can excavate a more complex, meandering narrative of ecclesiastical belief than can a simple developmentalist approach.

Finally, the simple distinction between the blameless, orthodox Church and her erring, violent members in the area of religious freedom only dulls the Church's necessary examination of conscience regarding her long complicity with the use of civic coercion in religious matters. The prim demarcation between the sinless Church and her sinful members cannot render justice to the enigma of the holy wars, the tortures, and the executions carried out in the name of the merciful cross.

DIGNITATIS HUMANAE AND A CATHOLIC SOCIETY: THE CONFESSIONAL STATE AS A PERENNIAL POSSIBILITY

Christopher Cullen, S.J.

We are so completely enmeshed in modern liberalism that we find it difficult to see that the modern liberal democratic state is an anomaly in the history of politics and religion. No society in human history, prior to modernity, attempted to function without religion, that is, without telling its citizens what they should live and die for, what gods to worship for survival's sake, and what is the purpose of life. For the ancients and the medievals, a society must have its protecting gods. Sacrilege and heresy are threats to the body politic, for they sow dissension among the citizens about the most fundamental questions of human life. Ancient and medieval societies believed it perfectly within their right to suppress those who refused right worship because these acts were attacks against the body politic itself. Religious liberty in *ancien régime* Europe generally reflected this attitude.[1] It is crucial to understand the extraordinary nature of a society without an official religion if one is going to appreciate how anomalous is modern liberalism. Ancient and medievals, both Christian and non-Christian, would be dumbfounded before the idea that a society has no official cult. Modern liberal democracy is very much *ad experimentum*, and there are clear signs that the experiment is going badly for the souls of men.

It is important to appreciate the anomaly that is the modern liberal state in order to understand the Church's long struggle to deal with it. From the Roman Emperor Theodosius I in 381 to the beheading of King Louis XVI in 1793, the Catholic Church was deeply involved with confessional states, the most important of which was that governed by the Frankish monarchy. The alliance of the Frankish monarchy and the papacy, often stormy, like a troubled marriage, was the foundation of medieval Christendom. After the beheading of Louis XVI in January of 1793 until the era of Vatican II, the papacy treated the modern liberal

---

[1] Religious liberty in Christian Europe, Catholic or Protestant, generally meant tolerance for Jews, hostility and sporadic suppression of Moslems, and active suppression of heretics.

state with hostility. No doubt, it hoped that this was all a bad nightmare from which it would awake. *Dignitatis Humanae* is at once the white flag and the olive branch to modernity. It is an olive branch offered, however, only after the liberal state had, in general, shed its anti-Catholicism and anti-clericalism.

The Church, of course, did not begin in 1965, and so I want to read *Dignitatis Humanae* mindful of the previous history and in the light of the *Catechism of the Catholic Church*, which is the most important doctrinal document on religious liberty since the Council. Hence, I am led to my current thesis: the decree of the Second Vatican Council on religious liberty, *Dignitatis Humanae*, does not preclude the possibility of a Catholic confessional state. There are two fundamental reasons why this is so. First, the document carefully avoids limiting the state to concern for mere public order. The council unambiguously affirmed that the state exists to insure the common good. The common good as understood in the Catholic tradition encompasses the virtuous life of the citizens, including the virtue of religion. Secondly, the document clearly teaches the obligatory nature of the truth. Those who have not found the truth are obliged in duty to seek it, and those who have found it are bound in duty to adhere to it. It is in this context, then, that the Council clearly presents religious liberty as a limited, not an absolute, right that must be set within due limits. Hence, the pursuit of, and adherence to, the truth allows the state in a Catholic society to defend and promote the truth of Jesus Christ and of the Catholic Church, while prescribing the right within appropriate limits. A confessional state in a predominantly Catholic society remains a perennial possibility.

Contrary to popular opinion, the Council was not an endorsement of Enlightenment liberalism and its understanding of constitutional order, so accurately characterized by Alasdair MacIntyre, as a "government [which] does not express or represent the moral community of the citizens, but is instead a set of institutional arrangements for imposing a bureaucratized unity on a society."[2] Liberalism tends to regard the state as a means of insuring personal freedom and thus as completely

---

[2] Alasdair MacIntyre, *After Virtue* (Notre Dame, Indiana: University of Notre Dame Press, 1981), p. 236.

separate from society.[3] The state exists to insure public order, which is often conceived in a reductionistic way as simply preserving one citizen from harming another. The Council did not endorse liberalism's laissez-faire state that exists for the sake of maintaining mere public order. It did not exile Catholics to living perpetually in societies that refrain from answering the most important questions of human life.

This paper attempts to address a theoretical question, namely, whether the Council left open the possibility of a confessional state. By asking this question, we hope to accomplish two tasks: (1) to illuminate ways that the teaching of *Dignitatus Humanae* is in harmony with the Church's long tradition of confessional states that began when the Roman Emperor Theodosius I made Christianity the official religion of the Empire around 381 and forbade pagan rites;[4] and (2) to highlight tacit misinterpretations of the text which read it only through the eyes of post-Enlightenment liberalism. This paper is not "a call" for a confessional state. It merely attempts to answer a theoretical question. It is a question posed ultimately for the sake of a larger, as yet, unaccomplished task: showing how the teaching of Vatican II's most radical document, *Dignitatus Humanae*, can be reconciled with the Church's tradition.

First, let us look at the key texts of *Dignitatis Humanae* itself. In *Dignitatis Humanae*, religious freedom is declared to mean:

> that all men should be immune from coercion on the part of individuals, social groups and every human power so that, within due limits, nobody is forced to act against his convictions nor is anyone to be restrained from acting in accordance with his

---

[3] Roger Scruton, *The Meaning of Conservatism*, Revised Third Edition (South Bend, Indiana: St. Augustine's Press, 2002), p. 38.

[4] It was the Roman Emperor, Theodosius I, who outlawed paganism. In 385, he renewed a prohibition against bloody sacrifices; in 391, he forbade all pagan ceremonies in Rome; in 392, he outlawed pagan worship, whether public or private. All of this was in addition to his active suppression of Arians in many different ways.

> conviction in religious matters in private or in public, alone or in association with others.[5]

The Council declared that the basis of this "right to religious freedom" is found in "the very dignity of the human person" as this is known by revelation and reason.[6]

This right to religious freedom includes two key elements. First, it includes a freedom of conscience, such that no one can be forced to act against his conscience in religious matters.[7] The Council gives as the reason for this the fact "that the practice of religion consists primarily of those voluntary and free acts by which a man directs himself to God." The freedom of conscience has long been recognized in the tradition of the Church. The second element is the free exercise of religion. It is this element that is more problematic in terms of the Church's tradition. The Council declared that to deny man "the free exercise of religion" is to do an "injustice" because man's social nature requires that he give external expression to internal acts of religion. The document proceeds to explain that this external expression of religion includes: (1) corporate autonomy for religious bodies, and (2) freedom of religious association. The document says:

> Therefore, provided the just requirements of public order are not violated, these groups have a right to immunity so that they may organize themselves according to their own principles. They must be allowed to honor the supreme Godhead with public

---

[5] Austin Flannery, O.P., ed., *Dignitatis Humanae* in *Vatican Council II: The Conciliar and Post Conciliar Documents: A Study Edition* (Northport, New York: Costello Publishing Company), par. 2.

[6] Ibid., par. 2.

[7] *Dignitatis Humanae*, 3: "It is through his conscience that man sees and recognizes the demands of the divine law. He is bound to follow this conscience faithfully in all his activity so that he may come to God, who is his last end. Therefore he must not be forced to act contrary to his conscience. Nor must he be prevented from acting according to his conscience, especially in religious matters. The reason is because the practice of religion of its very nature consists primarily of those voluntary and free internal acts by which a man directs himself to God. Acts of this kind cannot be commanded or forbidden by any merely human authority."

> worship, help their members to practice their religion and strengthen them with religious instruction, and promote institutions in which members may work together to organize their own lives according to their religious principles.[8]

Dignitatis Humanae restrains the civil authority from using coercive force or discrimination against either an individual or a religious body for religious reasons.

With this said, however, we must take careful note that *Dignitatis Humanae* does not declare that the state either is excluded from legitimate concern for the common good or is restricted to maintenance of mere public order. This is a crucial point, because if the state is concerned for the common good, then it must be concerned about the spiritual and moral welfare of its citizens. In other words, the common good of society includes the pursuit both of virtue and of the end of human life, i.e., union with God insofar as the virtues dispose man to the reception of beatitude. Among the moral virtues is the virtue of religion as a form of justice that involves rendering to God the worship due Him.[9] Since the Incarnation, this virtue demands the worship of Jesus Christ. The common good of society, then, would seem to include ensuring the conditions that would contribute to each of its members attaining his supernatural end – union with God. At the very least, society's pursuit of the common good would include preventing those things that positively hinder man's pursuit of his end.

In the middle of the Council in 1964, John Courtnay Murray wrote an article, "The Problem of Religious Freedom," which appeared in *Theological Studies*.[10] In it he implies that religious liberty entails the restriction of the state to the maintenance of public order. He implies

---

[8] *Dignitatis Humanae*, 4.

[9] This is a point that the *Catechism of the Catholic Church* makes very clear: "Justice toward God is called the 'virtue of religion' (*Catechism of the Catholic Church*, Second Edition [Citta del Vaticano: Lireria Editrice Vaticana, 2000], par. 1807; see also 1836, 1839, 2087). Also worthy of note is the following: "Adoration is the first act of the virtue of religion" (*Catechism*, 2096).

[10] John Courtney Murray, S.J., "The Problem of Religious Freedom," *Theological Studies* 25 (1964): 521.

that the common good lies outside the competence of what he terms "the constitutional state." Murray's remarks seem to constitute an attempt to give a classical liberal interpretation to the notion of religious liberty. He outlines three principles that make government constitutional, and then he asserts that "when government is based on them, it is based on the truth."[11] The first principle is the distinction between the sacred and the secular orders of human life; the second is the distinction between society and the state; the third is the distinction between the common good and public order. Public order, Murray claims, entails three goods: public peace, public morality, and justice. He says, "The power of the state is therefore limited to the maintenance of public order in a threefold sense."[12] What Murray calls the principles of constitutional government are what is usually meant by the modern liberal state.

The conciliar document, *Dignitatis Humanae*, however, does not demand that the Catholic accept "the constitutional government" for which Murray argued. It does not require the Catholic to accept the restriction of the state to the maintenance of mere public order. On the contrary, *Dignitatis Humanae* directly ties the civil authority of the state to the maintenance of the common good: "Therefore the civil authority, the purpose of which is the common good in the temporal order, must recognize and look with favor on the religious life of its citizens."[13] The state is not excluded from concern for the common good; on the contrary, the civil authority of the state is declared to have its very purpose in securing the common good. What is more, the document has a comprehensive definition of the common good: "The common good of society consists in the sum total of those conditions of social life which enable men to achieve a fuller measure of perfection with greater ease."[14] This definition clearly allows for traditional understandings of the common good that would include the spiritual

---

[11] Murray, "The Problem of Religious Freedom," p. 521.

[12] Ibid.

[13] *Dignitatis Humanae*, 3: "Postestas igitur civilis, cuius finis proprius est bonum commune temporale curare religiosam quidem civium vitam agnoscere eique favere debet."

[14] Ibid., 6.

and moral welfare of the citizens. In the context of a Catholic document, "the perfection of man" can be presumed to refer to the final end of union with God in everlasting life.[15]

The second reason why the decree on religious liberty leaves the confessional state as a perennial possibility is that it unambiguously places the right to religious liberty in the context of the obligatory nature of the truth and, therefore, presents the right as a limited, not an absolute, right. As already seen, the right is based on the dignity of the human person. But the Council closely ties the right to the obligatory search for truth:

> It is in accordance with their dignity that all men, because they are persons, that is, beings endowed with reason and free will and therefore bearing personal responsibility, are both impelled by their nature and bound by a moral obligation to seek the truth, especially religious truth.[16]

It is because of what human beings are that they have a moral obligation to seek the truth. This ordination to truth means that the human being is immune from coercion in religious matters. The right to religious liberty is directly tied to this ordination to truth. This is crucial for two reasons. One, the right only follows from an obligation – to seek the truth – and therefore is not absolute, but is ordered to the truth. Secondly, once the truth is found, the truth demands adherence and imposes moral obligations. The Council teaches: "They [men] are also bound to adhere to the truth once they come to know it and direct their whole lives in accordance with the demands of truth."[17] The right to religious liberty is a right that in no way absolves anyone from the duty either to seek for or to adhere to the truth. Hence, it is not an absolute right, but one subject to the truth. This means that (1) it cannot be exercised outside of the truth insofar as this truth can be known by reason; and that (2) it cannot be exercised in such a way that it contradicts the truth. The right is not rooted in radical liberalism's autonomous individual who may determine the purpose and meaning

---

[15] *Catechism*, 16, 260, 356.

[16] *Dignitatis Humanae*, 2.

[17] Ibid.

of human life for himself. The right is grounded in human nature insofar as it is inclined to the good of human reason, which has been ordered to the truth.

Furthermore, the right is always exercised in a concrete human society. "The right to freedom in matters of religion is exercised in human society. For this reason its use is subject to certain regulatory norms."[18] Hence, the Council taught that the right could not be prescribed when the just requirements of public order are not observed.[19]

In general, the *Catechism of the Catholic Church* presents a more tightly organized presentation of the same issues than are found in *Dignitatis Humanae.* The *Catechism* makes clear that the state's role is to ensure the common good: "Every human community needs an authority to govern it. The foundation of such authority lies in human nature. It is necessary for the unity of the state. Its role is to ensure as far as possible the common good of the society."[20] In this paragraph, the *Catechism* ties the governing authority of a society directly to the common good, thus rejecting a liberal reading of *Dignitatis Humanae.* This authority follows from the requisites of human nature itself.

Then, in a subsequent paragraph, the *Catechism* goes further and defines the nature of the common good: "By common good is to be understood 'the sum total of social conditions which allow people, either as groups or as individuals, to reach their fulfillment more fully and more easily.' The common good concerns the life of all."[21] The *Catechism* then goes on to explicate three necessary conditions for the common good: (1) "the common good presupposes respect for the person as such;" (2) "the common good requires the social well-being and development of the group itself;" (3) "the common good requires peace, that is stability and security of a just order."[22]

---

[18] Ibid., 7.

[19] Ibid., 2.

[20] *Catechism*, 1898.

[21] Ibid., 1906.

[22] Ibid., 1907-1909.

With regard to the first element, the document says, "Society should permit each of its members to fulfill his vocation. In particular, the common good resides in the conditions for the exercise of the natural freedom indispensable for the development of the human vocation."[23] The *Catechism* is attempting to correct a strictly liberal understanding of the common good. It ties the common good to the development of the human vocation. The distinctly human vocation is to union with God in Christ. This point is made clear in the first statement of the section of the *Catechism* on the "Communal Character of the Human Vocation:" "All men are called to the same end: God himself."[24] "The vocation of humanity is to show forth the image of God and to be transformed into the image of the Father's only Son."[25]

The *Catechism* quotes *Dignitatis Humanae* when discussing the first article of the Creed and the nature of the act of faith. The act of faith must be free. "To be human man's response to God by faith must be free, and... therefore nobody is to be forced to embrace the faith against his will. The act of faith is of its very nature a free act."[26] Faith cannot be compelled without destroying the very nature of the act.

The *Catechism* treats the right to religious liberty later under the first commandment, which prescribes the worship of God. By placing its treatment there, the *Catechism* presents the right as an aspect of the human duty to serve God. Here again the right is closely tied to duty. The duty to serve God implies a respect for other men's search for the truth about God. The *Catechism* says, "[This duty] does not contradict a 'sincere respect' for different religions which frequently 'reflect a ray of that truth which enlightens all men' nor the requirement of charity."[27] The *Catechism* is clear that:

---

[23] Ibid., 1907.

[24] Ibid., 1878. "Of all visible creatures only man is able to know and love his creator, . . . and he alone is called to share, by knowledge and love, in God's own life. It was for this end that he was created" (*Catechism*, 356).

[25] Ibid., 1877.

[26] Ibid., 160.

[27] Ibid., 2104.

> The right to religious liberty is neither moral license to adhere to error, nor a supposed right to error, but rather a natural right of the human person to civil liberty, i.e., immunity, within just limits, from external constraint in religious matters by political authorities.[28]

There are two key points about this passage. First, the *Catechism* reiterates that religious liberty is a negative or passive right - it is immunity from external constraint. It does not oblige the state to render recognition or goods to religion. It is not a positive or active right that necessitates support from the state. The second point here is that the *Catechism* makes clear that the religious-liberty right is not absolute, but only relative, and therefore bound by "just limits." It cannot be exercised outside of the limits of public order. This proposition is clear. But it also cannot be exercised outside the limits of the order of truth, the objective moral order:

> The right to religious liberty can of itself be neither unlimited nor limited only by a "public order" conceived in a positivist or naturalist manner. The "due limits" which are inherent in it must be determined for each social situation by political prudence, according to the requirement of the common good and ratified by the civil authority in accordance with "legal principles which are in conformity with the objective moral order."[29]

Presumably, then, the state would not be obliged to tolerate a religion that practices human sacrifice, as did the ancient Aztecs before the arrival of Hernan Cortés. Nor would the state have to tolerate a religion that practices temple prostitution, as did the ancient Canaanites; nor ones that advocate suicide for their members, such as certain medieval sects, as well as certain more recent ones. One can argue that these religions violate both the just limits of public order and the legal principles in conformity with an objective moral order.

---

[28] Ibid., 2108.

[29] Ibid., 2109.

The *Catechism* also makes clear that a right (*jus*) cannot be rooted in error. Murray points clearly to this fact in his notes on *Dignitatis Humanae*, published in English immediately after the Council: "Neither the *Declaration* nor the American *Constitution* affirms that a man has a right to believe what is false or to do what is wrong. This would be moral nonsense."[30] Murray makes clear that the right is not to be conceived as being rooted in liberalism's autonomous individual who may determine the purpose and meaning of human life for himself.

Nor can the argument be that the right to religious liberty is rooted in the sincere but erroneous conscience. This would still ground the right in error. The decree is clear that the basis for the right is man's dignity. A medieval Cathar might sincerely have acted from an objectively erroneous conscience that judged suicide a good act because this act liberates one from the body, but said Cathar cannot claim that such an erroneous judgment gives such a person a right to suicide. A bishop may sincerely act from an objectively erroneous conscience that judges suicide to be a justified act of protest against other unjust acts, but one cannot claim that this erroneous judgment gives the bishop a *right* to suicide.

Contrary to such interpretations of the document, the *Catechism* moves in the other direction. It explicitly calls for the public and legal recognition of Sundays:

> In respecting religious liberty and the common good of all, Christians should seek recognition of Sundays and the Church's holy days as legal holidays. They have to give everyone a public example of prayer, respect and joy and defend their traditions as a precious contribution to the spiritual life of society.[31]

Although this paper is not advocating a confessional state, one might find it helpful, as a theoretical exercise, to ask what a Catholic confessional state would look like in order to bring to light its consonance with the principles of *Dignitatis Humanae*. It is possible in

---

[30] John Courtney Murray, Notes to Declaration on Religious Freedom, in *The Documents of Vatican II*, trans. Walter Abbott (New York: Guild Press, 1966), n. 5.

[31] *Catechism*, 2188.

the current age to discern two very different models for a confessional state that are polar opposites. One model is found in certain Islamic societies, such as in Iran or in Saudi Arabia. Another is found in the Scandinavian countries, which are still technically confessional states, each with a state religion. The first model presents us with theocratic states that seem highly undesirable for a number of reasons and very problematic for the religious freedom that the Council decreed. The second model presents us with democratic states that are officially confessional but that do little to influence thoroughly secularized civil societies. A Catholic confessional state, without violating the religious freedom of its citizens, could re-introduce those principles eliminated at the birth of the liberal state: the pursuit of virtue and the recognition of transcendence. A confessional state, therefore, could (1) recognize the truth of the Catholic faith in its state papers, i.e., in an official capacity, thereby attempting to shape civil society by orienting it to a transcendent meaning and purpose; (2) affirm the human vocation to live the virtuous life; (3) enact laws that are in accord with the natural law and that prudently inculcate the virtues, especially the virtue of religion, such as what the *Catechism* calls for, namely, the public and legal recognition of Sundays and feasts; (4) require that the head of government and/or head of state be Catholic; (5) respect and defend the freedom of the Church (*libertas ecclesiae*) which is so highly sought by *Dignitatis huamae*; (6) actively support the works of the Church by various means, financial and otherwise (for example, a confessional state could support Catholic institutions that perform spiritual and corporal works of mercy, such as schools and hospitals); (7) shape the culture of such a society through education and censorship; and (8) secure and protect the borders from influences deemed detrimental to the common good. In short, the *cura ecclesiae* would fall within the competence of the state insofar as this affects civil society, that is, insofar as it affects the common good. The Church would work to sustain and foster the health of the body politic, without losing its own independence.

The thesis of this paper is that a Catholic confessional state remains a possibility even after *Dignitatis Humanae*. There are two reasons for this: (1) the decree does not remove the common good from the concern of the state, and (2) the right to religious liberty is not absolute but is prescribed by the obligatory search for truth and the limits of public order. In this light, *Dignitatis Humanae* appears more in harmony with the previous tradition and practice of Roman Catholicism. Whether or not such a state is desirable is another question.

The decree on religious liberty played a crucial role in the Church's struggle against communism. In the years since the Council, it seems to have also allowed the Church to guide a number of societies from dictatorships to democracy, in what Samuel Huntington calls "the third wave" of democratization in the history of the modern world – a wave that has been "overwhelmingly Catholic."[32] The great irony is that the Church has arguably become the single largest, transnational champion of ordered liberty. Ordered liberty does not preclude a Catholic confessional state.

---

[32] Samuel P. Huntington, "Religion and the Third Wave," *The National Interest* 24 (Summer 1991):29-42. The first wave lasted a hundred years and took place from the 1820's to the 1920's; the second started at the end of World War II and lasted until the mid-1960's; the third wave began with the end of the Portuguese dictatorship in 1974 and continues. "Since then democratic regimes have replaced authoritarian ones in more than thirty countries in Europe, Asia, and Latin America" (Huntington, p. 29). The first wave received its remote impulse from the Puritan Revolution in the seventeenth century and more immediate impulse from the American and French Revolutions. Most of the countries involved in this first wave were Protestant . The countries involved in the second wave were religiously diverse, but the larger number were Protestant. "In its first fifteen years the third wave was overwhelmingly Catholic" (Huntington, p. 30).

Freedom and Tolerance

Piotr Jaroszynski (Translator Hugh McDonald)

The word "tolerance" today is an integral part of our description of Western democracy. On the one hand, the word "tolerance" expresses an attitude of being open to the views of others in matters of world-view and religion. On the other hand, it has become a yardstick for determining whether a person fits in the world of our time. Intolerance is stigmatized as fundamentalism or even fascism. We may say that without tolerance there would be no democracy today, but the word unfortunately has also become part of the vocabulary of "political correctness."

The term "tolerance" began its career in the seventeenth century. Before that time it appeared in Latin in association with the virtue of fortitude. Apart from its literal meaning, it had a moral meaning. Tolerance was steadfastness. In its most literal sense, it referred to physical endurance. To tolerate something is quite literally to bear something, or to bear with something. By analogy, tolerance referred to endurance or steadfastness in the face of some evil. Part of the virtue of fortitude is the ability to put up a sustained resistance to evil, and so tolerance is very close to fortitude.

In the seventeenth century, the tolerance (or toleration) was extended to matters of religion and politics. At that time the religious conflicts that arose in the Reformation were still raging and were leading to political battles and even to bloody wars. On the twenty-fourth of May in 1689, the British Parliament passed the "Toleration Act" that allowed dissenting Protestants freedom of worship. The act particularly concerned Baptists, Congregationalists, and Methodists. Also in 1689, John Locke published the first volume of his *Epistula de Tolerantia*, in which he analyzed tolerance and touched the problems of the relation between politics and religion. Tolerance then acquired a religious, philosophical, and political status, but its most important context was matters of religion. The "Toleration Act." interestingly enough, did not extend to Catholics. The umbrella of toleration did not protect Catholics. Their religious practices were not tolerated, and they had no place in public life. Religious freedom was not something to be enjoyed by Catholics.[1]

Over time toleration extended beyond religion to the sphere of world-views until it became the first commandment (the "prime directive") in an ideological sense. Tolerance has today essentially changed the meaning of freedom. Freedom, in the classical sense, ends where evil begins, and evil was forbidden,[2] but today tolerance, not evil, sets the boundaries of freedom. Tolerance, however, has its own axiological system, its own system of values, and this is not in complete agreement with the Decalogue or with the classical ethics of natural law, which conforms with the Decalogue.

Today in the west the traditional ethics as upheld by Christianity is more and more in conflict with the ideological principle of tolerance. The perennial ethics for which Christianity has been a vehicle commands us to do good and avoid evil.[3] The ideological principle commands us simply to be tolerant.

"Evil" is neutered in this ideology. Instead of "evil," we are taught to speak of "differences," "diversity," and "minorities." We must be tolerant of anything different. When new laws strike at traditional principles and values, and offend the upright and well-formed conscience, the media is immediately prepared to re-educate us and reshape our attitudes. We are manipulated to speak and to think in terms of tolerance instead of in terms of good and evil. This manipulation begins in how we speak of moral matters. From there, it extends to the political arena and to civilization as a whole. By changing the way we speak, the media tries to change reality itself.

---

[1] When John Locke promoted his principle of tolerance, he left the door open for intolerance toward Catholics, ostensibly for political rather than for religious reasons.

[2] As in the words of the 19th century president of Ecuador, Garcia Moreno: "Freedom for everyone and everything, except for evil and evil-doers."

[3] This principle appeared in Cicero. St. Thomas Aquinas referred to it and wrote: ". . . bonum est faciendum et prosequendum, et malum vitandum:, *S.Th.* I-II, 94, 2. Cf. M. A. Krapiec, *Person and Natural Law* (Peter Lang, New York, 1993).

This attitude, that by using certain phrases we can actually change reality, is in fact a reversion to magic. The west is not merely going back to pre-Christian civilization, but it is turning its back on civilization as it looks to barbarism. Before Christianity, Greek and Roman thinkers and lawmakers had worked to refine their ideas of morality, but this heritage is rejected as well.[4] Aristotle had observed more than two thousand years ago that a man without morality is worse than a beast.[5] What can remain of a man's conscience if he can no longer distinguish between good and evil? If he has lost the ability to distinguish, he cannot be accountable for his actions. Is the ethics of our day supposed to be a system designed for people who are held to be morally incompetent? Is it a system designed for the morally insane?

What does it mean to be tolerant? The problem of tolerance was raised during the Reformation, and it primarily concerned religion. The principle of *cuius regio, eius religio* was that he who rules a land may also impose his own religion upon his subjects. In the face of this principle, statesmen looked for ways in which people of different religious confessions could coexist, how Catholics could live with Protestants, and vice versa. The Edict of Nantes was one of the most famous acts of tolerance, and from 1598 to 1685, it granted many rights to the Huguenots in a France that remained officially Catholic. Today, tolerance is more than a question of religion. Tolerance is a panacea for questions of morality, life-style, and world-view. The civilized man is a tolerant man, and he sees people who don't practice his kind of tolerance as primitive fundamentalists.

---

[4] The preamble to the Constitution of the European Union omits any mention of Christianity. It appeals to an indescript and general "religious heritage" ("[T]hey draw inspiration from the cultural, religious, and humanistic heritage of Europe, a heritage whose values are always present in it and which has rooted in the life of the society of Europe a perception of the central role of the human person and his inviolable and inalienable rights, and also respect for law.") There are many various religions in Europe today, but the identity of Europe after the fall of the Roman Empire was shaped by Christianity.

[5] ". . .if he have not virtue, he is the most unholy and the most savage of animals . . .," *Politics*, I, 1. 12.

What the word "tolerance" exactly means today is rather vague, because the word has become an ideological slogan. The slogan, in its extreme form, is a reversal of traditional morality. Tolerance means to do evil and avoid good! How else can we explain why perverts and criminals are protected? How can we explain the invasion of books and films that glorify evil and present blasphemies against Christianity? Tolerance has come to mean the ostracism of those who hold normal moral attitudes. In a more moderate form, tolerance does not urge people to support evil, merely to accept it and consent to it. It makes the good into something relative and subjective. The good becomes merely one of several options, a mere matter of taste. The question of good and evil is thus trivialized. Evil may not be condemned or rebuked, and so it is sheltered and strengthened. This is the ethics of the west today.

This ethics is based on an ideology that produces a social psychosis through the media and politics. Any public person who dissents from this ideology loses his position in public life. He is stigmatized or becomes a social non-entity. The ideology of tolerance has become one of the most important requirements of "political correctness."

It is interesting that unlike previous ideologies of the twentieth century such as Hitler's Nazism and the Communism of Marx, Lenin, and Stalin, the ideology of tolerance has no single author. While it does have binding authority, its authority is not connected with the name of any leader or founder. It exercises its authority impersonally as a kind of artificially produced social pressure. If someone disagrees with it, he does not know to whom he should direct his objections. Like every ideology, it grows out of something deeper, whether a philosophy or a type of civilization. In fact, political correctness as a tactic was developed by the leftist Frankfurt School. It was a tactic to advance communism by destroying the west from within, specifically by neutralizing those who dared to criticize Marxism. Political correctness was the tactic of changing the way people talk and think by teaching people that if they express their beliefs they are being disrespectful to others. They must avoid expressing their beliefs to make up for the injustices of the past. The Frankfurt School was founded in 1923, and in 1935 it moved from Germany to the USA.

Taking into account all that has been said, we have to face a basic ethical question today: will we choose the ethics of the good or the ethics of tolerance? In other words, we must define the moral principle that will be a real principle for all who live in the civilization that rests upon freedom.

The ethics of tolerance is a perversion of the ethics of the good. It is a caricature, but it is so cunning that the one ethics may be easily confused with the other. The ethics of tolerance is also a caricature of the virtue of Christian mercy and willingly cloaks itself in that garb.

The ethics of the good is rooted in classical Greek ethics. It is based on the idea that man can objectively recognize the good and choose it. This, however, is difficult in practice, and so people must be properly educated and formed. Each person must be educated and formed to develop his ability to recognize and choose what is good. Christianity explained the weaknesses of human nature in terms of the effects of original sin, and to overcome these effects, man needs more than education. Supernatural grace is necessary to do good, especially to attain the final end of life. The ethics of the good does not conceal the truth about man and his difficult moral condition.

The ethics of tolerance tries to dispense with this truth in the name of humanism. It permits man to do what he pleases without regard to good and evil. The ethics of tolerance undermines our ability to recognize and to choose objective goods. The good, like religion, is a private matter for the secular post-Protestant state. While the good is a private matter, evil in all its forms is publicly advertised. There is pressure from many sides to live at peace with evil and to accept it. This is what is meant by a tolerant man, while someone who does not accept evil is considered to be a fundamentalist.

The ethics of tolerance disguises itself as Christian mercy, but it is no such a thing. Christian mercy understands that someone may find himself in a bad situation, but it realizes that the person is still capable of willfully rejecting evil.[6] Mercy demands that we climb toward the

---

[6] "Accordingly the motive of 'mercy,' being something pertaining to 'misery,' is, in the first way, anything contrary to the will's natural appetite, namely corruptive or distressing evils, the contrary of which man desires naturally, wherefore the Philosopher says (Rhet., ii, 8) that 'pity is sorrow for a visible evil, whether corruptive or distressing.' Secondly, such like evils are yet

good. Tolerance accepts evil, and it even demands that we lower ourselves to its level. These are two different ethics, and they correspond to two different civilizations.

How is it that the ethics of the good and the ethics of tolerance are so easily confused? In both cases, we are dealing with a situation that evokes our pity. Tolerance wears the disguise of mercy, but it is not mercy. The emotion of pity must be first filtered through the intellect if we are to know whether it inclines us to virtue or to vice. This "filtration," namely, our intellect changing emotion into virtue, will depend on our intellect's ability to properly understand what is good and what is evil.[7] When people promote tolerance as a basic principle of action, they appeal not to the intellect, but to the emotions in an effort to evoke pity. People are led to think in this way: the poor murderer who must sit for so many years in isolation without his family; the poor deviant; the poor thief with no family or friends, unable to come and go as he wishes. As the difference between reprehensible and responsible behavior is erased, criminals are transformed into victims by evoking feelings of pity in violation of logic. When the feeling of mercy prevails over our ability to make rational judgments and over our ability to recognize causes and effects, mercy is quickly transformed into its opposite. Instead of healing evil, we leave the evil untouched, and so it grows all the more.

Another danger in failing to distinguish between the ethics of the good and the ethics of tolerance is that people will confuse their

---

more provocative of pity if they are contrary to deliberate choice, wherefore the Philosopher says (*Rhet.* ii, 8) that evil excites our pity 'when it is the result of an accident, as when something turns out ill, whereas we hoped well of it.' Thirdly, they cause yet greater pity, if they are entirely contrary to the will, as when evil befalls a man who has always striven to do well: wherefore the Philosopher says (*Rhet.* ii, 8) that 'we pity most the distress of one who suffers undeservedly,'" *S.Th.* II-II, 30, 1.

[7] "Mercy signifies grief for another's distress. Now this grief may denote, in one way, a movement of the sensitive appetite, in which case mercy is not a virtue but a passion; whereas, in another way, it may denote a movement of the intellective appetite, in as much as one person's evil is displeasing to another" *S.Th.*, II-II, 30, 3.

feelings with their conscience. Conscience is an act of rational judgment![8] It is an act of reason. The feeling of mercy is an emotion, a response of the sense appetite. The ideology of tolerance aims to eliminate the role of the intellect in moral judgment. The intellect is to be left unengaged with reality because the good is understood to be relative and subjective. The good will be irrelevant to the conscience because the emotions are more important, and pity is the most important. When the intellect is disengaged, people are easy victims for manipulation.

What are the practical consequences when the ethics of tolerance is dominant in particular areas of man's moral life? Ethics concerns the moral life of the individual. The good we should seek is not an abstraction or value. It is the concrete aim of our natural inclinations. When we speak of the three basic inclinations of our nature, we may speak as well of three ends or goods: the preservation of our life, the transmission of life, and our development as persons in the truth. The ethics of the good orders us to do good. This is the source of the imperative that we should respect human life from conception to natural death, that we should be solicitous of man's spiritual development, and that we should work for truth in the media, in politics, and in the schools. The ethics of tolerance, on the other hand, promotes suicide and euthanasia as an easy way to resolve the drama of human suffering. It promotes abortion as a way of ridding ourselves of unwanted children, and it also has no qualms about the use of deception and manipulation in public life, when this suits its aims.

In the economic order, the ethics of the good focuses on the family. The child comes into the world and develops within a family. His family protects his material existence and fosters his spiritual growth. The ethics of tolerance promotes alternative models of the "family:" the single parent, two adults of the same gender, alternative ways of bringing children into the world such as *in vitro* fertilization, often where the biological parents do not have any personal connection to the child. The promotion and legalization of "homosexual marriages" results from the application of the principles of the ethics of tolerance.

[8] ". . . for conscience may be resolved into *cum alio scientia* [that is knowledge applied to an individual case]" *S.Th.*, I, 79, 13.

The countries of the European Union are more and more intensely moving in this direction. There is a similar movement in North America, most notably in Canada.

In the political order, the ethics of the good views justice as the foundation of the political community, and there are three kinds of justice: commutative, legal, and distributive. Commutative justice concerns relations between individuals. Legal justice concerns relations between individuals and society or state. Distributive justice concerns relations between the society or state and individuals. Because social life is complex, the idea of social justice is complex. The perfection of society requires that these three types of justice should all go together. In the ethics of tolerance, on the other hand, we find reductionism. The ethics of tolerance accepts only one kind of justice, namely, any one of the three exclusively but understood only from the egoistic point of view. The other kinds of justice either do not exist or are regarded as unimportant. The ethics of tolerance is guided by the principle of the strong prevailing over the weak, whether it is the stronger individual, corporation, or state. In this way, the deepest meaning of social life is destroyed. Commutative justice concerns only the partners in their business agreements; it does not concern the nature of their businesses themselves. Legal justice is abused to promote economic environments connected with the circles of power. Distributive justice makes it possible to treat the state as the fiefdom of certain interest groups. Such a political system is sick, and these are mere illusions of justice.

In the relation between politics and justice, there is the danger that the most important aim of politics will be denied. Justice demands that we give to each what is due (*cuique suum*), but justice is inadequate when we think of what we each owe to our parents, what we have inherited from those who have gone before us, and what we have received from God. Yet our parents, our predecessors, and God are at the foundation of our existence. We see that these points of reference are denied in the West, especially now in the European Union. Not only is the role of the family and of parents undermined, but also the entire heritage of Europe is being rejected. Finally, society is shutting its eyes to God. The rights of children are increased while the rights of parents are diminished. Since the state is the source of laws and rights, children are more and more the property or wards of the state. Experiments with the preamble to the constitution show how the authors are trying to forget the two millennia of Christianity that essentially shaped the identity of Europe. In the absence of God, the whole legal and moral order drifts like a leaf in the wind, and the only remaining right is the right of the strongest concealed in legalism. The proposed constitution of the European Union refers neither to Christianity nor to God. This is the final effect of the civilization which is trying to take toleration as its first principle, a civilization which wants to stay without God and without its true western heritage.

The ethics of tolerance is a fusion of two seemingly opposed ideologies: liberalism and socialism. Liberalism is individualism. It treats our moral judgments as relative and as completely dependent upon the individual. Morality and religion thus become private matters. Socialism, on the other hand, is the ideology of the group. The idea of socialism is based upon the conviction that the true being, the true substance is society; individuals are only parts of the society like a hand or a leg is a part of a body. Liberalism, on the other hand, literally related to freedom, glorifies an individual as individual, undermining his relations to society. Liberalism with its proclaimed glorification of individual rights is the starting point. It draws people in, but eventually liberalism is swallowed up by socialism. Hobbes and Locke taught that, in socialism, the individual freely relinquishes his natural rights to the political authorities. This socialist state is superior to the individual. The socialist authorities determine the law and how the law is interpreted. The slogan of tolerance, then, is merely a tool for destroying the individual's ability to understand reality in terms of good and evil so that he will no longer react properly to good and evil. When our understanding is dimmed, the media can easily manipulate our social reactions without regard to good and evil. Tolerance is a way of manipulating society.

When we refer in our moral judgments to tolerance, as it is understood by modern man, we are eroding the ground we stand on, for we are losing contact with reality and reason. The fundamental moral questions are whether man is capable of objectively recognizing good and evil, and whether in recognizing them, he can take a proper stand toward them by making the right choices. The traditional western ethics of the good is based on a positive answer to these questions. Man can recognize objective good and evil, and he can take a proper stand by using his powers to choose rightly. The ethics of tolerance answers in the negative: man cannot know objective good and evil because good and evil are only subjective realities determined by him, and so either choice he makes is good because it is his choice, and not because it aims at the objective good.

The ethics of tolerance is the foundation of post-modern ethics. Post-modern ethics gathers together most of the destructive philosophical positions in western philosophy as it seeks to destroy the western heritage, especially Christianity. The ethics of the good enables man to live and act on the rational level rather than merely on the emotional, which can so easily miss the objective good and can so easily be manipulated. If morality is to be true and if men are to be free, then we must work to save the ethics of the good. We must recognize true tolerance, which has persons and the good of persons as its object, and never confuse it with indifference, which is only a step away from hatred for our neighbor.[9]

---

[9] "... Then as now, true Christians practiced this tolerance with regard to persons, which is quite simply an evangelical virtue. We must guard ourselves from confusing true tolerance with false tolerance. Is it a question of error? We must combat it with all our forces under whatever form it presents itself, just as it is our duty to combat evil everywhere that we find it. Man would abdicate his quality of being intelligent and moral if he were to act otherwise. Tolerance can only concern itself with persons and it consists in acting with kindness as we act toward equals. There is more, dear sirs, because after having determined the object of this virtue, it is important to define the motive. To be true, tolerance must be based on the feeling of charity and not on indifference in matters of belief or of religion. Many people imagine themselves to be tolerant. They are merely indifferent, which is not at all the same thing. Tolerance does not at all consist in being completely unconcerned about our neighbour under the pretext that we must leave to each his liberty to believe as he wishes. It does not concern in avoiding meddling even if it means his loss. You say you possess the truth, and you will not use all legitimate means to assure its benefits to your equals? You will not look to free them from their errors because you do not want to disturb their liberty of thought and action? You would leave them to run with merry hearts before a certain danger without enlightening them about the consequences of their acts? And you will call this exercising tolerance? But my dear sirs, that would be the most culpable indifference. True tolerance is always accompanied by zeal because it draws from charity the motives that inspire it" Msgr. Freppel, *Saint Cyprian,* (1873), 2nd edition, (Bray et Retaux, France), pp. 17-19.

Abortion and Ideology

Raymond Dennehy

A survey of the justifications advanced by scientists, philosophers, and other members of the elite class, such as judges, to justify the legalization of induced abortion reveals that they have abandoned rational inquiry in favor of ideology. For although their arguments have the trappings of the objectivity of scientific method and other marks of rational inquiry, it is clear that they subvert reason and manipulate evidence to actualize an ideal that they perceive to be above all rational criticism. This enslavement to ideology is but a reenactment of what happened in Nazi Germany and Soviet Russia to the detriment of science and philosophy, not to mention the degradation of human life.

Sophistical Arguments for Abortion

Two months after the U. S. Supreme Court rendered its decision in *Roe v. Wade,* when the public debate on abortion was white hot, a political cartoon appeared in the editorial section of what is now called *The San Jose Mercury News*, depicting two departed souls standing on a cloud and sporting the obligatory wings. All about them tiny fetuses, also sporting wings, are standing. One of the souls says to the other: "Fetus, Fetus. I never knew so many kids named 'Fetus'."[1] A couple of days later, the paper printed a letter to the editor from a representative of a local feminist group complaining about the cartoon's "insensitivity to women who have had abortions." A plausible interpretation of the cartoonist's motive is that, rather than intending to bruise anyone's feelings, his aim was to caricature what was then the recent entry of "fetus" into everyday language as a replacement for the term unborn baby. Thereby hangs a tale.

The success of the pro-abortion movement depended on diverting the public's attention from the fact that induced abortion is the direct killing of an innocent human being. Replacing "unborn baby" with "fetus" was a good start, for the latter term is sufficiently abstract to deflect public consideration from the homicidal consequences. But

[1] *San Jose News* (San Jose, CA, March 12, 1973).

changing the public's thinking about abortion would require more than making "fetus" the preferred term in everyday discourse. It would also be necessary to spread a fog of confusion over the positions of science on the status of the fetus. Bernard Nathanson writes that, before his conversion from pro-abortion advocate to champion of human life, he and his colleagues worked hard to convince people that it is impossible to determine when human life begins by insisting that it is a moral, theological, or philosophical question, not a scientific one.[2]

Planned Parenthood, under the leadership of the late Alan Guttmacher, was apparently so devoutly committed to this project of disinformation that neither he nor his organization was embarrassed by contradicting themselves. For example, before he had become a promoter of abortion on demand, Guttmacher wrote the following:

> We of today know that man is born of sexual union; that he starts life as an embryo within the body of the female; and that the embryo is formed from the fusion of two single cells, the ovum and the sperm. This all seems so simple and evident to us that it is difficult to picture a time when it was not part of common knowledge.[3]

He wrote these words in 1933. And as late as 1963, Planned Parenthood proclaimed essentially the same position in its official pamphlet: "Is birth control an abortion? Definitely not. An abortion kills the life of a baby after it has begun...." But by 1973, Guttmacher's writings show that he had apparently undergone a conversion:

> Scientifically all we know is that a living human sperm unites with a living human egg; if they were not living there could be no union.... Does human life begin before or with the union of the

---

[2] Bernard Nathanson, "Confessions of an Ex-Abortionist," http://www.aboutabortions.com/Confess.htn; also see his book, *Aborting America* (Garden City, N.Y.: Doubleday & Company, Inc., 1979).

[3] Quoted in Robert Marshall & Charles Donovan, *Blessed Are the Barren: The Social Policy of Planned Parenthood* (San Francisco: Ignatius Press, 1991), pp. 294-95.

> gametes, or with birth, or at a time intermediate? I, for one, confess I do not know.[4]

What could explain this change of thought? New discoveries in embryology since 1963? Hardly! All the evidence since then only confirms the conclusion that from the moment of conception a new individual human life is present.

This gestational agnosticism takes various forms. The practice of decking oneself out in the clothes of science while speaking the language of everyday people seems to exert a powerful attraction on those in the pro-abortion ranks. For example, *Psychology Today* offered a fascinating account of life in the womb. The article's blurb asserted enticingly: "Behaviorally speaking, there's little difference between a newborn baby and a 32-week-old fetus. A new wave of research suggests that the fetus can feel, dream, and even enjoy *The Cat in the Hat*. The abortion debate may never be the same."[5] However, if the researchers interviewed by the author of those words have anything to say about the debate, it *will* stay the same. Their responses indicate that they would prefer the cozy and secure habitat of politically correct ambiguity. For example, Johns Hopkins psychologist, Janet DiPietro doubts that fetal research sheds any light at all on the abortion debate:

> The essence of the abortion debate is: When does life begin? Some people believe it begins at conception; the other extreme believes that it begins after the baby is born, and there's a group in the middle that believes it begins at around 24 or 25 weeks, when a fetus can live outside the womb, though it needs a lot of help to do so.
>
> Up to about 25 weeks, whether or not it's sucking its thumb or has personality or all that, the fetus cannot survive outside of its mother. So is that life or not? That is a moral, ethical, and religious question, not one for science. Things can behave and

---

[4] Quoted in *Blessed Are the Barren*, p. 295.

[5] *Psychology Today*, October, 1998, p. 44.

> not be alive. Right-to-lifers may say that this research proves that a fetus is alive, but it does not. It cannot.[6]

Heidelise Als, a Harvard University psychologist, offers another example saying:

> Fetal research only changes the abortion debate for people who think that life starts at some magical point. If you believe that life starts at conception, then you don't need the proof of fetal behavior. Your circumstances and personal beliefs have much more impact on the decision....[7]

To be sure, data that suggest or even establish that the fetus responds to its mother's voice with a lowered heart-beat or that it might even dream does not allow the conclusion that it is a human being. One might obtain the same kind of data from the observed responses of animal fetuses *in utero.* But for a scientist to speak as though ignorant of the conclusions of embryology and fetology and, worse yet, to cast doubt on whether the human fetus is even alive by appealing to an alleged disagreement in popular opinion is both preposterous and shameless. If the question of when human life begins is one for ethics and religion but not for science, then what do embryologists think that they have been doing all these years? And notice how Heidelise Als responds to the question by shifting attention from the objective results of scientific observation to the subjective factors that influence peoples' positions.

Not even one with the scientific stature of a David Baltimore, winner of the Nobel Prize for cancer research and president of the prestigious California Institute of Technology, seems embarrassed by basing his argument for embryo stem-cell research on his subjective opinion regarding the status of the embryo: "*To me*, a tiny mass of cells that has never been in a uterus is hardly a human being – even if it has the potential to become human."[8]

---

[6] *Psychology Today*, p. 47.

[7] Ibid.

[8] David Baltimore, "Don't Impede Medical Progress," *The Wall Street Journal*, July 30, 2001; emphasis added.

Another gambit is to offer a philosophical argument tricked out in the clothes of science. Princeton biologist Lee M. Silver exemplifies a group of pro-abortion scientists who do not hesitate to state their position, for he admits that the embryo is alive and that it is human, but he denies that it is human life. Although he speaks as a biologist, it is clear his pronouncements on the status of the embryo are philosophical rather than scientific. The obvious question that one would put to Silver is "How can the embryo be alive, be human, and yet fail to be a human life?" His answer is based on his distinction between "*life in the general sense*" and "*life in the special sense.*" Here he draws upon the venerable Scholastic adage, "When faced with a contradiction, make a distinction." By "*life in the general sense,*" he means an individual thing "as a product of reproduction and evolution that uses energy to maintain self-defining information and organization. The inanimate becomes animate only upon achieving the ability to evolve." The second meaning of "life" pertains to beings whose cerebral functioning reaches the state of consciousness. That distinction allows Silver to say that the embryo is human, but no more so than "the cells that fall off your skin every day."[9]

What is key in Silver's argument is that it is philosophical rather than biological. Of course, he is perfectly free to philosophize as long as both he and his readers bear in mind that he is no longer speaking as a biologist. But the trouble with Silver's transition is that the status of the human embryo is the kind of question that Mortimer Adler would call "a mixed question." For it cannot be decided either by science alone or by philosophy alone. What human life is and when it begins is a matter for the sciences of embryology and fetology to tell us. The contribution of philosophy depends on an interpretation of the scientific data. But instead of starting with that data, Silver immediately waxes philosophical, conveniently bypassing the position of embryology that from the moment of conception there is individual human life. This raises a crucial question about the dichotomy he claims to exist between "life in the general sense" and "life in the special sense," a question that he fails to address. Since embryology

---

[9] Lee M. Silver, *Remaking Eden* (New York, NY: Avon Books Inc., 1997), pp. 25-26 & 48.

tells us that, from the moment of conception, no constituent part is added to the newly conceived individual life - that is, mammalian reproduction is characterized by continuity in development - how can the embryo be human life in "the special sense" at t2 when, by Silver's own admission, it is only human life in "the general sense" at t1?

What is implied in this argument is that the two embryonic stages constitute a difference *in kind*, so that the respect given the embryo having "life in the special sense" need not be given to an embryo having "life in the general sense." It is axiomatic that of two things that differ in kind what applies to one in the relevant sense does not apply to the other in that relevant sense. Thus, if the two stages of embryonic development constitute a difference in kind, it would follow that the kind of respect to which an embryo having "life in the special sense" is entitled cannot be claimed by any embryo having "life in the general sense." The trouble is that we have no examples in biology of any mammal changing from one species to another *in utero*. This means that "life in the general sense" and "life in the special sense" could constitute a difference only in degree, not in kind. But of two things differing only in degree, what applies to one in the relevant sense, applies necessarily to the other in the relevant sense. For example, a theorem that applies to the triangle as such, applies to all triangles, regardless of whether equilateral, right, scalene, etc.

Silver might, wittingly or not, be taking sides with the functionalist in the *substance vs. function* debate, arguing that because an entity called "substance" is not observable, all that counts in ontological and moral enquiry is a being's function. If so, he would show once again that he has left the domain of science for that of philosophy to embrace a variation of developmentalist argument of Mary Ann Warren and Michael Tooley.

When it comes to making distinctions in the face of contradiction, no group does it better than philosophers. Mary Ann Warren and Michael Tooley, for example, admit that the fetus is a human being, but they deny that it is a person. The purchase gained by this distinction is that it permits the justification of induced abortion while protecting the right to life of persons, since the latter have rights and fetuses do not. What signals the advent of personhood is when a being starts performing functions such as self-awareness, consciousness of pleasure and pain, desiring to remain in existence, etc. Since the fetus does none of these things, it is only a potential person; whereas, the mother is an actual person. The rights of an actual person trump the rights of a merely potential person.[10]

Here, the principle, *Operatio sequitur esse* (operation follows essence), must be given its due. In the *order of discovery*, function comes before substance because how a thing behaves, its peculiar functions, are the first things we know about it. But in the *order of reality,* its substance is primary because it is only in virtue of what that thing actually is that it has those functions, functions peculiar to its substantial nature. From the knowledge of what a thing does, we infer what it is. Because substance enjoys primacy in the order of reality, it is a reasonable assumption that a person is present from the moment of conception even though self-awareness, thinking, and consciously desiring to remain in existence have yet to appear. To frame matters in a more dialectical way, the instrumentalists have not demonstrated that the fetus is not a person. Even if you buy into their Cartesian assumptions about the nature of the human person, the most their argument can claim is to have produced a merely *probable* conclusion. But to justify abortion when there is no certainty as to whether the fetus is a person implies the willingness to kill an innocent human person.[11]

Judicial Semantics

On the afternoon of the day that the U.S. Supreme Court rendered its *Roe v. Wade* decision, it rendered its *Doe v. Bolton* decision. What makes the latter decision remarkable is that, in the process of justifying abortion to protect a woman's health, the court saw fit to change the meaning of "health." Henceforth, the word would take into account not only the woman's physical and mental well being but her social and economic circumstances and age as well.[12] This had the effect of rendering every induced abortion therapeutic. It thereby allowed

---

[10] Mary Ann Warren, "On the Moral and Legal Status of the Fetus," *The Monist*, Vol. 57, #1 (January, 1973); Michael Tooley,"Abortion and Infanticide," *Philosophy and Public Affairs*, 2/1 (1972).

[11] Raymond Dennehy, "Liberal Democracy as a Culture of Death: Why John Paul II Was Right," *Telos*, No. 134 (Spring, 2006), p. 58.

[12] *Doe v. Bolton*, 410 U.S. 179, 188 (1973).

physicians who performed abortions to avoid what would otherwise have been the awkward circumstance of explaining why, if the physician's task was to preserve health and life, they were deliberately taking human life. The court's decision was not the result of a stipulative definition of "health;" it did not decree that "henceforth 'health' shall mean the following...." Instead, it resorted to semantic legerdemain by subsuming the word under the broader term "well being" and then asking what the attributes of that term were. Having rightly determined that well-being takes into account not only physical and mental health but also decent social and economic conditions along with one's age at the time of pregnancy, the justices then reintroduced the word "health," only this time laden with the attributes of the broader term "well being." "Health" was henceforth "well being."

By elevating induced abortion on request to the level of a therapeutic procedure, the court's display of semantic creativity whitewashed the abortionist by conferring on him the title "healer."

Ideology vs. Knowledge

The above examples testify to the power that ideology can exert on the minds and hearts of its adherents, a power so great as to lead them to believe that the righteousness and urgency of their cause licenses them to transcend the injunctions of truth, open-mindedness and the evidence of everyday experience, science and philosophy. Yves R. Simon's masterful critique of the difference between ideology and philosophy illuminates the allure the former exerts, even on those who profess a formal and solemn dedication to seek truth.

> According to the familiar use of the word, an ideology is a system of propositions which, though undistinguishable so far as expression goes from statements about facts and essences, actually refer not so much to any real state of affairs as to the aspirations of a society at a certain time in its evolution. These are the three components which, taken together, distinguish ideology from philosophy. The notion of truth which an ideology embodies is utilitarian, sociological, and evolutionistic. When what is actually an expression of aspirations assumes the form of statements about things, when these aspirations are those of a definite group, and when that group expresses its timely

aspirations in the language of everlasting truth – then, without a doubt, it is an ideology that we are dealing with.[13]

To satisfy the criterion of being sociological, it is not necessary that an ideology be embraced by society as a whole. It is sufficient if a group within that society embraces it, for example, the medical profession, scientific community, or academics. Eventually, of course, the ideology will, more often than not, find its way into the larger society, especially when it is initially held by the teaching profession or the media. It was a common tactic of Marxist groups, knowing theirs was but a minority viewpoint, to gain control of the centers of education and the media in order to "educate" the populace.

The utilitarian characteristic only makes sense because ideology aims to achieve a certain result in society by altering or destroying and then rebuilding social, economic, and political institutions. Hence, Marx wrote: "The philosophers have only *interpreted* the world in different ways; the point is to *change* it."[14] Simon appropriately parallels ideological activity with what the Scholastics call "transitive activity," activity that has no meaning or value in itself but is undertaken entirely to achieve a specified effect. Once the effect is achieved, the activity loses its rationale. Because, for example, philanthropy seeks to aid the poor, the elimination of all poverty would render philanthropy meaningless.[15] Finally, ideology must be evolutionary, for its credibility depends on the conviction that its goal is progressive, that it signals an improvement and even the fulfillment of the existing state of things.

Most importantly, an ideology must be credible if it is to attract a following. That means that it must claim to be rationally grounded; hence, the materialism propounded by the Marxists was "scientific" materialism. Not to be left behind, the pro-abortionists cloak their

---

[13] Yves R. Simon, *The Tradition of Natural Law* (New York: Fordham University Press, 1992), pp. 16-17.

[14] *Karl Marx: Selected Writings in Sociology and Social Philosophy*, edited by T.B. Bottomore & Maximilien Rubel; tr. by T. B. Bottomore (Harmonsworth, Middlesex: Penguin Books, Ltd., 1963), p. 84.

[15] Jacques Maritain, *Scholasticism and Politics,* translation edited by Mortimer Adler (Garden City, New York: Image Books, 1960), pp.163-64.

unscientific and irrational ideology behind facades of scientific and rational integrity. Simon writes:

> Indeed, in order to fulfill its utilitarian, social, and historical function, an ideology must have the appearance of a philosophy and express itself in terms of universal truth. Sincerity is a thing which admits of many degrees, and if the adherents to an ideology did not believe with some sort of sincerity that they were adhering to incontrovertible facts and essential necessities, the ideology simply would not work.[16]

If it is taken as an incontrovertible universal truth that a woman's right to control her reproduction is primary, then easy access to legal and safe abortion becomes not only a moral imperative but a dictate of reason also. Granted the existence of some advocates of abortion on request who concede that induced abortion is the deliberate killing of a human being,[17] the abortion ideology could never have found social, political, and juridical acceptance if the evidence from the science of embryology had not been flouted in favor of claims that the moment when human life begins is unclear and subject to honest dispute among scientists, theologians, and philosophers, as in *Roe v. Wade*, which claims that human life/personhood comes into being at some designated time after conception. In any case, an ideology has a dynamism, a mad energy generated by commitment to an ideal for humankind, that persuades the ideologue that the highest of moral imperatives is to do whatever is necessary for the realization of that ideal, even if that means transcending the injunctions of truth in science and philosophy while maintaining the needed façade of truthful inquiry. All of which leads Simon to zero in on the heart of ideology and philosophy respectively: the object of an ideology is an object of "desire," while the object of philosophy is a "pure object."

> In contrast with ideology, the law of philosophy is altogether one of objectivity. The object of an aspiration is not a pure object;

---

[16] Simon, *Tradition of Natural Law*, p. 18.

[17] E.g., Naomi Wolf, "Our Bodies, Our Souls," *The New Republic* (October 16, 1995); Sally Markowitz, "A Feminist Defense of Abortion," *Social Theory and Practice*, Vol. 16, 1 (Spring, 1990).

> it is an object and it is something else, viz., an end, just as the object of transitive action is an effect. The object of cognition alone is a pure object; this is one of the best approaches to a definition of cognition. It is by being an end (or a way to an end) that the thing desirable takes on the capacity of object in regard to desire, and it is by being an effect that the thing effected (or to be effected) takes on the capacity of object in regard to transitive action. The object of an ideology is, in spite of appearances without which the ideology would not work, an object of desire. The object of philosophy is a pure object.[18]

When referring in this passage to an object of philosophy as a pure object, Simon clearly has in mind speculative knowledge – *knowledge for the sake of knowing* as opposed to practical knowledge – *knowledge for the sake of acting*: the lover of truth submits his act of knowing entirely to the object, projecting no desire to reshape or redefine it. The result is what is called objective knowledge. In contrast, the object of an ideology cannot be a pure object, since, for one thing, its existence is not independent of the ideologue, for it is an idea that he desires to realize in the world. For another thing, just because it is an idea that he desires to see in existence, it is inevitably laden with *his* desires. Although focused differently, Simon's construal of ideology is not that different from Karl Mannheim's: "ideology is a 'quest for reality," but one that is relevant only for practice; it is 'an instrument for dealing with life-situations.'"[19] Nor does it differ substantially from Henry D. Aiken, who writes that the nineteenth-century philosophers became involved in a gigantic task of ideological and cultural reconstruction which precluded the very possibility of doing philosophy in the time-honored 'rational' and 'objective' ways which had prevailed in Western philosophy since the time of Plato and Aristotle.

The primary and most obvious harm the pro-abortion ideology has already done is the deliberate killing of close to 49 million innocent human beings in the United States alone since *Roe v. Wade* in 1973. This

---

[18] Simon, *Tradition of Natural Law*, p. 21.

[19] Wm. Oliver Martin, *Metaphysics and Ideology* (Milwaukee: Marquette University Press, 1959), 1.

legally sanctioned practice strikes at the heart of democratic society insofar as it makes the primary constitutional right, the right to life, a negotiable item. Deliberately killing human beings is now allowed, under the authority of a constitutionally protected right to privacy, for morally irrelevant reasons. The grim consequences of this for human life, both inside and outside of the womb, are obvious, for the appeal to morally irrelevant reasons to justify killing means that no one is safe. Yves Simon makes this point with airtight logic:

> The prohibition of murder is not relative to any of the aspects in which men are unequal but to features pertaining to the unity of human nature. Murdering an ignorant person is just as much a murder as murdering a well-educated person; education does not matter and degrees of education make no difference. Murdering a colored man is just as much a murder as murdering a white man; the law prohibiting murder is in no way relative to such contingencies as color or other so-called "race" features. Murdering a cancerous patient is just as much a murder as murdering a healthy person; it is not on account of health that murder is prohibited but on account of universally human features, common to healthy and to diseased persons. *Murdering an unborn child is just as much a murder as murdering an adult man; the phase of life in which murder takes place is altogether incidental.*[20]

As acknowledged above, the first and most serious consequence of pro-abortion ideology is the widespread deliberate killing of innocent human beings. Another harmful consequence is the loss of trust and community. Rom Harré emphasizes the need for trust as a value in the scientific community:

> These actual standards of value are closely tied up with the idea of mutual trust. They invoke a certain measure of public reliability. Scientists believe that things personally unknown to them are as another scientist says they are. And this trust is itself based upon shared standards of work and adherence to the common moral order. 'Seek truth and eschew falsehood' is not a

---

[20] Yves R. Simon, *Philosophy of Democratic Government* (Chicago: The University of Chicago Press, 1951), p. 203; emphasis added.

> methodological principle but a moral injunction. It has to do with the conditions under which trust is maintained. Trust is not maintained by telling each other only literal truths. Under that constraint the members of the community would perforce remain forever silent. It is enough that they tell each other what they honestly believe to be the truth.[21]

But the injunction to honesty is not always observed among scientists, particularly when they commit themselves to purposes that collide with the evidence gained from their research. In 1866, Ernest Haeckel formulated his Biogenetic Law, otherwise known as the recapitulation theory: "Ontogeny [the embryological development of an individual] is a brief and rapid recapitulation [review] of the phylogeny [evolutionary history of the organism],"[22] which teaches that "the embryo of a complex animal goes through stages resembling its ancestors...."[23] Haeckel's theory attained textbook status and for decades was accepted as the explanation for the supposed fact that the human embryo has primitive gill slits. But Haeckel was guilty of outright fraud. In 1874, biologist Wilhelm His was able to demonstrate that to support his Biogenetic Law, Haeckel had purposely altered previous drawings of human and dog embryos.[24] Why did he tamper with the evidence? It seems that Haeckel was a true believer in Darwinian evolution,[25] perhaps remaining convinced that since the validity of evolutionary theory was beyond dispute, the distortion of lower truths was justified by the cause of service to that higher truth. But Haeckel was but a single person. What happens when a government throws its support behind deceitful intellectuals?

---

[21] Rom Harré, *Varieties of Realism, A Rationale for the Natural Sciences* (Oxford: U.K.: Basil Blackwell, 1986), p. 12.

[22] Percival Davis & Dean H. Kenyon, *Of Pandas and People: The Central Question of Biological Origins*, 2nd Edition (Dallas, Texas: Haughton Publishing Company, 1993), p. 129.

[23] Quoted in Eric J. Blievernicht, "Gill Slits in Human Fetuses?" http://rae.org/gillslit.html, p. 1.

[24] Ibid., p. 1.

[25] Ibid.

Nazi ideology is a case in point of what happens when ideology is allowed to trump knowledge. Two German Nobel Prize winning physicists, Philipp Lenard and Johannes Stark, led a group of "national researchers" in an effort to develop a German or Aryan physics, dismissing Einstein's relativity theory as "Jewish world-bluff." The two did not hesitate to hector and verbally intimidate colleagues who subscribed to relativity theory and quantum mechanics.[26] In 1936, the new rector of the University of Berlin instituted no fewer than 25 courses in racial science (*Rassenkunde*), purporting to supply scientific support for the Nazi claims of superiority of the Aryan race and the inferiority of the Jews,[27] when, in fact, the courses consisted of systematically distorted scientific claims. The replacement of inquiry and the love of truth with the specious certitudes of Nazi ideology produced a devastating result on the life and mission of the university:

> The teaching of the natural sciences, in which Germany had been so preeminent for generations, deteriorated rapidly. Great teachers such as Einstein and Franck in physics, Haber, Willstaetter and Warburg in chemistry, were either fired or retired. Those who remained, many of them, were bitten by the Nazi aberrations and attempted to apply them to pure science. They began to teach what they called German physics, German chemistry, and German mathematics. Indeed, in 1937 there appeared a journal called *Deutsche Mathematik*, and its first editorial solemnly proclaimed that any idea that mathematics could be judged nonracially carried "within itself the germs of destruction of German science.[28]

Science in the USSR fared no better. It was a Stalinist dogma that the science developed in the capitalist West was "bourgeois science." The communists hoped that Soviet science would eventually rival Western science and, in the end, surpass it. But even after the end of World War

---

[26]Leslie Stevenson and Henry Byerly, *The Many Faces of Science: An Introduction to Scientists, Values, and Society* (Boulder: Westview Press, 1995), p. 167.

[27]William L. Shirer, *The Rise and Fall of the Third Reich: A History of Nazi Germany* (New York: Simon and Schuster, 1960), p. 250.

[28] Ibid., p. 250.

II, it was clear that, with the exception of physics, the sciences in the USSR had not made any progress worth talking about. A major figure in the Soviet scientific program was the biologist, Trofim Denisovich Lysenko. In 1940, Stalin appointed him director of the Institute of Genetics of the USSR Academy of Sciences, and by 1948 he had managed to attain absolute control over Soviet biology. Having the might of the Soviet Union at his disposal, Lysenko succeeded in repressing support among Soviet biologists for the Mendelian doctrine of hereditary genetic transmission, despite its worldwide acceptance by the scientific community.[29]

If obstructing a nation's progress in scientific research is bad enough, the loss of trust among scientists is itself also a terrible price to pay. But the payment does not end there. The lies and distortions that permeate elitist circles is a malignancy that will sooner or later spread to the public sphere, especially when, like the abortion debate, it pertains to the daily lives of ordinary human beings. When mistrust runs rampant in the population, civic virtue slowly withers, for, as a plant needs water, civic virtue cannot live without mutual trust. And without civic virtue, there can be no community of persons. As Hannah Arendt observed, the inability of a people to tell fact from fiction is one of the conditions for the rise of totalitarianism. In an atmosphere of conflicting opinions and skepticism, the authoritarian leader assumes in the eyes of the public an attractiveness that he could never have had otherwise. In the midst of their confusion, the people look to him for guidance. It made no difference to the German people when the facts proved Hitler's wild assertions to be false; they continued to believe and follow him.[30]

Ideology's Internal Contradiction

The inspiration and energy of an ideology come far more from an object of will than of reason, despite the ideologue's claims to the contrary. August Comte and his followers preceded Karl Marx in the attempt to establish sociology as the dominant field of knowledge. But

---

[29] Stevenson and Byerly, *Many Faces of Science*, pp. 165-67.

[30] Hannah Arendt, *The Origins of Totalitarianism* (New York: Harcourt Brace Jovanovich, 1973), p. 305, n. 1, and pp. 373-74.

the attempt rests on a premise that is incompatible with the premise that philosophy's object is the "pure object." For, if the validation of a statement's truth is preponderant social affirmation, then, of course, a pure object of knowledge must be regarded as a fiction. Consider, for example, Karl Marx's claim that all consciousness is conditioned by the modes of human production[31] or Thomas S. Kuhn's claim that it is impossible to determine whether science makes progress because the paradigm of what constitutes science is composed of non-rational, non-scientific cultural components that change from era to era.[32] There can be no doubt that socio-economic forces shape human consciousness; we are, after all, social beings. But it is quite another thing to say that such forces exert so powerful an influence as to render the human intellect incapable of arriving at objective, ahistorical, transcultural knowledge. And while it is equally beyond doubt that our fundamental scientific outlooks of the universe have changed radically since the Ptolemaic system, it does not necessarily follow that this leaves us bereft of any way of judging whether science makes progress. The fact that we are capable of ever more precise and successful prediction in science is perhaps a reliable standard of progress.[33] At all events, anyone who embraces the view that science is the standard of all knowledge of reality and, at the same time, accepts the claim that the standard of scientific knowledge is not grounded in rational considerations but instead in broad psychological and social elements will find himself in the same camp as the Marxists, holding that all knowledge is socially conditioned.

The problem with sociologism is that it harbors an internal contradiction. This contradiction bedevils the sociology of knowledge in general. Consider the proposition of knowledge so dear to Marxists and sociologists: "All knowledge is socially conditioned." It is one thing to construct a universe of discourse, *D'*, in which all propositions are composed of terms that are assigned meanings on the basis of their

---

[31] *Karl Marx: Selected Writings*, p. 67.

[32] Thomas S. Kuhn, *The Structure of Scientific Revolutions*, 2nd ed. (Chicago: University of Chicago Press, 1975), Ch 2.

[33] W.H. Newton-Smith, *The Rationality of Science* (London: Routledge and Kegan Paul, 1981), pp. 38ff.

relation to all the other terms in that universe, so that *pd'1* cannot be understood apart from its position in relation to pd'2, *pd'3, pd'4* ... and they, in turn, cannot be understood apart from *pd'1*, etc. While it would be true to say that every proposition in that universe of discourse is "socially" conditioned and thus cannot be understood apart from the other propositions, the term "all propositions" applies only to universe of discourse *D'*. The latter constitutes an *object language* that depends on a *meta-language, D*, for its meanings. The meanings that the meta-language assigns to the propositions that comprise the object language need not pertain to the propositions that comprise the meta-language.

But when the term *all knowledge* is taken as unrestricted in its extension, then the statement, "All knowledge is socially conditioned," is itself socially conditioned. Since the statement is supposed to mean that because all knowledge is socially conditioned, it is, to that extent, not objective, one can infer that the statement itself is socially conditioned and, to that extent, not objective. If the sociologist of knowledge wishes to extricate himself from this muddle, he will have to show why the knowledge claims asserted by the sociology of knowledge are not socially conditioned, and this he cannot do without contradicting himself or admitting that the statement is false. That is the fatal weakness of ideology.

Rejecting the object of philosophy, the pure object, the ideologue is left only with his demiurgic drive to impose an ideal on the world, and for this he must claim that the meanings of institutions, practices, and realities, like human beings, are social constructions that, accordingly, have only the value that society confers on them. These characteristics express themselves today in the pro-abortion and feminist movements, and indeed both have a Marxist ring to them. The principal argument advanced by feminists is based on equality: women can never achieve the equality enjoyed by men until they have the power to control their reproduction. And true liberation requires not only economic equality but gender equality as well. But the latter goal will forever remain out of women's reach as long as social institutions rest upon the belief that gender is a biological imperative rather than a social construct. To show that it is the latter, Marta Llama presents us with a minimum of five genders: (1) men (persons with two testicles); 2) women (persons with two ovaries); 3) hermaphrodites (persons who simultaneously have one testicle and one ovary); 4) masculine hermaphrodites (persons with testicles but who also display other female sexual characteristics); 5) feminine hermaphrodites (persons with ovaries but who also display male sexual characteristics.)[34] Her point in adverting to this panoply is to support the contention of the gender feminists that the traditional division of the sexes exclusively into male and female is a social decree rather than a biological imperative since the other three manifestations of sexuality are equally real. Although the ontology of physical differences between men and women cannot be written off as social constructions, the psychological and intellectual differences can be explained as products of socialization. But this explanation requires buying into the feminist fable of a paradisiacal time long ago when male and female were the same in those parts of their being until the biological imperative of bearing and nursing children confined women to the home while men remained free to build culture.[35]

Therefore, the claim that all ontology is really ideological reveals itself as more dogmatic than rational. By its own admission, it is not an ontological proposition, since "All knowledge is socially conditioned" can only be a proposition about knowledge, not about things or events. Society's acceptance of propositions as "true" must therefore rest on pragmatism: the particular social construction produces results deemed desirable and is accordingly held to be "true" or "good." So the ideologist finds himself in the position of having to admit that pragmatism is a true philosophical proposition about human knowledge. But this conclusion is incompatible with any claim that pragmatism is not ideology; instead, it must be the philosophical foundation of ideology. An ironic outcome this: an ideological idea of ontological truth as really social truth rests on a non-ideological idea of truth about the nature of knowledge.[36]

The internal contradiction of the sociologism embedded in ideology thus fails to dissolve ontology, which remains independent of epistemic

---

[34] Babette Francis, "Is Gender a Social Construct or a Biological Imperative?" *Family Futures: Issues in Research and Policy*, 7th Australian Institute of Family Studies Conference, Sydney (July 24-26, 2000), p.2.

[35] Sherry Ortner, *Making Gender: The Politics and Erotics of Culture* (Boston: Beacon Press, 1996), Ch 2.

[36] Martin, *Metaphysics and Ideology*, p. 79, n.1.

claims. On the contrary, epistemology depends on things; *ontology precedes epistemology:* things are the measure of mind; mind is not the measure of things. That independence refutes, above all, the self-destructive statement, "all knowledge is socially conditioned." Philosophy's task is not to change the world but to discover the truth of things in the world, for example, the truth about unborn humans, as the premise for how they ought to be treated.

FAIRNESS, FREEDOM, AND RESPONSIBILITY

Montague Brown

It is natural and good to insist on fairness. If we have been unduly burdened with a task, we rightly object. We do not mind so much if others also have the same disagreeable task, but an unequal imposition of responsibility infringes on our freedom. It seems unjust that we should have to bear such an infringement. Sometimes the burden is by way of someone in need. When faced with situations where someone needs our help, what are our responsibilities?

To focus the discussion, let us consider the abortion issue and, in particular, the case of pregnancy through rape. There seem to be a couple of levels of unfairness here. On the first level, and most generally, two people are involved in causing a pregnancy, and only one has to carry the child to term. On a deeper level, the woman who is pregnant through rape is in no way responsible for becoming pregnant, yet her freedom will be dramatically curtailed if she brings the pregnancy to term. Why should her life have to be ruined? Nobody else has to bear this burden; it seems unfair that she should have to. More than this, she has suffered the obvious injustice of rape. How is this to be remedied?

Our discussion will be divided into three sections. In the first, we shall consider briefly the issue of abortion in general. In the second, we shall take up the special case of ending a pregnancy due to rape, looking at how it differs from other abortion cases and to what degree these differences are morally significant. In the third section, we shall consider the dimensions of freedom and responsibility in the special case of pregnancy due to rape and in our relations with others.

I

In this first section, let us sketch briefly the best arguments for insisting on including all stages of human life from conception to death under the umbrella of the right to life. If the zygote/embryo/fetus has an intrinsic right to life, such a right should never be directly violated. Thus, the zygote/embryo/fetus should never be subject to the direct attack of an abortion.

When Thomas Aquinas lays out the principles of the natural law, he holds that "good is to be done and promoted, and evil is to be avoided."[1] In the realm of moral responsibility, we have a more absolute duty to avoid evil than we do to promote the good. Thus is grounded that most obvious of moral absolutes: do not intentionally violate the good of innocent human life. Our responsibilities to promote the good of human life, which we shall discuss later, are much less specific, and apparently less absolute. For besides the good of human life, there are other goods which have intrinsic value, such as friendship, knowledge, and beauty.[2] So, promoting good is not equivalent to promoting the good of life. We are not all required to procreate; we are not all required to become doctors or nurses or researchers in the life sciences. We can, without being immoral, enter politics, study metaphysics, or write poetry.

Although it seems straightforward to say that we should never intentionally take the life of an innocent human being, the problem in abortion is not solved, for one can ask what constitutes a human being. Is there a stage of development before which the zygote/embryo/fetus (or, to follow such contemporary thinkers as Peter Singer, Michael Tooley, and Mary Anne Warren, the new-born child[3]) is not yet human?

---

[1] Thomas Aquinas, *Summa Theologica* (hereafter *ST*) I-II.94.2.c, 5 vols. translated by Fathers of the English Dominican Province (Allen, Texas: Christian Classics, 1981), 1, p. 1009.

[2] In *ST* I-II.94.2.c, Aquinas mentions the self-evident goods of life, procreation, knowledge, and orderly social life (friendship). Contemporary thinkers Germain Grisez and John Finnis, among others, have developed this theory, pointing out other basic goods found in the natural law tradition and elsewhere in Aquinas. For the basic principles of this theory, see Germain Grisez, *Way of the Lord Jesus: Christian Moral Principles*, 3 vols. (Chicago: Franciscan Herald Press, 1983-97), and John Finnis, *Natural Law and Natural Rights* (Oxford: Clarendon Press, 1980).

[3] These thinkers argue that a human being does not have a right to life until specifically human activities such as self-awareness, rationality, and freedom are exhibited, normally at about two years of age. Thus, they argue for the permissibility of infanticide up until this time. See Peter Singer, *Practical Ethics* (Cambridge: Cambridge University Press, 1979), pp.122-26; Michael Tooley,"Abortion and Infanticide," *Philosophy & Public Affairs*, 2, no. 1 (Fall 1972): 37-65; and Mary Anne Warren,"On the Moral and Legal Status of Abortion," *The Monist*, 57, no. 1 (January, 1973): 43-61.

The arguments in favor of denying the right to life to any stage of human life subsequent to conception are unconvincing, for these stages do not signal substantial changes, but only accidental changes.[4] Even Judith Thomson admits as much in her 1981 article "A Defense of Abortion."[5] The changes are in terms of things like quantity, quality, time, place, and relation, and not in terms of the kind of thing it is. Thus, just as my status as a human being is not changed by changes in my weight, my hair color, the time of day, my position in the room, or my relative dependence on others, so too the accidental changes from conception to birth, although more dramatic perhaps, do not change the kind of thing that continuously exists from conception to birth. Let us look briefly at the arguments from biology, philosophy, and law on this matter.

Embryologists universally agree that biological life begins at conception. At that point there is a being with its own unique and non-repeatable set of chromosomes. True, there could still be twinning, but that does not mean that we do not have an individual now - only that we will have two individuals then. The disagreement, when there is one, is more semantic than biological.[6] Without doubt, a new living being, which is neither sperm nor egg, exists at conception. The artificial procedure of conception known as *in vitro* fertilization makes this clear: the doctor imitates nature, forcibly joining sperm and egg to create new life, so that the infertile couple can have a child. The debate is about whether to call this zygote "human life." Philosophically, we can say that from the moment of conception there is a unique

---

[4] Aristotle distinguishes substance and accidents in his *Categories*. Specifically, "a substance as such is never truly said to vary in degree in time or as compared with another substance." Aristotle, *Categories* 5 [4a6] in *Aristotle Selected Works*, edited and translated by Hippocrates C. Apostle and Lloyd P. Gerson (Grinnell, Iowa: Peripatetic Press, 1982), p. 34.

[5] "I am inclined to agree, however, that the prospects for 'drawing a line' in the development of the fetus look dim." Judith Jarvis Thomson, "A Defense of Abortion, " *Philosophy and Public Affairs*, 1, no. 1 (Fall, 1971): 47-66, p. 47.

[6] See Dr. and Mrs. J. C. Willke, *Abortion: Questions and Answers* III.7 (Cincinnati: Hayes Publishing Co., 1990), pp. 40-43; and Patrick Lee, *Abortion and Unborn Human Life* (Washington, D.C.: Catholic University of America Press, 1996), pp. 69-73.

individual with his or her own life-force, the same life-force that will sustain the human being throughout his or her entire life. Without this unique life-force, there would be no growth or development. Sure the zygote/embryo/fetus depends on the mother for nourishment, but it does not depend on the mother for its ability to take the nourishment and transform it into growth. There is no substantial change – that is, change from one kind of thing (genus/species) to another – only accidental changes of quantity, quality, time, place, relation, etc.[7] Perhaps, one might argue, as did Aquinas, that there is a process of delayed hominization,[8] that the rational soul cannot be infused until the matter is sufficiently developed. If, as Aquinas argues, the rational soul is the only form of the human being,[9] then, before it is infused, there is no human being. There is some plausibility to this theory, but it is not a demonstrated fact or a necessary truth. How could it be since, as Aquinas makes very clear, the rational soul is immaterial and can exist on its own?[10] If this is so, then it could exist with a zygote as well. And in matters where there is some doubt, one should always take the morally safer course. Since it cannot be proven when the rational soul is infused, and killing an innocent human being is a grave moral wrong, we should give the benefit of the doubt to the zygote and consider it human. The clarity with which biology has shown the zygote to be the product of man and woman (and not from the male alone, as Aristotle and Aquinas thought) gives added reason to take the moment of conception as the definitive beginning of human life.

There is even a medical and legal distinction now in place related to biological death which, if consistently applied, could be used to define the moment human life begins. The distinction comes into play regarding the argument many hold which claims that an embryo, in the early stages, is just a bunch of cells. Since it is not wrong to remove a bunch of cells from the human body so that they die, as in surgery, so it

---

[7] Richard Werner makes this argument in his article "Abortion: The Ontological and Moral Status of the Unborn," in *Today's Moral Problems*, edited by Richard Wasserstrom (New York: Macmillan, 1979).

[8] Aquinas, *ST* I.76.3ad3, and *ST* I.118.2ad2.

[9] Ibid, I.76.3.

[10] Ibid, I.75.2.

is not wrong to remove the embryo so that it dies. In an article in *First Things*, Maureen L. Condic suggests that there is already a way of distinguishing human life from a bunch of living cells, worked out by those who have need of distinguishing the boundary of life and death at the end of life:

> The medical and legal definition of death draws a clear distinction between living cells and living organisms. Organisms are living beings composed of parts that have separate but mutually dependent functions.... The critical difference between a collection of cells and a living organism is the ability of an organism to act in a coordinated manner for the continued health and maintenance of the body as a whole. It is precisely this ability that breaks down at the moment of death, however death might occur.[11]

When we apply this same distinction to the beginning of life, we find that the embryo satisfies the same criteria as does life in its latter stages. "Embryos are in full possession of the very characteristic that distinguishes a living human being from a dead one: the ability of all cells in the body to function together as an organism, with all parts acting in an integrated manner for the continued life and health of the body as a whole."[12]

Given that one should never choose directly against the good of innocent human life and that embryos are innocent human lives, the conclusion that one should never take the life of an embryo logically follows.

II

There are, however, three cases that many people who consider abortion in general to be wrong count as exceptions. These are when the mother's life is in danger, when the pregnancy is due to rape, and

---

[11] Maureen L. Condic. "Life: Defining the Beginning by the End," *First Things* 133 (2003): 50-54, p. 52. See also, Germain Grisez, *The Way of the Lord Jesus*, Vol. 2 pp. 493-94.

[12] Condic, "Life," p. 52.

when the embryo is severely handicapped (or is likely to be so because of incest).

The last we should reject out of hand since to accept it is to accept a sliding scale in honoring human life. We are all defective in one way or another – if not physically, then emotionally, intellectually, and always morally. No two of us are exactly equal in intelligence, ability, and moral integrity. Since we do not accord adult human beings the right to life according to their perfection, neither should we accord rights on this basis to embryos.

The case of abortion as the only way to save the life of the mother is a complicated one. We allow that people have a right to preserve their lives: killing in self-defense is legitimate, though it must be only as a last resort.[13] Thus, abortion in the case of the mother's life being threatened could be a legitimate act if it could be shown that the intention is life-saving and that the death of the child is only an unintended side-effect that is accepted but not chosen. The issue is complex but moot in most cases, since it is nearly always possible to save both the life of the child and that of the mother.

The case for the legitimacy of abortion in cases of rape is the one on which I would like to focus. Happily such cases are very rare, for a variety of reasons: the woman is fertile for only a few days of her menstrual cycle; in many cases there is lack of penetration or premature ejaculation; and the trauma of rape often prevents the pregnancy from occurring.[14] Still, such pregnancies do sometimes occur, and we should ask whether these cases should be exceptions to the prohibition against abortion. On the face of it, the argument to permit abortion in pregnancies due to rape is less strong than in pregnancies that threaten the life of the mother since in the latter case what is lost and gained is a proportional good – human life. In rape cases, the good that is lost – human life – is not commensurate to the good that is gained (if it is indeed gained) – peace of mind, freedom from a dependent child, prevention of financial or emotional burden, etc.

---

[13] See Thomas Aquinas, *ST* II-II.64.7.c.

[14] See Willke, *Abortion*, 150.

The case of rape does, however, involve a moral dimension not found in the case of an action taken to save the mother's life – the injustice perpetrated on the woman. She is not pregnant by choice, nor was it an accident: she has been forced against her will. Normally, responsibility comes with freedom of choice. Only acts done by free choice can be right or wrong. This is Judith Thomson's point in her famous violinist analogy in "A Defense of Abortion": since you did not give your assent to the violinist (or his caregivers), you have no obligation to let him remain plugged into you. Nor, it seems, does the woman pregnant through rape have any responsibility to carry the child to term. We are responsible for our chosen actions and for the normal consequences they entail. But sexual intercourse in the case of rape is not the woman's action; it happens to her, but she does not choose it. This is unlike the case of accidental pregnancy, where the woman might plead that she did not intend to become pregnant. Her choice to engage in the act of sexual intercourse, which is naturally linked as cause and effect to the coming to be of new life, makes her responsible. In the case of rape, however, it does not seem that she is responsible for the pregnancy that such an action entails, nor for bringing that pregnancy to term.

As we begin a discussion of abortion in rape cases, it is essential that we admit fully and unequivocally that bringing the child to term is a burden on the woman. Moreover, it seems that it is not one she should have to undergo. There are really two instances of unfairness here: the rape itself, and the consequent requirement to bear the child. The rape is not only unfair; it is unjust. It violates the integrity of the woman as well as the good of orderly social life (and, in addition, the law). It also violates the good of procreation, for life is best brought into the world in the context of mutual love and support; that is, rape is a violation of the right of the child to come to be in a loving environment.

The second unfairness – the requirement that the woman should carry the child to term – is the particular one at issue in this paper. Why should she have to accept a burden that she did not freely accept? Here the relations between freedom, fairness, and responsibility are brought most closely into focus. After all, if someone arbitrarily throws a fifty-pound pack on my back, am I obliged to carry it? If someone promises that I will pay back his friend for the money he borrows, am I obliged to do so? Unless there are extenuating circumstances, the answer is "No" to each question. So why should a woman who is pregnant through rape be obliged to carry the child to term?

One critical difference between pregnancy through rape and these cases is that a child is intrinsically valuable, whereas the pack and the money are not. The act that frees the mother from the child (abortion) is a direct violation of the basic human good of life – the life of the child. But the woman might say that she does not want the child to die: she just does not want to undergo the imposition of carrying the child to term. She directly intends only the goods of freedom and peace of mind; the death of the child is an unintended side effect. If this imposition could be removed without killing the child, she would do it; but such a removal cannot be done, given the current state of medicine. Why should she have to carry this physical and emotional burden? She did not in any sense assent to it, nor was it in the normal course of things (such as a child's duty to help out around the house even though the child did not assent to being born).

One could argue that dying of cancer is not in the normal course of things, and yet the patient should not commit suicide. The patient did not freely accept the illness; on the contrary, she would undoubtedly be happy to be free from it. Nevertheless, because life is an intrinsic good, she is morally obliged to refrain from suicide as a way of escaping her suffering. Here, like the case of rape, the burden is of intrinsic value – the life of a human being who does not deserve to die. What is missing in this case, but present in the case of rape, is the willful violation of the woman. Human justice exists to address willful violations. Just as when I steal from you, the law requires that I pay you back to right the balance I have upset, so it seems some redress is due the woman who is pregnant through rape. But here, of course, is the important distinction: punishment is due the rapist who willfully violated the woman, not the child who is completely innocent of all wrongdoing; yet abortion kills the child. Clearly, the child should not pay the price of the violation with his or her life.

When presenting the precepts of the natural law, Thomas Aquinas says that, besides our strict obligation not to violate basic goods such as life, truth, and friendship, we also have an obligation to promote them. We are not merely supposed to refrain from hurting people; we are supposed to help them. In fact, although the requirement not to take innocent human life is more absolute than the requirement to promote human life, the negative insight into the strict prohibition against taking life is based on the positive insight into the good of life. We only know that violating life is bad because we know that life is good. Badness is always parasitic on good. We know a bad pen (one that blots or fails to write) by knowing what a good pen should be. We know a sick dog because we know what a healthy one should be. Likewise, we know the badness of violating life because we know life to be good. When Aquinas talks about this obligation to help others, he grants that we have no absolute obligation to help everyone in need. Since it is not possible to help everyone, we can have no obligation to do it. It is enough, he says, for us to help those we meet who are in great need and who have no one else to help them. "Since one cannot do good to all, we ought to consider those chiefly who by reason of place, time, or any other circumstance, by a kind of chance, are more closely united to us."[15] Not everyone in need has the same claim on our aid. "If, however, it is easy to see how he can be otherwise succored, either by himself, or by some other person still more closely united to him or in a better position to help him, one is not strictly bound to help the one in need."[16] However, because of the fact that until viability, at least, the mother is the only one who can help this child, it seems that she has a strong obligation to do so.

We said at the outset that our positive obligations to help others are not as strict as our obligations not to harm others. But it seems that in some cases the positive obligation approaches the same level of absoluteness as the negative. Consider the following scenario: Suppose I'm walking on the beach minding my own business, thinking of some metaphysical problem or just enjoying the beautiful day. As I'm walking along, I come upon a young child lying face-down in a tide pool struggling to get out. Can I just walk on by thinking of my problem or enjoying the day and do nothing, or am I obliged to help the child up? Clearly, I am obliged to help the child. In the first place, the need is dire – life is at stake. In the second place, I am the only one around. And in the third place, it is easy for me to save the child. When these three

---

[15] Augustine, *On Christian Doctrine* I.28, quoted in Aquinas, *ST* II-II.71.1c, 3; p. 1491.

[16] Aquinas, loc. cit.

things come together, the positive obligation to save life approaches the absolute status of the prohibition against taking life.

It is not my fault: I did not mean for the child to fall into the pool. Nor was I doing anything irresponsible that might have led to the scenario. Nevertheless, I cannot just mind my own business: I am morally obliged to help the child. The case of pregnancy through rape is similar. It is not the woman's fault: she did not mean to get pregnant. Nor was it her irresponsibility that led to the pregnancy. Still, the child is in dire need: if the mother does not continue the pregnancy, the child will die. The mother is the only one who can help: given the current state of medicine, we are not able to take the embryo from the mother's womb and keep it alive until it can live on its own.[17] And it is relatively easy for the woman to continue the pregnancy. It is not that carrying a child to term is as easy as my reaching down to raise the head of the drowning child, but carrying a child to term is the normal way that new lives are brought into the world.

There is, however, the difference that, not only is the pregnancy not chosen by the woman (as I did not choose that the child should fall into the pool and be drowning), but the pregnancy was against the woman's will. Thus, it is doubly beside her free intention. Still, the intrinsic value of the child and the sole ability of the mother to save the child indicate her responsibility. In any case, it is not the child's fault that the mother is pregnant. It is not the child who acts against the woman's will. The rapist is guilty of a grave injustice and should be severely punished, but the child is entirely innocent.

There are many other cases in our lives where obligations come our way to which we did not agree beforehand. Consider the case of the responsibility we have to care for the elderly or the disabled – in particular those in our families. This is perhaps closer to our particular case since, just as the woman did not ask or consent to be pregnant, so we did not ask or consent to be born. We never freely agreed to have parents, so why should we be responsible for them? Yet clearly we have

---

[17] It is possible that, in time, we may be able to do so. If so, the obligation for the mother to carry the child to term would be significantly reduced since she would not be the only one who could keep the child alive.

obligations to them, and special ones at that, since they are our parents. Admittedly, this example does not involve an injustice, as in rape cases.

But, ultimately, unfairness or injustice does not change the obligation. It seems unfair that innocent bystanders who did not look for trouble should have to try to stop a mugger from beating up an old lady. Yet clearly, if they do nothing when they could have helped, they are morally and legally culpable. And why should a particular generation of young men have to risk their lives to defeat the uninvited aggression of Japan and Nazi Germany in World War II? Yet those young Americans who did not ask for the fight were obliged to defend their country and to go to the defense of our allies in Europe. So too in the case of pregnancy due to rape: the injustice is irrelevant to the responsibility of the bystander or citizen soldier. If there is a mugging or a war, although they had nothing to do with starting it, they must act to protect the common good. Although we clearly recognize the hardship that bystanders and soldiers face when they protect us, we think it is proper that they should do so. Is it fair that these people in particular should have to risk their lives or die for their fellow citizens? Not in particular, but someone must do so at times of crisis if the commonweal is to be protected. There is an unfair burden here, but it is their job to shoulder this responsibility. So, too, it is an unfair burden for a victim of rape to carry the child to term; nevertheless, it is her duty to shoulder the responsibility for the good of the child and of the community.

III

It has often been said that the goods intended by abortion due to rape – the healing, the peace of mind, the restoration of freedom – are actually not met by getting an abortion. Patrick Lee presents a number of important arguments on this issue in his book *Abortion and Unborn Human Life.*[18] These are points in addressing what seem to be the obvious positive reasons for having the abortion. But I would like to suggest another here – the goodness, for others and for oneself, of freely accepting the responsibilities which come our way.

---

[18] Lee, *Abortion,* pp. 123-24.

At issue in our discussion are two very different notions of freedom.[19] One stems from the social-contract tradition. On this view, our responsibilities are self-imposed, and we should be free *from* all responsibilities except those to which we agree. We give up our right to do anything we please in order to live in a society; therefore, we are obliged to obey the laws of that society. There are no other licit claims on our freedom. On this basis we should be free from any externally imposed responsibilities (much at play in our contemporary world). The second kind of freedom is quite different. It is a freedom *for* responsibility. That is, it is the ability to accept willingly and make our own those responsibilities we have to others. Often these responsibilities are externally imposed, not dependent on a prior assent from us. Such responsibilities are those we have for our parents and for our fellow human beings beyond just avoiding hurting them. But our willingness to accept them is a mark of moral maturity, of love in action.

The first kind of freedom and responsibility seems to be a kind of minimum for living in society; however, society itself cannot survive if this is all we have. If our relations with others are based merely on our prior assent, then all obligations to our parents and elders are void. And all responsibility to God is void, too. We did not agree to be born or created. But our obligations to be grateful to, to respect, and to honor parents and God are fundamental, for without parents and God we would not exist, nor would we have any goods at all.

The argument for this obligation has two premises, one from practical reason and one from theoretical reason. The practical premise is that we should be grateful for good done for us. This is a corollary of the self-evident principle that we should do good and avoid evil. Since I know that I seek the good and would be happy if I found it, if someone gives me the good, I should appreciate that gift. If you share your lunch with me when I forget mine, I should thank you. If you save my life, I should be grateful. But parents have given us life (a great good), and God has given us all goods including parents. The theoretical premise is

[19] These two kinds of freedom are distinguished by Germain Grisez and Russell Shaw in *Beyond the New Morality: The Responsibilities of Freedom* (Notre Dame: University of Notre Dame Press, 1980), ch. 1.

that we received our life from our parents and (needing more metaphysical proof) that we receive all good things from an ultimate source, the God the Creator. This we know theologically, but we can also know it philosophically, as demonstrated by Augustine, Aquinas and others (based on arguments from Plato and Aristotle).[20] Together these two premises imply that we should repay the good that parents and God have done for us. Since we cannot do this in kind, we do it by showing gratefulness and respect. In the case of what is owed to God (everything), we can pay nothing back (since He needs nothing); therefore, we should show our gratitude by giving to those around us.

Without gratitude for what we have been given, we can find no reason to give to others, except self-interest. Self-interest breaks down quickly as a basis for social life. For if self-interest guides us, then we do not care for other people in any sense for their own sakes. Therefore, as soon as we are able to renege on our promises to them without negative repercussions, we will do so. Such a basis for communal life is precarious at best. Certainly it is not a true community where there is free unity of wills.

To realize that "there but for the grace of parents and God go I" is to see one's being in the world in an entirely new light. Our role is not to avoid the effort of communion with others – striving for the least effort and the most pleasure. Rather, our role is to transform the disordered and unjust into the order of justice and love. Those who accept undeserved and even unjust suffering and turn it to the good, exercise their freedom in the fullest sense. In the first place, turning something to good must be a free choice, for there are no fully moral actions that are not free. Secondly, turning suffering toward the good takes enormous effort and willed sacrifice: there is no reason to believe that the person does so for selfish motives.[21] Through the free acceptance of

---

[20] See Aquinas, *ST* I.2.3.

[21] That is, unless one means by selfishness the rarefied meaning Aristotle gives it in Book IX of the *Nicomachean Ethics.* Here he points our (rightly, ultimately) that to be selfish in the most precise sense of the word is to care for what is most one's self, which is oneself as free and intelligent, rather than subject to the whims of pleasure or fancy. This self is benefited by virtuous action. The community benefits and the individual agent benefits.

responsibility in love, they transform the accidental into the ordered and the maliciously intended into acts of love. The free acceptance of suffering imposed on one against one's will takes what is disordered and transforms it through the order of intelligent will. The free acceptance of suffering due to injustice and malicious intent envelops what is evil within the generosity of love. The pregnant rape victim's acceptance of the advent of a new life works in both ways. This is a great good for society and a great good for the individual. In addition, it recognizes the clear truth that the child is entirely innocent and "infinitely" loveable.

To accept such suffering and hardship is a tall order, whether it be bringing a child to term, risking one's life for fellow citizens, or caring for infirm parents. Those who do accept it are rightly thought of as heroic. But they also commit themselves to the meaningful exercise of their freedom for the sake of others. This is a great moral good for the individual agent and a great political good for the community. And it is an opportunity to share in the providence of God,[22] which is worked out through the free gift of self to others - even to the point of death.

Conclusion

We must never minimize the burden that a woman who is a mother through rape faces. That would be a great injustice. However, neither should we minimize the injustice done to the child if the child is aborted. Given that the mother is the only one who can preserve the life of this child, she has a duty to do so. But when she does so, she should be recognized for her heroism (particularly since our current societal norm dictates that in such a situation one chooses abortion). She deserves our wholehearted support. But lest she see her responsibility as a mere duty and burden, we should emphasize the

---

But this is not the normal sense of selfishness, nor is it the Hobbesian sense that underlies the social contract theory of morality.

[22] This is a participation in Providence in the sense that Providence is the free act of God, not based at all on our merits, and turning evil to good (e.g., rape to the birth of a child); it is also a free act of charity, guided by the recognition of moral obligation, but not determined by biological or sociological necessity.

deeply meaningful and enriching act of selflessness that she performs. Such free self-giving is indeed a great treasure for others, but also for her. Aristotle says that friendship (which is a greater good than justice since if all were friends, there would be no need of justice, but just people still seek friends[23]) is more in giving or loving than in receiving or in being loved. If we honor friendship, then the one who gives achieves it more than the one who receives.[24] Though the giving comes in response to suffering, uninvited and unjustly perpetrated, it transforms the disordered into the ordered, the malicious into the loving, and the meaningless into the providential.

---

[23] Aristotle, *Nicomachean Ethics*, VIII.1.

[24] Ibid., VIII.10.

Contributors

Sr. Terese Auer, O.P., is a member of the Dominican Sisters of St. Cecilia Congregation, Nashville, Tennessee. She received her master's degree and doctorate in philosophy from the Center for Thomistic Studies at the University of St. Thomas in Houston, Texas. She has taught at the high school and college levels for the past 30 years. Sr. Terese is currently in charge of the bioethics department at the new Pope John Paul the Great Catholic High School in Dumfries, Virginia.

Montague Brown is the Richard L. Bready Professor of Ethics, Economics, and the Common Good at Saint Anselm College, in Manchester, New Hampshire. His areas of interest are medieval philosophy, metaphysics, ethics, and philosophy of mind. He has published five books as well as numerous articles in his areas of interest. His most recent book is *The Restoration of Reason: The Eclipse and Recovery of Truth, Goodness, and Beauty* (Baker Academic, 2006).

Fr. Romanus Cessario, O.P., priest of the Eastern Province of the Dominicans, currently serves as professor of systematic theology at St. John's Seminary, Brighton, Massachusetts. His thesis, *Christian Satisfaction in Aquinas*, was directed by the late Colman O'Neill, O.P., and published in 1982; a revised version, *The Godly Image* (St. Bede's Press/Fordham University Press), appeared in 1990. Fr. Cessario has published many articles on dogmatic and moral theology as well as on the history of Thomism. His books include *The Moral Virtues and Theological Ethics* (University of Notre Dame Press, 1991), *Perpetual Angelus: As the Saints Pray the Rosary* (Alba House, 1995), *Christian Faith and the Theological Life* (1996) and, in collaboration with Kevin White, a translation of the fifteenth-century Dominican theologian John Capreolus's *Treatise on the Virtues* (2001) (both published by Catholic University of America Press). His *Introduction to Moral Theology* (2001) inaugurated the multi-volume Catholic Moral Thought series at CUA Press. His most recent book is *A Short History of Thomism* (Catholic University of America Press, 2004; French edition, Paris, 1999). Fr. Cessario serves on the editorial boards of several journals and is senior editor of the monthly worship aid *Magnificat*. For the last two decades he has lectured extensively in both the United States and Europe.

Gavin T. Colvert is Associate Professor of Philosophy and Director of the Ecumenical Institute at Assumption College in Worcester, Massachusetts. He has published articles in the areas of ethics, political philosophy, philosophy of religion, and medieval philosophy. He is currently working on a study of the historical and contemporary importance of virtue and law in Aquinas' ethical and political theory.

Rev. John J. Conley, S.J., holds the Francis X. Knott Chair in Philosophy and Theology at Loyola College in Maryland. He specializes in ethics, aesthetics, and modern French philosophy. Recent books include *The Suspicion of Virtue: Women Philosophers in Neoclassical France* (Cornell University Press, 2002) and *Jacqueline Pascal: A Rule for Children and Other Writings* (University of Chicago Press, 2003).

John A. Cuddeback received a Ph.D. in Philosophy from The Catholic University of America. He is chairman of the Philosophy department at Christendom College in Front Royal, Virginia. He teaches, writes, and lectures in ethics, especially on the topics of friendship and law.

Fr. **Christopher Cullen**, S.J., is Associate Professor of Philosophy at Fordham University. He is the author of *Bonaventure* (Oxford, 2006), and other publications that include, "Alexander of Hales" in *The Blackwell Companion to Philosophy in the Middle Ages* (Blackwell, 2003); "John Peckham" in *Encyclopedia of British Philosophy* (Continuum, 2006); "Scholastic Hylomorphism and Western Art," in *Beauty, Art, and the Polis* (CUA, 2000). From 2001-2004, he was Vice President of the American Maritain Association and the conference organizer for the AMA's conferences at Princeton, University of Chicago, and Emory. He is also Associate Director of Fordham's Center for Medieval Studies.

Raymond Dennehy is Professor of Philosophy at the University of San Francisco. He is a frequent guest on local radio and television for discussions of current biomedical topics, such as abortion, physician-assisted suicide, and embryonic stem-cell research. He has written *Reason and Dignity*, *Anti-abortionist at Large*, and *Soldier Boy: The War Between Michael and Lucifer*, as well as editing *Christian Married Love*.

Heather McAdam Erb is Professor of Graduate Philosophy, Catholic Distance University (Hamilton, Virginia). Her doctoral dissertation at the University of Toronto focused on the metaphysics of Thomas Aquinas. She has taught graduate and undergraduate philosophy at Fordham University, philosophy and religious studies at Penn State University, St. Francis University, and Mount Aloysius College. Dr. Erb has published numerous essays, articles, and chapters in international collections (including a recent *festschrift*) reflecting her main scholarly interests, which include the metaphysics and spirituality of Aquinas. She has contributed to the renaissance of Thomistic studies in Eastern Europe through publications and seminars for Lithuania Christian College, and is currently engaged in collaborative research focusing on interdisciplinary topics in Aquinas studies.

Desmond J. FitzGerald, Professor Emeritus, University of San Francisco, studied with Anton C. Pegis in 1947, while obtaining his M.A. from the University of Toronto. Later, while teaching at USF, he earned his Ph.D. at The University of California, Berkeley, working with Richard Popkin on Descartes. More recently, he has written on Gilson and Maritain, whose lectures he attended at St. Michael's in the 1940s.

Francis Cardinal George, O.M.I., Ph.D., S.T.D., entered the Missionary Oblates of Mary Immaculate on August 14, 1957. He studied theology at the University of Ottawa, Canada, and was ordained a priest on December 21, 1963. He earned a master's degree in philosophy at the Catholic University of America in Washington, D.C. in 1965 and a doctorate in American philosophy at Tulane University, New Orleans, Louisiana in 1970. In 1971, he received a master's degree in theology from the University of Ottawa in Canada. During those years, he also taught philosophy at the Oblate Seminary, Pass Christian, Mississippi (1964-69); Tulane University, New Orleans, Louisiana (1968); and at Creighton University, Omaha, Nebraska (1969-73). He was Provincial Superior of the Midwestern Province for the Oblates (1973-74). He was Vicar General of the Oblates in Rome from 1974-86. He returned to the United States to coordinate the Circle of Fellows for the Cambridge Center for the Study of Faith and Culture in Cambridge, Massachusetts (1987-90). During that time, he obtained a Doctorate of Sacred Theology from the Pontifical Urban University, Rome (1989). Pope John Paul II appointed him Bishop of Yakima in Washington on July 10, 1990, and then appointed him Archbishop of Portland in Oregon on April 30, 1996. On April 8, 1997, Pope John Paul named him the eighth Archbishop of Chicago. He is the first native Chicagoan to serve as Archbishop of Chicago. On January 18, 1998, Pope John Paul II announced Archbishop George's elevation to the Sacred College of Cardinals. In November 2007, Cardinal George was elected president of the United States Conference of Catholic Bishops.

Carson Holloway is Assistant Professor of Political Science at the University of Nebraska at Omaha, where he teaches political philosophy, constitutional law, and American government. He is the author of *All Shook Up: Music, Passion, and Politics* and *The Right Darwin: Evolution, Religion, and the Future of Democracy* (both with Spence Publishing). He is currently at work on a book on modern political philosophy and the social thought of Pope John Paul II, to be published by Baylor University Press. His scholarly articles have appeared in *The Review of Politics*, *Interpretation: A Journal of Political Philosophy*, and *Perspectives on Political Science*.

Brian W. Hughes is Assistant Professor of Theology at the University of Saint Mary, Leavenworth, Kansas. Dr. Hughes holds a Ph.D. in Theology from Boston College. He has published articles on Newman and is currently working on a book about the place of theology in the Catholic university.

Piotr Jaroszynski holds the Chair of the Philosophy of Culture at the John Paul II Catholic University of Lublin, Poland. He works within the framework of classical philosophy. He belongs to the American Catholic Philosophical Association, American Maritain Association, Gilson Society, and the International Society of Thomas Aquinas. He has written numerous articles and several scholarly books, including *The Controversy Over Beauty* (1992; 2002 in Polish), *Metaphysics and Art* (Peter Lang, 2002), *Science and Culture*

(Rodopi, 2007), and *Ethics: The Drama of the Moral Life* (Alba House, 2003), as well as many books for a broader public. For his textbook, *Ethics: The Drama of the Moral Life*, he received the personal thanks of Pope John Paul II.

David J. Klassen has a B.A. and an LL.B. from the University of British Columbia. He practiced law in Vancouver, British Columbia from 1983 until he began his studies in philosophy in 1998. He completed his M.A. at The Franciscan University of Steubenville in 2000. His master's thesis deals with Hans Kelsen's critique of natural law theory. He completed his Ph.D. in Philosophy at The Catholic University of America in 2007. The title of his dissertation is, "Thomas Aquinas and Knowledge of the First Principles of the Natural Law." His research interests include metaethics, jurisprudence, and philosophy of the person.

Steven A. Long received his undergraduate degree from the University of Toledo (1976) and his MA in philosophy from the University of Toledo (1978). He pursued postgraduate study at the University of Leuven in Belgium at the Institute for Philosophy. While in Belgium he also undertook private studies with Fr. Jan Walgrave, O.P., the renowned Newman scholar and Thomist. He pursued further studies at the Catholic University of America in Washington, D.C., receiving his pontifical doctorate in philosophy in 1993. He publishes widely in journals such as *Revue thomiste*, *The Thomist*, the English-language edition of *Nova et vetera*, the *International Philosophical Quarterly*, *Communio*, *Louvain Studies*, and *The National Catholic Bioethics Quarterly*. He lectures in the United States and Europe and is an associate editor of the English-language edition of *Nova et vetera*. He is the author of *The Teleological Grammar of the Moral Act*, published by *Sapientia Press*. A collection of his essays, tentatively titled *Thomistic Disputations*, has also been accepted for publication and is forthcoming from *Sapientia Press*. Dr. Long currently teaches natural law and metaphysics as an associate professor of theology within the Graduate Theology School of Ave Maria University in Naples, Florida.

Ralph Nelson began teaching philosophy and political science at the University of Windsor in 1961, and continued on there as emeritus professor. His research and publications were in the areas of moral, social, and political philosophy, and in democratic theory. Author of numerous articles on Yves R. Simon and Jacques Maritain, he published in such journals as *Semiotica*, *Canadian Journal of Political Science*, *Comparative Politics*, *Publius*, *Science et esprit*, and *International Philosophical Quarterly*. He was co-editor of Yves R. Simon's *Foresight and Knowledge* (1996).

Peter A. Pagan received a bachelor's degree in philosophy from the University of California, Berkeley (1989), and a doctorate in philosophy from Fordham University (1997). His doctoral dissertation was on the question of man's final end in the thought of Thomas Aquinas. He has taught at Fordham University (1995), Wheeling Jesuit University, West Virginia (1996-2003), and Aquinas College, Nashville, Tennessee (2003-present). The recipient of various academic awards and grants, including a WJU scholar-in-residence grant (2003), he has served on both the Program Committee and the Executive Committee of the American Maritain Association. His articles appear in previous volumes published by the American Maritain Association, in *The Thomist*, and in *The National Catholic Bioethics Quarterly*. His research interests include philosophical theology, philosophical psychology, natural law theory, philosophy of nature, and the interface between science and theology.

Alice Ramos is Professor of Philosophy at St. John's University in Queens, New York, where she has taught since 1987. She holds a Ph.D. in French Literature from New York University, and a Ph.D. in Philosophy from the University of Navarra, Spain. Her publications include a book written in Spanish entitled: *Signum: De la semiótica universal a la metafísica del signo* (EUNSA), and two edited books: *Beauty, Art, and the Polis* (2000), and *Faith, Scholarship, and Culture in the 21st Century* (2002), both volumes edited for the American Maritain Association and distributed by the Catholic University of America Press, and over forty articles in areas such as Thomistic metaphysics, Kantian ethical theology, Alasdair MacIntyre's ethical enquiry, and Christian anthropology. She is the recipient of grants for scholarly work both in the United States and in Europe. A past president of the American Maritain Association (2002-2004), she is currently on the executive committee of the Maritain Association, and a member of the executive council of the American Catholic Philosophical Association. Her present research focuses on the foundations of ethics and on the transcendentals in Aquinas, especially beauty.

Fr. **James V. Schall**, S. J., is a professor in the Department of Government at Georgetown University. His books include, among others, *The Life of the Mind*, *Roman Catholic Political Philosophy*, *The Sum Total of Human Happiness*, and *The Regensburg Lecture*.

Index

A

B

C

D

G

H

I

Printed in the United States
212598BV00002B/2/P

9 780966 922677